GREAT
SCOTTISH
HEROES

Stuart Pearson, after many varied careers over decades in law enforcement, education, government and business, has finally found his calling in writing. His first book *Bittersweet: The Memoir of a Chinese Indonesian Family in the Twentieth Century* (released globally in 2009) was published by Singapore University Press to much critical acclaim, and was nominated for the New South Wales Premier's Prize for Literature in 2010. *Great Scottish Heroes* is his third book; his second (with Bob Mitchell), *Blood on the Thistle: The tragic story of the Cranston family and their remarkable sacrifice in the Great War* was published in the summer of 2014, to universal approval and strong sales. He is married, and lives in Sydney, Australia.

STUART PEARSON

GREAT SCOTTISH HEROES

FIFTY SCOTS WHO SHAPED THE WORLD

JB

JOHN BLAKE

www.johnblakepublishing.co.uk

www.facebook.com/johnblakebooks ⬛
twitter.com/jblakebooks ⬛

First published in paperback in Great Britain in 2015

ISBN: 978-1-78418-375-2

British Library Cataloguing-in-Publication Data:

A catalogue record for this book is available from the British Library.

Design by www.envydesign.co.uk

Printed in Great Britain by CPI Group (UK) Ltd

1 3 5 7 9 10 8 6 4 2

© Copyright Stuart Pearson 2015

The right of the Stuart Pearson to be identified as the author of this work has been
asserted by him in accordance with the Copyright, Designs and Patents Act 1988.

Papers used by John Blake Publishing are natural, recyclable products made from
wood grown in sustainable forests. The manufacturing processes conform to the
environmental regulations of the country of origin.

Every attempt has been made to contact the relevant copyright-holders, but some were
unobtainable. We would be grateful if the appropriate people could contact us.

CONTENTS

INTRODUCTION   IX

CALGACUS (FIRST CENTURY AD): Mythical leader of resistance   1
    to the Roman Empire

SIR WILLIAM WALLACE (c. 1270–1307): Freedom fighter   8
    for Scottish independence

ROBERT THE BRUCE (1274–1329): Warrior for Scottish   15
    independence, King of Scotland

JOHN KNOX (1514–1572): Religious reformer and founder   20
    of Presbyterianism

MARY, QUEEN OF SCOTS (1542–1587): Tragic monarch   26
    of Scotland

JOHN NAPIER (1550–1617): Mathematician who invented   33
    logarithms

JAMES VI OF SCOTLAND AND I OF ENGLAND (1566–1625):   37
    First King of Great Britain and Ireland

DAVID HUME (1711–1776): Philosopher, historian and essayist   41

FLORA MACDONALD (1722–1790): Unlikely Jacobite hero   48

ADAM SMITH (1723–1790): Philosopher and pioneer of classical 56
economics

JOHN KNOX WITHERSPOON (1723–1794): Minister and 63
educator who shaped America's early thinking

NIEL GOW (1727–1807): Fiddler, composer and champion of 70
Scottish folk music

ROBERT ADAM (1728–1792): Great Neoclassical architect 73

JAMES WATT (1736–1819): Inventor and mechanical engineer 76

JOHN PAUL JONES (1747–1792): Spiritual father of the US Navy 82

SIR HENRY RAEBURN (1756–1823): One of Scotland's most 91
significant portrait painters

THOMAS TELFORD (1757–1834): Civil engineer and noted 94
builder of roads, bridges, rail and canals

ROBERT BURNS (1759–1796): National poet of Scotland 97

LACHLAN MACQUARIE (1762–1824): Colonial Governor who 104
set Australia on its path to prosperity

SIR ALEXANDER MACKENZIE (1764–1820): Fur trader and 112
explorer who completed the first east–west crossing
of Canada

CHARLES MACINTOSH (1766–1843): Chemist and inventor of 116
waterproof fabrics

CAROLINA OLIPHANT, LADY NAIRNE (1766–1845): Collector 120
and writer of Scottish songs and ballads

SIR WALTER SCOTT (1771–1832): Writer, lawyer, poet 124
and historian

ROBERT STEVENSON (1772–1850): Civil engineer and famed 128
builder of lighthouses

THOMAS COCHRANE, 10TH EARL OF DUNDONALD 134
(1775–1860): Naval hero and founder of the navies of
three countries

SIR DAVID BREWSTER (1781–1868): Inventor, mathematician, 142
physicist and science writer

DAVID LIVINGSTONE (1813–1873): Missionary, explorer of   146
   Africa, crusader against the slave trade

MARGARET OLIPHANT (1828–1897): Prolific Scottish novelist   152
   and writer

ISABELLA ELDER (1828–1905): Philanthropist, promoter of   156
   women's education and benefactor of the poor
   of Glasgow

ANDREW CARNEGIE (1835–1919): Industrialist and prodigious   161
   philanthropist

JOHN MUIR (1838–1914): Naturalist and founder of   165
   national parks

SIR JAMES DEWAR (1842–1923): Chemist and physicist   173

ALEXANDER GRAHAM BELL (1847–1922): Eminent scientist   176
   and inventor

KATE CRANSTON (1849–1934): Businesswoman and patron   179
   of the arts

ROBERT LOUIS STEVENSON (1850–1894): Novelist, travel writer   182
   and anthropologist

SIR PATRICK GEDDES (1854–1932): Philosopher and pioneer   186
   of town planning

DOUGLAS HAIG, 1ST EARL HAIG (1861–1928): Supreme   190
   commander of the British Imperial armies on the Western
   Front during the First World War

DR ELSIE INGLIS (1864–1917): Surgeon and suffragist   198

CHARLES RENNIE MACKINTOSH (1868–1928): Architect who   204
   pioneered the 'Glasgow Style' of design in Scotland

JOHN BUCHAN, 1ST BARON TWEEDSMUIR (1875–1940):   211
   Novelist, historian and Governor General of Canada

DANIEL LAIDLAW (1875–1950): Piper who won a VC at the   215
   Battle of Loos in, 1915

SIR ALEXANDER FLEMING (1881–1955): Biologist and   219
   discoverer of penicillin

HUGH DOWDING, 1ST BARON DOWDING (1882–1970):   225
The mastermind behind victory in the Battle of Britain in
the Second World War

JOHN LOGIE BAIRD (1888–1946): Scientist and pioneer   233
of television

SIR JOHN 'JACKIE' STEWART (B.1939): Three-times World   236
Champion Formula One racing driver

SIR ALEX FERGUSON (B.1941): One of football's most   240
successful managers

ANN GLOAG (B.1942): Businesswoman and major charity   242
donor

HAZEL COSGROVE, LADY COSGROVE (B.1946): Scotland's first   245
female Supreme Court judge

SUSAN BOYLE (B.1961): International singing sensation   250
and inspiration

JOANNE ROWLING (B.1965): Best-selling author, who inspired   255
youth to read for pleasure

BIBLIOGRAPHY AND SOURCES   261

INTRODUCTION

When I was commissioned to write *Great Scottish Heroes*, the first two questions that sprang to mind were definitional. What defines being a Scot, and then, what does the word 'hero' mean?

The first question can be answered fairly quickly and easily. In this book, a Scotsman or Scotswoman is defined by a person's birth or adoption. In other words, if a person was born in Scotland then they are automatically a Scot. If they were born elsewhere but had chosen to live in Scotland and adopt its culture, heritage, laws and customs, then they are a Scot by adoption. This last point is relevant for two of the people I've included in my list of fifty great Scottish heroes; Joanne (J. K.) Rowling and Elsie Inglis. In the case of J. K. Rowling, she was born near Bristol in England but adopted Scotland when she took up residence in Edinburgh in 1993 – though, in fact, her connections with Scotland go beyond residency: her mother was part Scots, Rowling's maternal great-grandfather having been born on the Isle of Arran.

Elsie Inglis was born in India during the time of the British Raj. Her father was in the employ of the Indian Civil Service (British India) and later the Chief Commissioner of the province of Oudh. Both parents were Scottish and when Elsie's father retired, the family, including fourteen-year-old Elsie, returned to live in Scotland, specifically Edinburgh. With both women, I contend that even though they were not born in Scotland, they have adopted Scotland as their homeland.

The second definitional issue that needs to be addressed is the meaning of the word 'hero'. The word has become much overused in modern society. When a sport star scores the match-winning goal or runs a personal best, that person is called a hero by the press and media. In artistic terms the hero is the central character in a story, play or film. When emergency workers in uniform save lives, the public often declare them to be heroes. In some countries it can also be the name of a sandwich!

But can an inanimate object, a character in a book and people merely doing the job they were trained and paid for, really be heroes?

According to the *Collins English Dictionary* a hero is a person who is 'idealised for possessing superior qualities in any field'. The *Oxford English Dictionary* says, 'a person, typically a man, who is admired for their courage, outstanding achievements, or noble qualities'. Finally the *Macquarie Dictionary* defines a hero as, 'a person of distinguished courage or performance'.

From these three sources the common features are:

Courage + noble qualities = role model for others

I have tried to select men and women from Scotland's past and present who exemplify the characteristics of being courageous and having noble qualities. Synonyms that could be used interchangeably with courage and nobility would be influential, noteworthy, remarkable, outstanding, important, significant, memorable, striking, impressive, uncommon or exceptional. I hope that the fifty Scots I have chosen not only provide interesting reading, but also role models for people everywhere.

One more issue that must be addressed is the actual selection of the people who appear in the following pages. If people had to select their own list of fifty great Scottish heroes, I dare say there would be little unanimity. Everyone would have listed different names and no two lists would match exactly.

So it is for me. The fifty names I have chosen represent my choice and my choice alone. It was not forced on me, nor was it the work of a committee. If anyone takes issue with my selection, they are perfectly welcome to publish a list of their own!

In truth I could have picked a hundred great Scottish heroes, possibly even two hundred. There are so many Scots who have made significant contributions to the world that it is unfortunate such a large number must be omitted.

Scotland is a country about the same size as Serbia or the Czech Republic. It has a population similar to Singapore's or Finland's. Yet it has produced as many Nobel Prize winners as South Africa, Belgium and Hungary, all of which have greater populations and a larger land mass.

Scotland is a small nation that punches above its weight in many fields of human endeavour, such as exploration, theology, science, philosophy, economics, medicine and the arts. Scotland has enjoyed and continues to enjoy a disproportionate influence over the rest of the world.

A large number of biographies in this book coincidentally

fall within Scotland's golden age of progress, called the Scottish Enlightenment (approximately 1700–1800). During this 100-year period, Scottish thought, discoveries, courage, inventions and enterprise not only changed Britain, but also the world.

* * *

And what is there not to love about a country whose official animal is the imaginary unicorn and whose official flower is a prickly weed (thistle)?

STUART PEARSON

CALGACUS (FIRST CENTURY AD)

MYTHICAL LEADER OF RESISTANCE TO THE ROMAN EMPIRE

No statue exists for this person and no archaeological evidence has yet been found to confirm that he ever lived. His name only appears in one piece of ancient writing by Tacitus, the first- century Roman senator and historian. However, if Calgacus did not exist at all, what he represented was as real as if he had actually lived.

In AD 80 Gnaeus Julius Agricola, the Governor of the Roman province of Britannia, decided to invade and annex the land to the north of his territory in what is called Scotland today. Northern tribes beyond the border were raiding and plundering the newly conquered province of Britannia and threatening to undo much of the good work of Romanising and developing the province.

At this stage the Romans had been in Britain for only forty years and their control over the province was by no means assured. Just twenty years earlier Boudicca, warrior Queen of the Iceni tribe, had led a bloody revolt against Roman occupation that had almost caused Emperor Nero to abandon Britannia altogether. In order to secure a strong northern frontier, Agricola decided he must subdue these northern tribes, which were collectively called the Caledonii.

Leading an army of some 10,000 legionnaires, 8,000 auxiliary infantry and 3,000 auxiliary cavalry, Agricola marched north from Eboracum (modern-day York) building forts and roads as he went. Meanwhile, the Roman fleet was sent ahead to raid the coast and provide supplies. Agricola was determined to do a thorough job, so he designed the campaign to take years, not months. If successful, he might even earn great honour back in Rome by subjugating the barbarian north and adding a new province to the Empire.

While he was finalising his plans to conquer the last remaining parts of mainland Britain (and some say the surrounding islands known today as the Hebrides), he fought many small battles to subdue the tribes of the Scottish Lowlands. The route he pioneered through Scotland was so cleverly chosen that numerous southern invaders would also choose this course during their campaigns in Scotland for the next 1,500 years.

One site, a Roman fortress at Inchtuthill, Perthshire was used as the advanced headquarters for Governor Agricola in his campaign against the Caledonii. It housed over 5,000 soldiers and covered such a large area that, had the occupation continued, Inchtuthill (known by the Romans as Pinnata Castra, or Fortress on the Wing) may have grown to become the Roman capital of a new Scottish province, called Caledonia.

Eventually by AD 83 Agricola had reached the River Tay, which one first-century Roman commander described as where 'the world and all created things come to an end'. North of this region, the Roman general found increased resistance from a large confederation of tribes that were ably led by a man called Calgacus.

In the life of Agricola by his son-in-law the Roman historian Tacitus, we are told that Calgacus (from the Celtic *calg-ac-os* for 'Swordsman') was a chieftain of the Caledonian confederacy united in armed opposition to a Roman invasion of what is known today as northern Scotland. Tacitus described him as, 'the most distinguished for birth and valour among the chieftains'. Thus, Calgacus became one of the first Scots to be named in written history.

He initially fought a determined resistance to the Romans in a series of skirmishes as the Roman legions marched further into northern Scotland, reaching as far as the River Spey in present-day Moray, and possibly even further.

The Caledonii continued to attack the extended Roman supply and communication lines and, according to Tacitus, the Romans only managed to beat them off with difficulty.

When Agricola's troops captured many of the storehouses holding the Caledonians' recently gathered harvest, Calgacus had to choose between fighting or letting his people starve in the forthcoming winter.

In the late summer or early autumn of AD 83, the Romans heard about a gathering of a huge number of Caledonii on a hill named by Tacitus as Mons Graupius (a name erroneously transcribed later as Mons Grampius – giving rise to the modern Grampian mountains). This was the final showdown that the Roman general was hoping for. The moment when he would break Scottish resistance forever.

Tacitus writes that the Scots numbered approximately 30,000 warriors. Calgacus also had a sizeable number of war chariots, which he placed in front of his troops ready to send them downhill to smash the Roman's front line. Agricola was at a disadvantage of having to fight uphill, but he had 3,000 of some of the finest auxiliary cavalry waiting on his flanks to intercept and neutralise the threat from the slow-moving chariots. He also had 8,000 allied auxiliary infantry drawn up from all parts of the Empire. These he lined up in front of at least two Roman legions (10,000) held in reserve.

It appeared that Calgacus had the odds in his favour. He had the advantage of numbers (30,000 as against 21,000) and was in a superior position on higher ground.

The precise location of the battle is unknown but archaeologists and historians have suggested several locations. One of the first to have been put forward was Raedykes in Aberdeenshire, the site of a large Roman camp situated where the Grampian foothills come closest to the sea to form a narrow corridor. However, this location would appear to be too far south as there were several more Roman camps constructed further north along the coast of north-east Scotland almost all the way to Inverness.

A large marching camp subsequently discovered near the hills of Bennachie in Aberdeenshire seems a more probable setting. The terrain satisfies Tacitus' description of the battle, with room for an extended Roman line that still allows for the movement of cavalry. The slope opposite the camp is steep enough to provide a defensive position for massed Caledonii.

More northerly still is the Pass of Grange, overlooked by Knock Hill near Keith, in Moray County as another potential site. Here, the Grampian mountains again come close to the sea and there is an approach to the Moray Firth. It is an advantageous site to defend and less than twenty kilometres from sheltered anchorage, where Agricola's fleet could have waited. But the nearest Roman camps so far uncovered in this location seem too small and too removed from the supposed battle site. Further sites, such as Gask Ridge on a hill west of Perth, as well as locations as far afield as the counties of Fife and Sutherland have been suggested. To date, no definitive proof of location for where the battle was fought has been found.

Tacitus conceived a speech which he claimed Calgacus had uttered to his warriors before the Battle of Mons Graupius. It is now widely regarded as a complete fabrication, but nevertheless the speech did accurately echo sentiments that have since been expressed by Scots for millennia. According to Tacitus, Calgacus roused his troops to fight by saying:

I have a sure confidence that this day . . . will be the beginning of freedom to the whole of Britain. To all of us slavery is a thing unknown; there are no lands beyond us, and even the sea is not safe, menaced as we are by a Roman fleet.

To us who dwell on the uttermost confines of the earth and of freedom, this remote sanctuary of Britain's glory has up to this time been a defence. Now, however, the furthest limits of Britain are thrown open, and the unknown always passes for the marvellous. But there are no tribes beyond us, nothing indeed but waves and rocks, and the yet more terrible Romans, from whose oppression escape is vainly sought by obedience and submission. Robbers of the world, having by their universal plunder exhausted the land, they rifle the deep.

If the enemy be rich, they are rapacious; if he be poor, they lust for dominion; neither the east nor the west has been able to satisfy them. Alone among men they covet with equal eagerness poverty and riches. To robbery, slaughter, plunder, they give the lying name of empire; they make a solitude and call it peace.

The battle started with Calgacus launching his heavy war chariots, but Agricola countered by sending in his cavalry to disperse them.

This would be the last time that war-chariots, which had dominated Bronze and Early Iron-Age battlefields, would be deployed in any large numbers in combat. Larger, more powerful horses were now being used more effectively by Romans as cavalry.

An exchange of missiles then took place before the 8,000 auxiliary troops in the Roman front line attacked uphill, closing with the Caledonians to neutralise the latter's longer swords. Then the Roman cavalry re-engaged to attack the Caledonian flanks, which caused their line to falter. At this crucial moment, four Batavian auxiliary cohorts from Rome's provinces in Germania and two Tungrian cohorts from Gaul, led a decisive assault on Calgacus' centre, causing them to break and flee.

By Tacitus' account, the battle cost the lives of 10,000 Caledonians and just 360 auxiliary infantry troops. The Roman legions in reserve played no part in the battle. The remaining 20,000 Caledonians simply melted away into the hills. No mention was made of the death or capture of Calgacus, so it was assumed that he was among those who survived, and whose lurking presence in the mountains helped ensure the Romans never did conquer Scotland. Frustrated by the never-ending hit-and-run tactics of the local tribes, the Romans soon withdrew to the south.

Even though they failed to tame the warriors of northern Britain on this occasion, the Romans still celebrated a great triumph back in Rome. Nor was it the end of Rome's desire to conquer Scotland. Over the next 130 years the mightiest military force in the world at the time made at least three further attempts to subdue the tribes residing in what is present-day Scotland. In one attempt the Romans even built a second barrier to try to secure their gains: the Antonine Wall built between the years AD 142 and 154 across the central belt of Scotland; it was abandoned after just eight years of service.

After initial gains, every campaign ultimately ended in failure. Either the legions of Rome were recalled to deal with conflict elsewhere in the Empire, or the soldiers were worn down through guerrilla tactics by a people who simply would not concede defeat.

The tribes were too fierce, the land too difficult, plus there was nothing there that made the effort worthwhile. By AD 212, the Romans finally had enough and withdrew permanently back 160 kilometres to the first barrier they had erected – Hadrian's Wall – a strongly defended fortification built a hundred years earlier to keep out the northern tribes. There, the Romans remained for another two centuries and never set foot in Scotland again.

Even the fourth-century Roman soldier and historian, Ammianus Marcellinus, was moved to write about the continuing troubles in Northern Britain, saying in his *Res Gestae*: 'The wild tribes of the Scots and the Picts broke their undertaking to keep the peace, were causing destruction in those areas near the frontiers, and the provincials, exhausted by the repeated disasters they had already suffered, were caught in the grip of fear.' Whether Calgacus did or did not exist, he personified the pugnacious, independent attitude befitting a Scottish hero that has become a national trait of Scotland ever since. Throughout the Roman, Viking, Norman and English invasions, the Scottish people have remained fiercely independent.

A millennium later another Scottish independence fighter, William Wallace, epitomised the same characteristics as Calgacus before the Battle of Stirling Bridge in 1297 – quoted by the nineteenth-century historian Patrick Fraser Tytler in his *History of Scotland* as saying, 'We come here with no peaceful intent, but ready for battle, determined to avenge our wrongs and set our country free! Let your masters come and attack us, we are ready to meet them beard to beard.'

SIR WILLIAM WALLACE
(c.1270–1307)

FREEDOM FIGHTER FOR
SCOTTISH INDEPENDENCE

Very little is known of William Wallace's early years, but it is thought that he was born around the year 1270 in either Elderslie, a small Scottish village near Paisley in Renfrewshire, or Ellerslie in the neighbouring Scottish county of Ayrshire. The Wallace family had roots in both locations, where they owned land.

There is almost no reliable information about William Wallace's early life. He is said to have spent his childhood at Dunipace, near Stirling, under the supervision of his uncle, who was a priest. Wallace probably led a comfortable and peaceful life as the son of a nobleman.

When Wallace was growing up, King Alexander III ruled Scotland. His reign had seen a period of peace and economic stability. In 1286, King Alexander died after falling from his horse leaving as his only heir a three year-old granddaughter, Margaret, in Norway. The nobles of Scotland established a government of guardians to look after Margaret until she reached maturity and awaited her arrival by ship from across the North Sea.

Unfortunately Margaret fell ill on the voyage and died in the Orkney Islands without reaching the Scottish mainland. This threw the Scottish monarchy into a crisis, with several powerful and influential Scottish families claiming the throne. With Scotland threatening to descend into civil war, King Edward I of England was invited to arbitrate on accession in 1292. At a great feudal court held in the castle at Berwick-upon-Tweed, he declared John Balliol to have the strongest claim and therefore to be the next King of Scotland.

His choice was not as simple as that. John Balliol may have had the strongest claim, but he also had the weakest character. King Edward had designs on Scotland himself and deliberately chose Balliol whom he thought he would be able to subjugate with ease. In 1296, he summoned King John to London to stand before him like a commoner and pledge support for his military actions against the French. However, Scotland and France had signed a military alliance of their own against England only the year before. Insulted that he would have to repudiate the recently signed treaty as well as by his treatment before Edward, the Scottish king renounced his homage to the English throne and returned home to Scotland in haste to prepare for the inevitable war that would follow.

He did not have to wait long, as a month later Edward stormed Berwick-upon-Tweed, which was then part of Scotland, and sacked it. Moving further north along the coast, the traditional route of all invaders since the Romans, the Scots were decisively defeated in the Battle of Dunbar in East Lothian. Three months later, with English troops easily subduing the rest of Scotland, King John formally surrendered his Kingdom to England. He was then taken into custody and imprisoned in the Tower of London and King Edward declared himself ruler of Scotland. Edward also started appointing English noblemen to important positions of authority in Scotland. In effect, Edward was turning independent Scotland into a vassal state.

Resistance to Edward's actions began immediately and the first act definitely known to have been carried out by Wallace was in 1297 when the twenty-seven-year-old William and about thirty followers burned down the Scottish town of Lanark and killed its English sheriff, William de Heselrig in 1297. Common people started flocking to Wallace's banner and, supported by ever-increasing numbers of men, he attacked English strongholds across central Scotland. Rebellions were now beginning to break out throughout Scotland from the Highlands to the Lowlands.

Edward had completely misjudged the mood of the Scottish people, but he could not do anything about it personally as he was away in France with his army fighting the French. However, he was not entirely without options and he sent his ablest nobles north at the head of a large force to crush the rebels.

On 11 September 1297, an English army confronted Wallace and his men at the Forth River near Stirling. Wallace's forces had grown into an army, but he was still vastly outnumbered. The English had to cross a narrow bridge over the Forth before they could reach Wallace waiting for them on the other side. Seizing this strategic opportunity, Wallace held off the attack until almost half of the English soldiers were across and then he fell upon them with everything he had. Half of the English were trapped on one side of the bridge and could not retreat, while the other half of the English army on the opposite bank could only watch helplessly. The ensuing battle was a massacre, with the English losing an estimated

5,000 English infantrymen and 100 cavalry for the loss of perhaps a few hundred Scots. It was a shattering and humiliating defeat for the English.

After the battle, Wallace and his co-leader (Andrew Moray, who had been leading a parallel rebellion in Scotland's north-east) were jointly named as 'Guardians of Scotland' in the name of King John Balliol, who was still imprisoned in the Tower of London. However, Moray, who was severely wounded in the battle, died of his wounds in late 1297, leaving Wallace effectively in charge of Scotland. It was at this time that a council of elders knighted Wallace for his victory at Stirling Bridge. Now at the head of a large, if ill-disciplined, army of supporters, and emboldened by his performance at Stirling Bridge, Sir William Wallace decided to cross the border and attack England while King Edward was still in France.

Wallace's attacks on England were cruel and very destructive. It has been said that it was more like barbarians pillaging and looting the countryside, than an organised military incursion into enemy territory. But Wallace had his reasons for such brutality; he needed to quickly restock Scotland's coffers with booty plundered from England's northern counties of Northumberland and Cumberland and he needed to show King Edward that, unlike John Balliol, Sir William Wallace was not a person to be trifled with.

In early 1298, Edward returned with his army from France and immediately set out for Scotland determined to crush any opposition once and for all. Wallace cleverly avoided any confrontation and fought a guerrilla-like withdrawal back into the heartland of Scotland, destroying the countryside as he went. This forced Edward and his powerful army deeper and deeper into Scotland, with his supply lines becoming stretched. When Wallace sensed that the advantage had swung in his favour, he made preparations at Falkirk (midway between Glasgow and Edinburgh) to do battle with the English.

The type of battle tactics successfully employed by Wallace were quite common throughout Scotland at the time. It involved closely packed rows of men in a circle presenting long wooden stakes or metal pikes towards the enemy in every direction. It resembled a prickly hedgehog and was called a 'schiltron'. While these formations remained intact, they were virtually impregnable against heavy cavalry, but King Edward did not come north with just cavalry, he had found a new weapon he used to great effect in France – the longbow.

Edward did not engage the schiltrons with his cavalry as Wallace anticipated, but stood some distance off and used his archers, of which there were several thousand, to rain arrows down on the unarmoured Scottish infantry. It was a slaughter. Wallace's men fell like leaves in autumn and gaps started appearing in the massed formations of schiltrons. Only then did the English king send in his heavy cavalry, who smashed their way through the gaps, causing the Scots to break and run.

It is estimated 2,000–3,000 Scots died on the battlefield that day in 1298. Wallace barely escaped, but his military reputation as a brilliant leader and tactician had been shattered.

He resigned his guardianship in December 1298 and was succeeded by Robert the Bruce (later King Robert I). William then disappeared for the time being from the pages of history.

It is said by some that he went to France in an attempt to gain military support to continue the struggle against England, but there are only vague scraps of evidence supporting this. In truth, nothing is really known of his activities or whereabouts for almost the next five years.

SIR WILLIAM WALLACE (c.1270–1307)

In the meantime, Edward set about securing his authority over Scotland once again, by sending more nobles and soldiers north to subdue the persistently restless population. He also engaged in the tactic of buying off Scottish nobles with the promise of more wealth and land in return for their loyalty. In England he was given the nickname of the 'Hammer of the Scots'.

However, in 1304 Sir William Wallace is recorded organising several skirmishes with authorities in the Scottish Borders and central belt of Scotland. He had returned to his favourite tactic of engaging the enemy where he was weak and melting away before he could respond in strength. King Edward was furious when he was informed Wallace was back, and realised that he could well be the match to light yet another rebellious uprising, unless he was stopped before his popularity spread.

Even with a damaged reputation arising from his defeat at Falkirk, William was still undoubtedly popular with the common people who saw him as a freedom fighter. But he was not so universally admired by the Scottish nobles, many of whom had already thrown their lot in with the English king.

Wallace evaded capture for over a year as he continued his hit-and-run tactics, but a Scottish noble betrayed him for a large reward and turned him over to King Edward in 1305. Wallace was transported to London and tried for treason in a show trial. If found guilty, there was only one penalty for treason and King Edward made sure that this was indeed the verdict rendered by the court.

The King wanted more than just a guilty verdict though: he wanted Wallace's execution to be a demonstration of Edward's awesome power. Wallace was stripped naked and dragged through the streets of London to a public venue for his execution. There he was hanged until the rope had almost strangled him to death, but at the last moment he was cut down. Then his genitals were removed by knife and he was disembowelled while still alive. His intestines were burnt on a brazier before him and then he was beheaded. But this was still not enough for King Edward.

All four limbs of Sir William Wallace were cut from the body. His head was placed on a pike on London Bridge and his limbs were displayed separately in four northern towns as a reminder of the fate that befalls those who oppose the King of England. But Edward's show of strength backfired. Rather than subdue the Scottish people, his treatment of Wallace inflamed them. Robert the Bruce (*see* p. 15), the man who became Guardian of Scotland after Wallace, was stirred into action. He took up the cause of independence that would ultimately lead to Scotland becoming a sovereign nation again and he being crowned Robert I, King of Scotland.

Wallace holds a very special place in the hearts of Scots people and in 1869 a huge stone monument was erected to him very close to the site of his victory at Stirling Bridge. In the minds of many Scots today, Sir William Wallace sacrificed his own life in the cause of Scotland's freedom.

ROBERT THE BRUCE,
KING ROBERT I (1274–1329)

WARRIOR FOR SCOTTISH
INDEPENDENCE, KING OF SCOTLAND

Robert the Bruce (also Robert Bruce and later Robert I of Scotland) was born, possibly at Turnberry Castle, Ayrshire, into the noble and influential Bruce family. The death of King Alexander III of Scotland in 1286 and that of his only successor, the infant Margaret, on her way back from Norway, set in train a chain of events that would cause Robert to play a central role in Scotland's history. A role which still influences Scotland today.

Rival claimants emerged to claim the vacant Scottish throne, including the powerful Bruce family, and King Edward I of England was asked to arbitrate. The English ruler had designs of conquering his northern neighbour for himself, and appointed a weak and compliant nobleman in John Balliol to rule Scotland. Balliol was less compliant than the king had assumed and eventually stood up for the Scots people in the face of the English king's demands. In 1296 Edward attacked Scotland – with the support of the Bruces –

and after delivering a crushing defeat, forced Balliol to abdicate and surrender Scotland to him. Edward started ruling Scotland from London as if it were a province of England.

Scots resistance to Edward's rule broke out the following year led by another Scot, William Wallace (*see* p. 8), and grew into a widespread revolt. Wallace won a victory over Edward's army at Stirling Bridge in 1297 and was declared a Guardian of Scotland. The following year Edward invaded Scotland again, this time defeating Wallace at Falkirk. Wallace went underground but was eventually captured and, in 1305, tried, hung, drawn and quartered in London.

Robert the Bruce supported the cause for independence and when Wallace withdrew from public office, Robert stepped forward to become the next Guardian of Scotland, along with an arch-rival, John Comyn, a nephew of Balliol and contender for the throne. The two could not work together and in 1299 a third party was appointed as Guardian, allowing Robert to resign.

Edward I invaded Scotland again in 1301 and 1303 to force Scottish nobles to pledge their allegiance to the English crown, yet Edward never quite trusted their oaths of fealty, particularly that of Robert the Bruce, whom Edward regarded as duplicitous.

Robert was biding his time waiting for the right moment to strike, but first he had to deal with John Comyn's rival claim to the still vacant throne of Scotland. In 1306, Robert invited Comyn to Dumfries for discussions and there the usual disagreements over each other's claim quickly led to a heated argument during which, it is said, Robert drew his dagger and stabbed John Comyn, who died soon after. Robert moved quickly to reduce the Comyn family's power by seizing much of their lands in southern Scotland. He also confessed to the Bishop of Glasgow who conveniently gave

Robert absolution for the killing, on the condition that Robert would promote the Roman Catholic Church, when he became King of Scotland.

Robert the Bruce became Robert I when he was crowned King of Scotland a few months later, but the English then persuaded the Pope in Rome to excommunicate him from the Catholic Church. However, Edward I was not content for religious matters to take their course: he was a man of action who would not stand idly by while Scotland slipped out of his grasp. His reaction was swift and predictable.

In 1306, he raised another army and invaded Scotland yet again. The two armies met at Methven, near Perth, resulting in a crushing defeat for Scotland.

Robert I became a wanted outlaw and most of his family were captured. Two of his brothers and a number of his supporters were hung, drawn and quartered. His sisters were imprisoned, one of them held in a cage that hung out from the castle walls for up to four years. Robert wintered on an island off the coast of Ireland. It is here that myth and reality blur, for legend has it that while at his most despondent he saw a small spider trying to spin a web in the cave he was hiding in on the island of Rathlin. Time after time the spider tried and failed, but when all seemed hopeless the spider managed to finally succeed. Robert took this as a sign that he should never give up the fight to free Scotland from the yoke of English domination.

After a year of being on the run, a year in which Edward had unleashed terror in Scotland, Robert came out of hiding. Aided by loyal and capable followers, he won the first of many victories over the English. The more defeats he inflicted on Edward's soldiers, the more that Scottish supporters flocked to his cause. He held his first parliament in 1309 and by 1314 he had taken back much control of Scotland.

In 1307, Edward I died while making preparations to once more raise an army and take it north to crush Scottish impudence. His son Edward II promised to complete the task but he was not as determined or as ruthless as his father. He was also slower. It took Edward II several years to gather his forces, during which Robert waged a ceaseless and brilliant guerrilla campaign against the English troops that were occupying less and less of Scotland.

In 1314, a huge English army finally arrived in Scotland and camped at Bannockburn, preparing to relieve nearby Stirling Castle, which was the last English stronghold in Scotland and under siege from Robert. The Scottish king then did something unexpected. Faced with two opposing forces, one in the castle and the other on the plains outside, he decided to attack rather than withdraw.

The resulting Battle of Bannockburn in 1314 would go down as one of the defining moments in Scottish history. Facing 20,000 English soldiers on the boggy ground below Stirling Castle Robert's 7,000 Scottish troops inflicted an overwhelming defeat on the English. Edward II only just managed to escape the battlefield, but most English knights and soldiers did not. Up to 10,000 Englishmen were killed at the battlefield or hunted down in the rout that followed as soldiers fled back to the English border some 150 kilometres away.

Robert I now turned the tables on the English and launched devastating raids into northern England. He even invaded Ireland, where his brother was crowned king by exuberant Irish anxious to gain their own independence.

King Robert also achieved diplomatic victories. In 1320, Scottish nobles and influential people submitted the Declaration of Arbroath to Pope John XXII in which they asserted that Robert was their rightful monarch and pressed Scotland's status as an independent kingdom. Four years later, the Pope recognised Robert as king of an independent Scotland and withdrew the excommunication order imposed earlier.

The Declaration of Arbroath is one of the most important documents ever written, being the first ever declaration of independence by any nation, and containing remarkably advanced ideas in the areas of nationhood and kingship: arguably providing some of the intellectual background to the later American and French Revolutions.

In 1327, the English deposed Edward II in favour of his son, Edward III, who had no desire to continue the fight against Scotland. In Edinburgh and again in Northampton, Edward III concluded a peace treaty by which England renounced all claims to sovereignty over Scotland. The peace treaty successfully concluded Scotland's thirty years of wars for independence. Robert had achieved everything he had set out to do.

King Robert I of Scotland died at his house in Cardross in 1328 of a serious illness described by some as leprosy. He requested that his heart be taken to the Holy Land, but it only got as far as Spain where his trusted friend, Sir Douglas Stewart, was slain in fighting with the Moors. It was returned to Scotland and buried in Melrose Abbey, while the rest of Robert's body had already been buried in Dunfermline Abbey. Robert I left behind a well-ordered nation at peace with its neighbour for the first time in decades. Unfortunately, that peace would be broken within the year and warfare would continue at irregular intervals over the next three centuries.

JOHN KNOX (1514–1572)

RELIGIOUS REFORMER AND FOUNDER OF PRESBYTERIANISM

It is generally accepted that John Knox was born in Haddington, East Lothian around 1514, where a statue in his honour was erected in the late 1900s outside a school in his name.

His father, William Knox of Haddingtonshire, was a farmer who had survived the disastrous Scottish defeat at the Battle of Flodden (1513). Knox was probably educated at the grammar school in Haddington. At this time, the priesthood was the only path open for those whose inclinations were academic rather than mercantile or agricultural. He was educated in Divinity by John Major, who was regarded as one of the greatest scholars of his time. Major taught at both the universities of Glasgow and of St Andrews during the time that Knox was being taught, so it is uncertain which university he attended.

Around 1540, Knox was ordained into the Roman Catholic priesthood, then the only officially sanctioned religion operating in

Britain. Rather than taking up a position in a parish, he became a tutor to two wealthy families located around Edinburgh. It is thought that he was influenced by the heads of these households who had secretly embraced the ideas of religious reformation that was sweeping Europe at the time.

In 1544 Knox became close friends with, and indeed a bodyguard to, George Wishart, a religious reformer who had just returned from Europe to spread the Reformation in his native Scotland. Wishart was arrested by the Catholic Church, tried for heresy and burnt at the stake.

At the time the Catholic Church owned more than half the land in Scotland and received an annual income that was estimated to be eighteen times greater than that of the Crown. It was also one of the most corrupt churches in Europe with many priests openly taking bribes and having common-law families. Alcohol abuse and lack of spiritual vigour seemed endemic and finally Knox had had enough. He publicly professed his belief in the Protestant faith and fled to St Andrews which was then a place of refuge for a growing band of Protestant reformers.

In July 1547, St Andrews was seized by the French, and Knox became a galley-slave for the next nineteen months. There he experienced hardships and miseries which are said to have permanently damaged his health. Staunchly Catholic, France was unrelenting in its suppression of the preaching of Reformation that was spreading through the rest of northern Europe at the time. The French on board the galley threatened the Scottish Protestants with torture if they did not give proper signs of reverence when mass was performed on the ship.

Knox refused to kiss a statue of the Virgin Mary, throwing it in the sea when his captors were not looking. The captors did not discover who had actually thrown the statue overboard, but rather than punishing everyone it was felt wiser to ignore the provocation. Later in life when recalling this incident in his memoir, John Knox took great delight in writing that there were no more attempts after that to submit the Scots to 'idolatry', as he put it.

The English Government, recently converted to its own form of Protestantism, eventually intervened to release Knox and the other prisoners, but he felt he could not return to Scotland as the Catholic Church there had launched a purge of all Nonconformist preachers. For the next ten years he submitted to voluntary exile which was shared equally in England and on the continent. While in Europe he met with the great religious reformer John Calvin, with whom he had similar ideas and who preached an increasing radical liturgy to the English-speaking refugee congregation in Geneva.

In August of 1555, Knox returned to Scotland where he preached an Evangelical doctrine in various parts of the country. He also married Margery Bowes, daughter of Richard Bowes, captain of Norham Castle located on the border between Scotland and England. But the timing of Knox's return was not favourable. In 1556, he was summonsed to appear before a Catholic court in Edinburgh to answer a charge of heresy. Remembering the fate of his predecessor Wishart only twelve years earlier, Knox wisely returned to Geneva with his new wife and his mother-in-law. He had been in Scotland for only nine months.

Back in Geneva again, Knox resumed his ministry and published a criticism against Mary of Guise, the mother to the future Queen of Scotland, whom Knox believed was wrong to adhere to her Catholic faith. The treatise was called, *The First Blast of the Trumpet Against the Monstrous Regiment of Women*. In it he wrote 'to promote a woman to bear rule, superiority, dominion or empire above any realm is repugnant to nature, contrary to God.' Even though his words were aimed at Mary of Guise, when Elizabeth Tudor became Queen of England later the same year, she was deeply offended and never forgave him.

Knox returned to Scotland in 1559, and the following year the Scottish Parliament with the guidance and urging of Knox enacted legislation ('Confession of Faith') which replaced Catholicism with Protestantism as the official national religion of Scotland. Knox was appointed minister of St Giles, Edinburgh, the main church in Scotland and, assisted by five other ministers, drew up the *Book of Discipline* outlining important doctrinal issues and establishing regulations of the new Church. This new Church was based on Knox's own experiences in Geneva and heavily borrowed from the work of John Calvin.

At its root, the new religion rejected the authority of the Pope and the entire hierarchy of the Catholic Church and insisted that no man should come between an individual and God. Priests were replaced with ministers and each parish was governed by a Kirk Session (elders) instead of Bishops, Archbishops, Cardinals and ultimately the Pope.

The new Church placed great importance upon education and performing good deeds. To this day followers of the Church of Scotland (often called Presbyterians, from the late Latin *presbyter* meaning 'church elder') still consider it is important to improve society through social justice and reform. Education, hard work, frugality, and performing good deeds was the Protestant work ethic that John Knox laid as the foundation stone of the Church of Scotland.

The Catholic Mary, Queen of Scots (*see* p. 26) returned from France in 1561 and was subjected to an unrelenting onslaught from

Knox who was at the peak of his powers and influence. Although unsuccessful in persuading Mary to recant her Catholic faith, the torrid and sometimes vitriolic haranguing from both the pulpit and in person showed the rest of Scotland that a humble minister was not afraid to stand up to a queen. It was about this time that Knox started writing his major work, *The History of the Reformation in Scotland*. It would take him another six years to complete and unfortunately highlighted a vain streak in his character by emphasising his own contribution at the expense of the efforts of others.

Shortly after returning to Edinburgh, John Knox lost his much-loved and helpful young wife, Margery, who left him two sons. But it was only a few years later that he married a second time, which drew much unwanted attention to himself. First, the bride was Margaret Stewart, who was remotely connected to the royal family, but even more so, she was only seventeen, while he was fifty. Margaret would eventually bear him three daughters.

At this time the Reformer lived a very laborious life. Knox was much engrossed with the public affairs of the national Church, and at the same time devoted to his work as a parish minister. In 1571 he suffered what would now be considered a stroke and his physical activities slowed significantly. For the next year he lived in a house provided by the local Edinburgh authority, surrounded by family and friends.

Knox died in 1572, leaving his wife and five children very little money. True to his creed, he lived frugally and it was only the awarding of a stipend from the Scottish authorities that saved his surviving family from poverty. He claimed proudly in his will, 'None have I corrupted, none have I defrauded; merchandise have I not made.' At his funeral the Regent of Scotland said of him, 'Here lyeth a man who in his life never feared the face of man. Who hath been often threatened with dagger, but yet hath ended his dayes in peace and honour.'

It would have been easy for the Anglican Church of England to have become the national religion of Scotland when the Catholic Church was removed in 1560. After all, the Church of England had been in power since 1534 and was well-placed to expand north across the border. The singular great contribution to Scotland's history is that John Knox created a home-grown Scottish Presbyterian religion to replace Catholicism, rather than Anglicanism.

For assuring the dominance of a Scottish religion, Knox contributed to the formation of a uniquely Scottish character where hard work, frugality, education and the performance of good deeds still dominate the culture and mindset of Scotland today.

But an even greater reason for including John Knox in the list of Scottish heroes is the fact that the Church of Scotland, which he founded, has extended its reach far beyond Scottish boundaries.

Scotsmen and Scotswomen imbued with the Protestant work ethic of Presbyterianism have spread their considerable influence to all reaches of the globe – setting up churches, schools, hospitals, governments and businesses wherever they went. The Church that the firebrand preacher John Knox of Haddington created and the beliefs he built into it from the beginning has gone on to influence the minds, bodies and spirits of countless millions around the world.

Presbyterian beliefs have even influenced the constitutions of several countries, including America, where the Declaration of Independence and the Constitution were framed by many Scottish Protestants who had risen to prominence in America.

MARY, QUEEN OF SCOTS
(1542–1587)

TRAGIC MONARCH
OF SCOTLAND

Mary was born at the magnificent Linlithgow Palace, in West Lothian, Scotland. It was the royal house of the Stewarts and was set in parkland overlooking a loch on the main road between the strategically important castles in Edinburgh and Stirling. Mary was the daughter of King James V of Scotland and his second wife Mary of Guise, originally from Lorraine, France. She was also in line for the throne of England as she was the granddaughter of Margaret Tudor and was next in line after the children of Henry VIII.

Her father, James V, had been wounded at the defeat of the Scots army at the Battle of Solway Moss on 24 November 1542 and he died six days after the birth of his daughter. There were no other children to take the throne, so Mary was crowned Queen of the Scots at Stirling Castle a few months later in 1543, while still a baby. A relative and claimant to the Scottish throne, James Hamilton, 2nd Earl of Arran was appointed Mary's regent.

At this time in Scotland, the reformation of the Church was just beginning and although many nobles had rejected Catholicism in favour of becoming Protestants, some conversions were cynical and insincere. James Hamilton, the infant queen's guardian, was a case in point. He was nominally a Protestant who had been arranging the marriage of Mary to Prince Edward, the son of Henry VIII and Protestant heir to the English throne.

However, a pro-French and pro-Catholic faction led by Mary's mother, Mary of Guise, gained ascendency in the Scottish court and withdrew from marriage discussions with England. Hamilton then changed sides and secretly met with the Catholic Cardinal Beaton of St Andrews, recanted his conversion to Protestantism, and commenced arrangements for an alternative marriage of the young queen to the Catholic Dauphin (heir to the French throne), the future King Francis II.

Henry VIII of England was not impressed and invaded Scotland twice to enforce the marriage between Mary and his son Edward, in what became known as the 'Rough Wooing'. Between 1544 and 1550, much of south-eastern Scotland was devastated, in particular Edinburgh, Musselburgh, Haddington and Dunbar. If anything, English aggression drove Scotland further into the arms of their old ally the French.

Meanwhile, in Scotland, matters between Protestant and Catholic had come to a head. With Protestant England wreaking havoc in south-east Scotland and Catholic France being sympathetic, Beaton thought the time was right to crush Scottish Protestantism once and for all. He had several heretics arrested, tried and in the case of the Protestant leader – George Wishart – executed. But he had misjudged the mood of the people. In 1546, he was dragged from his bed at St Andrews and assassinated. From this point on, the influence of Catholicism in Scotland started to wane in favour of a local form of Protestantism championed by a thirty-two-year-old firebrand preacher and self-appointed leader of the new Scottish Church, John Knox (*see* p. 20).

In 1547 and again in 1548 victories by the English during the Rough Wooing resulted in Mary having to be moved repeatedly for her own safety. Henri II of France offered a safe haven for Mary and troops to repel the English in return for a formal written agreement that Mary would marry his son and heir to the French throne. The agreement was duly signed and Mary was sent to France along with her mother and a small retinue of court followers. The conflict was only brought to a halt when a sizeable French force landed in support of Scotland and Henry VIII of England was told that Mary was now in France and formally promised in marriage to the Dauphin of France.

Over the next decade Mary and Francis (François in French) grew up together in the court of France and when fifteen and fourteen respectively, were married in Notre Dame Cathedral to much pomp and ceremony.

In 1559, within a year of their marriage, Henri II, the old King of France died as a result of an accident and was succeeded by Francis II, which automatically made Mary queen of both France and Scotland. Many in France realised the marriage and the sudden elevation of Francis to the throne was a great political victory over France's arch-enemy Britain. The joining of the royal households of France and Scotland meant that France, the much stronger of the two kingdoms, had effectively gained access to the northern third of Great Britain. This presented France with the delicious possibility of a classical pincer attack on England from the directions of both France and Scotland.

Unfortunately, before any plans could be put in place, King Francis II of France died suddenly in 1560 from an ear infection, leaving Mary an eighteen-year-old childless widow. She was then stripped of her French crown in accordance to the marriage contract entered into less than two years earlier. She had little choice but to leave France and return to Scotland, a country that had undergone many changes in the twelve years Mary had been away. However, before she arrived, the Scottish Parliament took the opportunity of legislating Protestantism as the state religion and started what would become known worldwide as the Presbyterian Church. When Mary stepped ashore on Scottish land in 1560, she was a Catholic monarch of a Protestant country.

In a strange twist of fate, with the death of England's Henry VIII in 1547 and the accession of young Elizabeth I to the throne of England, Mary was now heir presumptive to the English throne. As both queens settled into their separate reigns a slow realisation began to grow on Elizabeth that Mary was a threat to her longevity on the English throne.

In Scotland, Mary made it clear from the day of her return she would continue to practise her Catholic faith, much to the displeasure of John Knox who took to berating her publicly. Normally this type of direct offence to a monarch during the sixteenth century would result in the arrest of the culprit, or worse, but Mary tolerated Knox's outbursts without the slightest intention of changing faith.

One of her first tasks as a widowed and childless queen was to find a husband to continue the Stewart line. (She chose to spell the name 'Stuart' to ensure it was correctly pronounced by the French; the two spellings became interchangeable for a time.) Despite other potential marriages into the royal houses of France, Spain and even England, she married her first cousin, Henry Stewart, Lord

Darnley, in 1565. Darnley was a hopeless choice and Mary married him out of love against the advice of almost everyone in the Scottish court. Mary even had to go to the extreme step of putting down a small rebellion organised by some nobles who were violently opposed to this union.

It did not take long for Lord Darnley to prove what everyone, except the Queen, suspected. Within months he was carousing with drinking partners, breaking out into fits of violence and whoring through the brothels of Edinburgh. Driven by jealousy against Mary's Italian secretary, David Rizzio, Darnley and a handful of co-conspirators, brutally murdered Rizzio at Holyrood Palace in front of Mary. It was 1566 and Mary was six months pregnant at the time.

Thinking that a coup was unfolding and her own life was under threat, Mary fled to Dunbar Castle, where the Earl of Bothwell met her with a hastily assembled army of 4,000 which she then used to hunt down the perpetrators. The wrongdoers were rounded up in short order and begged the Queen for forgiveness. Unusually, their request was granted, perhaps because the Queen could not bring herself to execute her own husband.

In 1566 Mary gave birth to James, who would eventually unite the royal households of Scotland and England as James VI of Scotland and James I of England (*see* p. 37). A few months later, Darnley, now suffering from syphilis and anxious to seek a reconciliation with Mary arranged to meet at a house just outside Edinburgh's city walls to sort matters out. On the night of 10 February 1567 while Mary was attending a wedding, a huge gunpowder explosion blew the house to bits. The next morning the bodies of Darnley and a manservant were found in the courtyard. Their deaths were not caused from the explosion, but either from strangulation or being smothered.

Rumours started flying about Edinburgh that implicated Bothwell; Catholics; agents from overseas and even Mary herself in Lord Darnley's murder. Bothwell was arrested and trialled but no prosecution witnesses turned up (they had been bought off) and Bothwell was acquitted. A few months later Mary accompanied Bothwell to his castle in Dunbar where she stayed for some weeks. Some said Mary had been abducted and raped, others said she went willingly as they had become lovers some time earlier.

Whatever the truth of this strange episode, it inflamed an already incendiary situation. To add even further fuel to the scandal, Bothwell obtained a lightning divorce from his wife of only a year and within a week married Mary in 1567. This was too much for the people of Scotland who were revolted by the thought that their Queen had possibly married her husband's murderer who had also possibly abducted and raped her. Underlying everything was Mary's adherence to Catholicism in the face of John Knox's furious opposition to her and her faith.

A large force of scandalised Scots confronted Mary and Bothwell and arrested them. She was imprisoned in Loch Leven Castle, Perthshire, an impregnable fortress in the middle of a large loch. There she was given the choice of abdicating in favour of her one-year-old son, James VI, or being put to death. She chose to abdicate, but within a year had escaped from her prison and raised an army to take back her throne; however, she was defeated at the Battle of Langside in 1568.

Rather than escape to France, she unwisely chose to flee to England, where she was promptly imprisoned by Queen Elizabeth, who by now quite clearly regarded Mary as a threat to her throne. Mary never returned to Scotland, and never saw her son again. Instead, she spent the following nineteen years in captivity in various English castles. Elizabeth would have quite happily allowed Mary to live in comfortable captivity for the rest of her life, but with breathtaking naivety, Mary allowed herself to become involved in plots to kill Elizabeth, forcing the Queen of England eventually to sign her death warrant in 1587. Less than a week after, the executioner's axe fell on her slender neck at Fotheringhay Castle in Northamptonshire.

At one point, Mary Queen of Scots reigned over two nations: Scotland and France and could have quite easily ruled over two more – England and Ireland – if circumstances had taken a slightly different course. But a lack of political prowess, three failed marriages and an intense rivalry with the Queen of England meant she died almost as dramatically as she lived: executed in 1587, with all her possessions burnt by order of the English Government.

In effect, the story of Mary Queen of Scots is both a personal tragedy for the Queen and a national tragedy for Scotland as both were preyed upon by people and forces much more powerful than either could resist.

JOHN NAPIER (1550–1617)

MATHEMATICIAN WHO INVENTED LOGARITHMS

Napier was born into a wealthy and influential family on the outskirts of Edinburgh, where their ancestral home of Merchiston Castle stands. Napier's father – Sir Archibald Napier – was Master of the Scottish Mint and carried the title of 7th Laird of Merchiston.

Napier was tutored at home before being sent, at the age of thirteen, to the University of St Andrews, where he became interested in theology. He then travelled to Europe to continue his studies. In 1571, when he was twenty-one, Napier returned to Edinburgh and the following year married Elizabeth Stirling, daughter of the Scottish mathematician James Stirling. They had two children together before Elizabeth died in 1579. Napier later married Agnes Chisholm, and they had ten children. On the death of his father in 1608, Napier inherited the family estates and moved with his wife and children to Merchiston Castle, where he was to live the rest of his life.

It was his writing on non-mathematical matters that first brought Napier to public notice. In 1593 he published a book criticising Catholicism, entitled *A Plaine Discovery of the Whole Revelation of St John*. Napier was strongly anti-Catholic, as was the entire Napier family, and being independently wealthy allowed John to indulge himself in vitriolic writing. Most of Europe was in religious turmoil at the time as Catholicism and Protestantism fought over the hearts and minds of the people. Scotland itself had only adopted Protestantism in 1560 and yet many Scots still craved for the return of the Catholic Church as the official state religion of Scotland. At the time there were rumours of a threatened invasion of Scotland by Catholic Spain and this fuelled his fanatical passion. The rumours proved false and Napier turned his attention to managing his father's estate.

As a person of intense curiosity and intelligence, he paid much attention to improving the productivity of Merchiston estate. He experimented with fertilisers, improved drainage and constructed devices to more accurately survey the extent of his land. He was also an amateur astronomer and it was while engaged upon the difficult task of calculating large astronomical numbers that an idea came to him to simplify the process, as he explained in his book *Mirifici logarithmorum canonis descriptio*: 'Seeing there is nothing that is so troublesome to mathematical practice . . . than the multiplications, divisions, square and cubical extractions of great numbers, which besides the tedious expense of time are for the most part subject to many slippery errors, I began therefore to consider in my mind [how] I might remove those hindrances.'

Napier would spend the next twenty years perfecting his idea into a branch of mathematics called logarithms.

Napier realised that all numbers could be expressed in what

is now called exponential form, meaning 8 could be expressed as 2^3 and 16 as 2^4. What made logarithms so useful was the fact that multiplication and division could be reduced to simple addition and subtraction. For example, 10^2 multiplied by 10^5 can be expressed at $10^{(2+5)}$ or 10^7. Much easier than 100 times 100,000.

Napier first wrote about this discovery in 1614, using Latin which was then the normal language of scientific writing. The book was titled *Mirifici logarithmorum canonis descriptio* (*A Description of the Wonderful Canon of Logarithms*). It was a brilliant and revolutionary breakthrough in mathematics. Henry Biggs was the leading mathematician in England at the time and he was so impressed by Napier's innovation that he travelled four days from London crammed in a coach to speak with him in Edinburgh. This led to a cooperative improvement in which logarithms became based on the figure 10.

Napier was not infallible though. He applied his mathematical expertise to the Book of Revelation in the Bible and predicted that the end of the world would come in either 1688 or 1700. His own death in 1617 prevented him discovering the error in his calculations.

Napier presented a mechanical means of simplifying calculations in his *Rabdologiae* (*Study of rods*), published in 1617. He described a method of multiplication using 'numbering rods' with numbers marked off on them. The reason for publishing the work is given by Napier in the dedication, where he says that so many of his friends, to whom he had shown the numbering rods, were so pleased with them that they were already becoming widely used, even beginning to be used in foreign countries.

Napier, however, will be remembered for making one of the most important contributions to the advancement of knowledge.

He passed away in 1617, just as his reputation as one of the world's greatest mathematicians was beginning to take form.

Today one of Edinburgh's universities, Napier University, is named after him and is built around his family home of Merchiston Castle.

Virtually all major advances in scientific achievement over the past 500 years, especially if they involved laborious and accurate calculations, would have been very difficult, if not impossible, without Napier's discovery of logarithms. Whether it was nuclear energy, astronauts landing on the moon, epidemiological studies to prevent plagues, stock market analysis or Einstein's Theory of Relativity – all were achieved through logarithms.

JAMES VI OF SCOTLAND AND I OF ENGLAND (1566–1625)

FIRST KING OF GREAT BRITAIN AND IRELAND

James (full name Charles James Stewart) succeeded to the Scottish throne when he was just thirteen months old, after his mother Mary, Queen of Scots (*see* p. 26) was forced to abdicate in his favour. Being under age, he was supposed to be assisted in his reign by a regent until he became of age to rule on his own. In reality his guardians (he ended up with no less than four) often treated him as a pawn in their own schemes to grab power. James grew up in Stirling Castle where his youth and adolescence was manipulated, sometimes threatened and always far from normal.

The first regent was the Queen's half-brother, James Stewart, 1st Earl of Moray who had forced Mary to abdicate. He was murdered in 1570 by supporters of Mary, Queen of Scots. The Earl of Lennox, grandfather of the young James was appointed regent in his place, but he too was killed when another group of supporters of Mary raided Stirling Castle a year later and shot him. The third regent died of a mysterious illness in 1572 and was replaced by James Douglas, the 4th Earl of Morton.

In many respects the Earl of Morton was an energetic and capable regent and mentor of James VI. He settled a bruising civil war and ushered in a period of relative calm in Scotland. But his influence came to a sticky end when he was belatedly convicted of complicity in the murder of Lord Darnley, an event that had occurred thirteen years earlier. It was James VI who signed Morton's death warrant and in a further strange ironic twist Morton was executed by the same primitive guillotine which he had personally introduced into Scotland.

James, now fifteen years of age, decided that he was old enough to rule on his own. Apart from the precarious nature being a ruler of Scotland was at the time, it could be said that the various influences on James helped him grow up to be a shrewd, wary intellectual who managed to reconcile the warring factions among his nobility with such success that he has been described as 'the most effective ruler Scotland ever had'.

As well as being the son of Queen Mary of Scotland, he was also the great-great-grandson of Henry VII of England. When Elizabeth I, the last Tudor monarch of England and Ireland died without issue in 1603, King James VI of Scotland then assumed the title of James I, King of England and Ireland and ruled conjointly.

The separate kingdoms were individual sovereign states, with their own parliaments, judiciary and laws, but James managed to negotiate his way through the inconsistencies and differences with a high degree of skill. He wanted a strong centralised authority and was a major advocate of a single parliament for England and Scotland. However, this proposal was rebuffed by both the English and Scottish parliaments.

Under his reign, the 'Golden Age' of Elizabethan literature and the performing arts continued, with James supporting playwrights such as William Shakespeare and Ben Jonson. Poems from John Donne and Walter Raleigh were making people sigh and philosopher Sir Francis Bacon was writing about deep, thought-provoking issues. James contributed to the growing pool of British literature by writing two books himself, confirming he was a talented scholar in his own right.

Perhaps his greatest achievement in the field of arts was his sponsorship of an English-language version of the Bible to make it accessible to all his subjects. In some places in the English-speaking world the Authorised King James Version of the Bible (published in 1611) is still used today. The period of his reign in England was named the Jacobean era (after the Latin form of the name James) and was used to signal a dynastic change in the ruling house of the monarchy from Tudor to Jacobean.

There were two standout features of his reign that were to have lasting consequences on Britain for centuries. One initiative can be viewed in a positive light, while the other has only caused long-lasting turmoil.

In 1606 James VI granted a charter to establish the first permanent British settlement in the New World. It was called Jamestown in honour of the King and would lead to many new colonies being established along the eastern coast of North America. A century and a half later the now prosperous colonies would declare their independence from Britain and go on to become the most powerful nation in the world.

His other initiative was not as successful. James was a committed Protestant and he encouraged the migration of Protestants from Scotland and England to Ireland by giving out land grants and titles, an action which suppressed and in some cases dispossessed the Catholic Irish. The Irish sectarian conflicts which have plagued Ireland for centuries can be traced back directly to this scheme instigated by James.

King James died in 1625, after a series of illnesses, leaving three adult children behind: Henry, who died of typhoid at eighteen, Elizabeth and Charles (who succeeded to the Crown and became King Charles I). James was nearly fifty-nine years old when he died and had been a king for all but one of these years.

DAVID HUME (1711–1776)

PHILOSOPHER, HISTORIAN AND ESSAYIST

Hume, regarded as one of the most important figures of the Scottish Enlightenment in the second half of the eighteenth century and also in the history of Western philosophy, was born into a moderately wealthy family in Edinburgh. He had an older brother and a younger sister. David's father was a lawyer and estate-owner, and the young Hume spent much of his time shared between Edinburgh and the family's rural property, called Ninewells, near Chirnside in the Scottish Borders.

When Hume was only two his father passed away, leaving his wife to raise the three children. When it was realised that David was a highly gifted and intelligent lad, he was sent off to Edinburgh University at the age of about eleven. It was presumed by his mother that the young Hume would study law, but he had other ideas. He studied Latin and Greek, and read history and literature, but it was the writings of classical philosophers, especially Cicero, that caught his attention and sowed the seed of what would become his lifelong obsession.

As far as Hume was concerned, the university was a place for learning rather than somewhere to be taught. He said, 'There is nothing to be learned from a professor, which is not to be met within books.' He completed his studies in record time and left the university at the age of fourteen (or fifteen in some biographies) to continue his lifelong quest for knowledge in the real world.

He appears to have had an uneventful adolescence, but even at this early age he was beginning to draw some tentative conclusions about life. When he was only eighteen years old, he complained that anyone familiar with philosophy realised it is embroiled in 'endless disputes'. Hume believed philosophers advanced theories to fit their pre-existing beliefs, rather than based on observing human nature. The youthful Hume resolved to avoid this mistake in his own work.

In 1734, when in his early twenties, Hume worked for a few months in Bristol earning a living as a clerk for a sugar importer, after which he moved to France to continue developing the ideas which were forming in his mind. He finally settled in La Flèche, in Anjou province (now Pays de la Loire). The great French philosopher, Descartes had attended the Jesuit Collège Royal Henry-Le-Grand there a century before, and the educational institution was still a magnet for young thinkers when Hume arrived. Hume learnt French, debated with the students and the Jesuit teachers who ran the college and, between 1734 and 1737, drafted *A Treatise of Human Nature*, which was to be the first of many pieces of writing that would come from his insightful and powerful mind.

Hume returned to England in 1737 to ready the *Treatise* for the press, at the insistence of his publisher, deleting some of the more controversial aspects of his ideas from the manuscript. When published in 1739, *Treatise of Human Nature* was not a commercial success, but it did attract criticism that would continue repeatedly for the rest of his life.

Beginning with the concept that one's ideas of the world should be based on observation (an early form of scientific research) which then leads to a conclusion, Hume wrote in *Treatise* that he observed that mankind was driven by desire, not reason. Even though his logic was sound and his observations strong, this was a radical, even a dangerous revolutionary concept at the time. The prevailing thought was that man was a rational creature, struggling to follow God's predetermined yet unknown path for us all. Hume rejected this, saying famously, 'Reason is, and ought only to be, a slave of the passions.'

In essence, Hume placed the irrational and emotional man at the centre of his thinking and believed the best way to understand this creature was through scientific study and observable fact, not blind faith.

Along with rejecting the prevailing God-centred construct of the universe, Hume also rejected the concept of God itself and in a world that was so totally absorbed with religion, this was a step too far for many conservative and devout people. A number of contemporaries denounced his writings as works of scepticism and atheism. Without God at the centre of the universe and our understanding of it, we have nothing and would be nothing, they argued. Hume responded that it was perhaps God that did not exist and in this way the debate very quickly went from one of philosophy to one of religion.

Returning to his home in Ninewells, Scotland, Hume published two volumes of *Essays, Moral and Political* in 1741 and 1742. In it, Hume proclaimed the dominance of human reason over religious faith at a time when religious dogma was followed by most people without question. The publications were modestly successful and with it, his reputation as a courageous modern thinker grew. And so too did the opposition.

In 1745, Hume applied for the Chair of Ethics and Pneumatical Philosophy (today it would be known as Psychology) at Edinburgh. His reputation provoked much vocal opposition and his application was eventually rejected, even though he was the most qualified candidate. Six years later, in 1751, Hume stood for the vacant Chair of Logic at Glasgow, only to be turned down again. He never held an academic post.

He was one of forty-two men of the Edinburgh Defence Volunteers to turn out to oppose the Jacobite army in 1745 and in that same year he accepted a position as tutor to the twenty-five year old 3rd Marquess of Annandale in 1745. Having already demonstrated his opposition to the Jacobite Rebellion, it was probably safer for Hume to wait out developments in the relative safety of the Marquess's estate at Craigie Hall, Linlithgow in the Scottish countryside. Unfortunately the young Marquess was mentally unstable (he would later be declared a lunatic) and Hume managed to extricate himself from this situation a little over a year later.

Next, Hume accepted an invitation from his cousin, Lieutenant-General James St Clair, to be his Secretary on a military expedition against the French in Quebec. But the fleet never left England. Finally, in 1748, Hume accompanied St Clair on a lengthy diplomatic mission to Austria and Italy at the same time when his *Philosophical Essays concerning Human Understanding* was released in Britain, which was reworked and reprinted as part of a larger piece of work published as *An Enquiry concerning Human Understanding* (1748).

In 1751, this *Enquiry* was joined by a second, *An Enquiry concerning the Principles of Morals*. Hume described the second *Enquiry* as his best work. More essays, under the heading of *Political Discourses* appeared in 1752.

In 1753 he was offered the position of Librarian to the Edinburgh Faculty of Advocates, a relatively obscure and modestly paid position, but which did provide him with the opportunity to work steadily on another project that had been forming in the back of his mind for some time.

The *History of England* was a massive undertaking comprising a million words dealing with Great Britain from the invasion of Julius Caesar to the Glorious Revolution of 1688 that would be issued in six volumes from 1754 to 1762. It became the bestseller of its day and produced enough income finally to make Hume independently wealthy.

But even as a librarian, he ruffled conservative feathers by banning certain books he disagreed with. Amid controversy and even an abortive attempt to have him excommunicated from the Church of Scotland, Hume resigned in 1756.

By 1763, the ever restless Hume decided it was time for a break and accepted the position of secretary to the British Ambassador to France. Hume's reputation had preceded him and he became the 'darling' of the Parisian gentlemen's clubs and salons. His time in France coincided with the very early rumblings of what would become the French Revolution in 1786. He had lengthy discussions on politics, life, religion and society with the leading French intellectuals of the day, including Voltaire and Rousseau, and found his stay in Paris most stimulating. Refreshed and reinvigorated, he returned to Britain in 1766.

Hume spent a year in London in the public service as Under-

Secretary for Scottish Affairs in Westminster and finally returned to Edinburgh in 1769, where he would stay for the rest of his life. He built himself a home in Edinburgh's New Town where he enjoyed dining and conversing with influential men and women of the city. During this period he was considered by many to be the intellectual force behind the Scottish Enlightenment that was taking shape with Edinburgh at its epicentre.

When not entertaining, Hume spent considerable time revising his previous material and working on his next major piece, *Dialogues concerning Natural Religion*, which was published by a nephew in 1779, three years after Hume's death.

He was diagnosed with intestinal cancer in 1775 and prepared for the inevitable with the same customary cheer and goodwill that characterised his life. On his deathbed Hume said he did not fear death, although he must have been in much pain. By all reports he died in 1776 satisfied with what he had achieved in his life. He was entombed on the east side of Calton Hill overlooking Edinburgh's New Town.

Hume's four major philosophical works – *A Treatise of Human Nature* (1739–1740), the *Enquiries concerning Human Understanding* (1748) and *Concerning the Principles of Morals* (1751), as well as his posthumously published *Dialogues concerning Natural Religion* (1779) – remain widely and deeply influential to this day. In addition, Hume also wrote a number of books on topics ranging from history to biography.

David Hume's primary project was to develop a science of human nature, a science stripped of dogma and based on observable fact and careful argument. His theories were the immediate forerunner to the views of John Stuart Mill. He thus paved the way for cognitive science, a vibrant interdisciplinary enterprise combining philosophy, psychology, neuroscience, and artificial intelligence. But his ideas extended well beyond the individual mind, into fundamental questions about morals, society, political and economic behaviour, and religious belief.

Hume's influence was evident in the moral philosophy and economic writings of his close friend Adam Smith (*see* p. 56). Kant reported that Hume's work woke him from his 'dogmatic slumbers', and Jeremy Bentham remarked that reading Hume 'caused the scales to fall' from his eyes. Charles Darwin regarded Hume's work as a central influence on his theory of evolution.

In the twentieth century it was Hume again who inspired first Bertrand Russell and then Karl Popper in their explorations of the meaning of life.

Now, in the twenty-first century, Hume remains the most fertile and provocative of all the great thinkers. He continues to influence ideas in epistemology, ethics, metaphysics, philosophy of action, language, religion, and even mathematics.

A recent poll of academics voted Hume as the Scot who had made the greatest impact on Scotland in the last thousand years. This is a huge statement, but it is nevertheless an understatement. Hume was not just important to Scotland; his influence has shaped, directed and led thinking around the entire world. It would be more accurate to say David Hume was a Scot who had one of the greatest impacts on the world over the past thousand years.

FLORA MACDONALD
(1722–1790)

UNLIKELY JACOBITE HERO

Flora was born on the island of South Uist in the Outer Hebrides of Scotland's west coast. She was the daughter of Ranald MacDonald, a tenant farmer and minor leader of the MacDonald clan, who died when she was just two years old. Her mother subsequently married a distant kinsman. When Flora was thirteen, a friend of her mother invited Flora to share the same education she was giving her own daughter. Flora moved to Nunton on the nearby island of Benbecula and there came under the notice and protection of the Chief of the MacDonald clan, another Ranald MacDonald, who had been educated in France where he had become acquainted with Charles Edward Stewart, the exiled young pretender to the British throne.

The MacDonalds were a powerful Highland clan with one of the largest number of followers spread throughout the islands of the inner and Outer Hebrides. After Ranald MacDonald returned to Scotland from France and became Chief of the MacDonald clan (full title, 18th Chief and Captain of Clanranald), he openly declared his support for Prince Charles and the Prince's campaign to be restored to the throne of Britain, by force if necessary.

The Scottish Royal family of Stewart (alternatively Stuart) had ruled the Kingdoms of England, Wales Ireland and Scotland from 1603 until the fourth Stewart in succession was removed in 1688 because of the family's strong links to France and Catholicism, and replaced by William from the Dutch House of Orange. The dethroned king and his descendants had never accepted the family's removal from power and in 1715 there had been an unsuccessful attempt to seize the throne by armed struggle. By 1745 it was clear to many that the next generation of Stewarts was on the point of a similar attempt.

After James II was deposed in 1688, the Stewart cause and its supporters, whether backing James in 1715 or his son Charles in 1745, were commonly and derogatorily referred to as Jacobites.

In the 1740s, Flora spent three years in Edinburgh continuing her education, learning how to make polite conversation and conduct herself in the best Edinburgh society. It would be called a 'finishing school' in today's terms. In early 1745, there was much agitation and unrest across Scotland as it was rumoured that the return to Scotland of Prince Stewart, or Bonnie Prince Charlie as he was better known, was imminent. Meanwhile, Flora, now twenty-three, went back home to the island of Benbecula in the Outer Hebrides.

Suddenly, in July 1745 the Prince did actually return, landing in western Scotland where many Highlanders enthusiastically flocked to his banner, while others refused to do so. Nevertheless, having gathered a small army of some 4,000 men, Charles Edward Stewart, the Bonnie Prince, marched to Edinburgh with more supporters swelling the numbers along the way. This included

Ranald MacDonald of Clanranald who was one of the first to swear his allegiance to the Prince.

He and hundreds of his clansmen would remain at the Prince's side, right through to the Battle of Culloden a year later.

The capital rose in wild enthusiasm for the Stewart Prince (although the Castle garrison steadfastly refused to acknowledge him) and shortly after, the Jacobites won a crushing victory over King George's troops at the Battle of Prestonpans. Prince Charles, at the head of what he believed was now an invincible army, struck south to march on London and reclaim his throne. But what followed was a series of failures, misjudgements and internal squabbles, compounded by poor leadership. Prince Charles and his followers were forced to strategically withdraw from England, and wait out a bitterly cold winter in the Scottish Highlands.

In April 1746, in one last attempt to revive their failing fortunes, the Jacobites decided to attack the approaching armies of King George outside Inverness at a place called Culloden Moor. This would be the last pitched battle fought on British soil. It was a hopelessly one-sided battle with sword against musket, and after just forty minutes of slaughter, the Jacobite army was decisively beaten. The Prince managed to escape the battle and with a price of £30,000 on his head, became a hunted man desperate to make his way back to the western islands of Scotland where it was hoped he could pick up a ship for France.

In truth the Rebellion of 1745 was a complete hotchpotch of conflicting interests and agendas. There were as many Scots fighting for George II as there were fighting for Prince Charlie. There were Catholics and Protestants on both sides of the conflict. Scottish Lowlanders and Highlanders supported each cause and sent troops to each side. The French supported, armed and funded the Jacobites, while mercenaries from Germany and Austria fought for King George. There were Irish troops on both sides as well. Finally and most bizarrely, there were even Englishmen fighting and dying on both sides in the rebellion (a regiment of several hundred soldiers had been raised in Manchester that fought on the Jacobite side, while thousands more English soldiers battled for King George).

Underneath the surface of this conflict there were great tectonic changes taking place in society. Britain was changing from an agricultural economy to an industrial one. People were leaving the country and moving to the cities (or overseas) for a better life. A new middle class was emerging that the poor aspired to join, but the upper class felt threatened by. Specifically, in Scotland, the clearing of the Highlands had begun because landowners had found sheep were now more valuable than people. Two centuries of universal, free education was creating the 'Scottish Enlightenment', which would usher in a period of incredible intellectual breakthroughs in Scotland during the second half of the eighteenth century. Society was becoming more tolerant, more democratic and more educated, but, in the cities, also more crowded and unhealthy.

In this context, the Rebellion of 1745 could be seen as the last hurrah of a bygone era; an era of absolute monarchy, religious intolerance and an economy based on the dominance of agriculture and the supremacy of semi-feudal landlords. It was the last bright glow of a flame already fading fast before it was finally extinguished.

But none of this would have even been thought of by young Flora MacDonald when in June 1745 the Prince and a small retinue of supporters unexpectedly turned up seeking refuge and assistance from the MacDonald household at Nunton on the island of Benbecula. The Prince's companion, Captain O'Neill had a plan for the Prince's escape but it required Flora's willing co-operation.

The government had rightly suspected that the Prince might make his way back to the western islands of Scotland for that was where his greatest support was located. They flooded the islands with troops who were systematically scouring every house and barn. The Prince had hidden in a cave for several days prior to arriving at the MacDonald household.

With every ferry and landing-place being guarded and every channel and loch patrolled by boats it was going to be difficult getting the Prince off the island, but there was no choice if he wanted to avoid capture and probable execution. Captain O'Neill's plan was to disguise the Prince as Flora's maidservant and get him on a boat over to the Isle of Skye where there were not as many troops. From Skye, the Prince would journey to nearby Raasay Island where it was thought (later proved falsely that there was a French ship waiting for him.

Flora thought the scheme 'fantastical', but was persuaded to go ahead from a sense of clan loyalty and perhaps by the entreaties of the Prince himself. The commander of the local militia was her stepfather, Hugh MacDonald and she convinced him to issue travel passes for herself, two servants and a crew of six boatmen to sail across to Skye. One of the two servants was meant to be an Irish maid, called 'Betty Burke'; in reality it was Prince Charles Edward Stewart dressed as a female.

The party set sail from Benbecula on 27 June 1746 across the 65 kilometres of open sea to the island of Skye. It rained, then stormed and the small boat was almost swamped by mountainous waves, but after a perilous overnight journey they could see the headlands of Skye.

Just as they were about to make landfall, a detachment of government troops saw them and started firing at them. Flora and her small party were forced back to sea to find another suitable place to land further along the coast. Later that same day they landed safely at Kilbride on Skye and the Prince was hidden in rocks while Flora MacDonald organised assistance for him in the neighbourhood. It was arranged that he be taken to Portree on Skye and from there to Raasay. Before continuing on his journey alone, Charles gave Flora a locket with his portrait and promised they would meet again. She never saw him again.

After another two months of being on the run, Prince Charles eventually made it back to France, sailing from the mainland coast on 20 September 1746. On his return to France, Prince Charles Edward Stewart was the hero of Europe. The story of his bold expedition and romantic escape made him the biggest celebrity of his time. Unfortunately, his life afterwards was one long disappointment. In 1748, he was expelled from France and spent the next forty years involved in, and creating, conspiratorial mischief wherever he went. In the end he died in Rome in 1788, a broken alcoholic, deserted by his wife and followers.

Back in Scotland, Flora MacDonald thought she might have got away with her part in the audacious escape plan, but idle and drunken boasting by the boatmen brought her under suspicion. She was arrested and brought to London for trial, and was imprisoned in the Tower of London, for a time under sentence of death. But when the Act of Indemnity of 1747 pardoned all who were involved in the abortive rebellion, Flora was allowed to return home a free woman.

However, the story of Flora MacDonald does not end here. In 1750, at the age of twenty-eight, she married Allan MacDonald, a captain in the British army. The couple lived on the Isle of Skye where she gave birth to five sons and two daughters.

In 1774, Flora and her family emigrated to North Carolina in the then British colonies of North America. In this regard she was no different from the thousands of other Highland Scots who were willingly or enforcedly leaving their land in search for a better life overseas. During the American War of Independence, Flora's husband, Captain MacDonald, served with the 84th Regiment of Foot (Royal Highlanders) on the British side of the struggle. Flora took an active role in the conflict recruiting Scots living in the colony to support the British Government. Captain MacDonald was captured by the American forces at the Battle of Moore's Creek Bridge (1776) and was held prisoner for two years until released in a prisoner exchange.

After her husband was taken prisoner, Flora remained in hiding while the American Patriots ravaged her family plantation and took all her possessions. When her husband was released from prison late in 1778, they realised there was no future for British loyalists in North America and she returned home with at least some of their sons and daughters to Scotland in a merchant ship. Once the American War of Independence was over, her husband Allan returned to live with her at the family estate in Kingsburgh on the Isle of Skye.

On her return to Scotland, Flora became a celebrity for the folk in the Scottish Highlands. Many romanticised her role as the pretty young maiden who helped her handsome young prince, some even hinting there might have been a physical relationship between them.

Flora MacDonald died at her estate in Kingsburgh in 1790, aged sixty-eight. She was buried in the local cemetery and a statue was erected to her memory in the grounds of Inverness Castle. Perhaps the most enduring legacy the world has of Flora MacDonald is a song that was first published in 1884 and has gone on to be sung the world over. 'The Skye Boat Song' was written by Sir Harold Boulton to an old Scottish tune and deals with Prince Charles's escape on a boat over the seas to Skye. Flora MacDonald figures in the second verse of the tune.

FLORA MACDONALD (1722–1790)

Loud the winds howl, loud the waves roar,
Thunderclaps rend the air;
Baffled, our foes stand by the shore,
Follow they will not dare.

Chorus:
Speed, bonnie boat, like a bird on the wing,
Onward! the sailors cry;
Carry the lad that's born to be King
Over the sea to Skye.

Though the waves leap, so soft shall ye sleep,
Ocean's a royal bed.
Rocked in the deep, Flora will keep
Watch by your weary head.

[*Chorus*]
Many's the lad fought on that day,
Well the claymore could wield,
When the night came, silently lay
Dead on Culloden's field.

[*Chorus*]

For a woman who had during her youth actively participated in a rebellion against the ruling monarch of Britain, it might seem ironic that most of Flora's sons went on to become officers in the British navy and army, while her husband whom she married only three years after being pardoned for aiding Prince Charles to escape, was a serving officer in the British Army.

ADAM SMITH (1723–1790)

PHILOSOPHER AND PIONEER OF CLASSICAL ECONOMICS

Adam Smith was born in Kirkcaldy, Fife in Scotland, the son of a customs officer who had died shortly before Adam was born. Among his friends in Kirkcaldy were Robert Adam and his brothers, who went on to become a family of famous Scottish architects (*see* p. 73). After studying at the Burgh School of Kirkcaldy, he moved from Fife to Glasgow University at the age of fourteen to study moral philosophy. He excelled and in 1740 gained a scholarship to study at Balliol College, Oxford University. However, Smith was not impressed with the teaching at Oxford, which he found dull and boring, being given by tutors who showed little interest in teaching.

Six years later he returned to Edinburgh University to become a lecturer in Rhetoric, which he did so successfully he was appointed to the Chair of Logic at Glasgow University in 1751. He was only twenty-eight years of age.

ADAM SMITH (1723–1790)

The Smith household of his youth was devoutly Christian, but at Oxford he appeared to have lost interest in formal religion and instead adopted a belief in a more natural and personal God that did not require dogma, ritual or miracles. Many other philosophers and thinkers of the time in Europe, Britain and America were influenced by this personal religious philosophy, which it is said helped shape the Enlightenment period of western thought as well as providing the intellectual underpinning for both the French and American Revolutions.

The following year he changed to Professor of Moral Philosophy in 1752. It was about this time that he met Scottish philosopher David Hume (*see* p. 41) who held similar beliefs about many matters, including liberty, free speech and philosophy. The friendship between the two would last a lifetime and go on to become the foundation of the Scottish Enlightenment which flowered in the latter half of the 1700s. The intellectual and personal friendship between Smith and Hume may have been the reason why Smith moved from teaching Logic (the science of reasoning) to Moral Philosophy (dealing with morals and ethics).

Smith's lectures became widely attended and attracted students from all over Europe. He remained in the city for twelve years, at a time when Glasgow was the fulcrum of the tobacco trade between America and Europe. He became a keen observer of human behaviour and one of the conclusions he drew was that an element of mutual benefit was present in how humans interacted with one another. The baker makes money from selling his bread, but the buyer satisfies his hunger by buying the bread. In 1759, Smith expanded on this theory in his first major work, *Theory of Moral Sentiments*, which was published in London to favourable reviews.

There were great social changes taking place in Scotland and the rest of Britain at the time. The Industrial Revolution was beginning to gather momentum. Questions about the rights of the people were being asked. Smith was observing it all unfold in front of him and gradually he became more interested in the political and economic implications of these changes – what would later be coined political economics.

He asked what role government should play, if any, in the lives of its citizens. How should one design these new things called factories; to favour the worker, or the employer, or both? One of the key discoveries Smith observed, was that labour appeared to be the prime factor in productivity and profitability. The prevailing theory of economic philosophy at the time (itself a field of study in its infancy) strongly argued that a nation's wealth rested on how much gold and silver it possessed. However, Smith concluded it was founded instead in the number and quality of its labour force.

In 1763 Smith was offered a well-paid position as tutor to the young Duke of Buccleuch, who came from an extremely wealthy and influential family residing in the Scottish Borders. It was an offer that Smith willingly took on as a test for both student and master. The eighteen-year-old Henry, 3rd Duke of Buccleuch was intelligent, confident and Eton-educated. Smith was forty-one and somewhat reticent and awkward in company. Between 1764 and 1766 Smith and his pupil travelled widely across Europe, coming into contact with many renowned academics of the day, including Voltaire, Rousseau and several others. The young Duke of Buccleuch is credited with helping his tutor socialise and come out of his shell. In turn, Smith fired the Duke with a passion for knowledge. The two would remain lifelong friends, with the Duke expanding that close circle to include Sir Walter Scott (*see* p. 124) in later life.

With a generous pension for life granted to him by the grateful

Duke, Smith returned to Kirkcaldy in 1766 and spent the next decade writing his great work *An Inquiry into the Nature and Causes of the Wealth of Nations*, which was published in 1776. It was deliberately written for the general reader, rather than academics, making it more accessible, more popular and therefore more successful. Apart from consorting with the great philosophical minds of Scotland such as Hume, Smith visited London frequently to discuss his ideas with interested men in literary circles and public life, including Benjamin Franklin, who was greatly impressed with Smith's concepts and wished to introduce them back into the American colonies.

It is not an overstatement to say that *Wealth of Nations* has become one of the most influential books ever written. It was originally published as a five-book series and sought to reveal the nature and cause of a nation's prosperity. As he began to explain the layers of society and human activity, the world's understanding of how society worked started to grow. Smith was an insightful, highly intelligent and keen observer, so his conclusions were powerful, compelling and world changing. For example, he developed the concept of a self-correcting 'invisible hand' at play in all human activity. This concept has largely been ignored by subsequent economists, but for Smith it was at the core of his observations.

These ideas reflect the concept that each person, by looking out for him or herself, inadvertently helps to create the best outcome for all. 'It is not from the benevolence of the butcher, the brewer, or the baker, that we can expect our dinner, but from their regard to their own interest,' Smith wrote in *Wealth of Nations*.

By selling products that people wanted to buy, the butcher, brewer and baker hoped to make money. If they were effective in meeting the needs of their customers, they would enjoy the financial rewards. While they were engaging in their enterprises for the purpose of earning money, they were also providing products that people wanted. Such a system, Smith argued, created wealth not just for the butcher, brewer and baker, but for the nation as a whole.

If an individual business collapsed, another would automatically take its place. If prices rose too much for one product, people would attempt to find a substitute elsewhere. Industries rose and collapsed, only to be replaced by other industries that would also go through the same lifecycle.

Because the economy was essentially self-correcting, it did not require for the most part the heavy hand of government intervention. In this regard he was a firm believer in a 'laissez-faire' free market (little or no government intervention). Yet even here, he accepted there were limits. He was opposed to monopolies (as they worked against a free market), slavery, imperialism and obscene inequality. He supported proportional taxation that taxed the wealthy progressively more than the poor. It is regrettable that these days many modern economists selectively (mis)use Smith's ideas to promote their own view of a world completely free of any governments whatsoever. Extreme capitalism was never advocated by Adam Smith.

He promoted free trade as a way to increase national wealth at a time when this concept was radical, even political heresy. The common belief at the time was that nations should build tariff walls around themselves to prevent inexpensive imports and protect domestic industries. Smith argued forcefully and cogently that this was bad policy for importers and exporters alike. Two centuries later many people, particularly politicians, continue to ignore Adam Smith's theories and argue instead for a return to high tariff walls and domestic industry protection.

ADAM SMITH (1723–1790)

In 1778 Adam Smith was appointed Commissioner of Customs in Scotland and moved with his mother from Kirkcaldy to live in Edinburgh near Edinburgh's Royal Mile. He was still living in Edinburgh when he died twelve years later in 1790. He was buried in the churchyard of Canongate Kirk, off the Royal Mile. The grave has become a place of pilgrimage for economists all over the world.

Smith was elected Lord Rector of Glasgow University in 1787. This position has changed over time, but in the late 1700s was effectively the Head of the University who was voted into the positon by every student, teacher and office holder for a period of two years. In Smith's case it was mainly a ceremonial positon to acknowledge his contribution to the advancement of knowledge and the fact that when he was much younger, he had been a student at Glasgow University.

He continued to write, up until his death, but much of his later work was lost when, at his request, his portfolios, manuscripts and volumes that he was preparing for publication were burnt after his death. The only major work to survive was *The Theory of Moral Sentiments* (1790). There is a lingering feeling that a great deal of valuable work that would have benefited the world was lost in accordance to his will.

His greatest legacy was providing the intellectual foundation for the birth of the modern academic discipline of economics. Smith's work would continue to be refined and expanded by other brilliant philosophers and economists over the next two centuries, and at times even contorted and misconstrued to suit various political agendas. For example, the entire Communist movement of the twentieth century and the suffering to humanity that followed this warped ideology was born from the ideas of Marx and Engels, who wrote *Das Capital* (1867, 1885, 1894; the fourth volume was published in the early twentieth century). It was claimed these writers were following in the path of Smith. This was wrong. Smith fervently believed in the supremacy of the individual over the state and would have been horrified how his ideas had been perverted to enslave, not liberate, millions of individuals.

Adam Smith was a hugely influential political economist and moral philosopher whose ideas helped shape the beliefs of his own contemporaries as well as generations that followed. At the core of economics today are the observations of Adam Smith, still penetrating through the unknown like a beacon on a hill; still showing us the way forward to a better future.

JOHN KNOX WITHERSPOON
(1723–1794)

MINISTER AND EDUCATOR WHO
SHAPED AMERICA'S EARLY THINKING

B orn in in the small village of Gifford, East Lothian, he was the eldest son of eight children to the local Presbyterian Minister and his wife Anna. It was claimed, though never proved, that the family's lineage could be traced back to John Knox, the famous Scottish Protestant reformer of two centuries earlier. John Witherspoon received the finest education available to a bright young gentleman of that era.

He was home taught by his very literate and very devout mother and then attended the grammar school in nearby Haddington, Scotland. Witherspoon proceeded to Edinburgh University, where he attained a Master of Arts and went on to complete four years of divinity school at St Andrews University to follow in the family tradition of entering the Church. When he took holy orders in 1743, Witherspoon was only twenty years old.

His first appointment was as Presbyterian Minister to the

Church of Scotland in the parish in Beith in North Ayrshire. He would stay for twelve years at Beith, during which he married Elizabeth Montgomery, who would bear him ten children, five of whom survived to adulthood. During his ministry at Beith, Witherspoon also authored three noted books on theology, including *Ecclesiastical Characteristics* (1753), and gained a wide reputation for his religious writings.

In 1757, he moved to Paisley, a small town then in transition to becoming an industrial town that would eventually be the centre of the world-famous paisley textile design industry. He enjoyed the confidence of a growing congregation at the Laigh Kirk in Paisley, yet still found time to write. In 1764, he received an honorary Doctorate in Divinity from St Andrews University in recognition of the contribution he was making to theology.

Unknown to Witherspoon, a number of his serious and thoughtful publications had made their way across the Atlantic Ocean to the British North American colonies. And people there were taking notice.

In 1766, two representatives from the College of New Jersey approached Witherspoon offering him the position of that institution's sixth president. The college was founded in 1746 as a liberal arts university open to any person of any denomination, although all previous five presidents were Protestant ministers as one of the main purposes of the college was to act as a Presbyterian seminary.

At the time the best-educated men were often to be found among the clergy and Witherspoon was acknowledged as one of Scotland's best-educated ministers. At first, he declined the position because his wife feared crossing the sea and being separated so far from her family. However, she was gradually persuaded that the voyage would be safe and certainly in her husband's interest. In 1768, the Witherspoon family consisting of parents and five surviving children arrived in America.

Just as importantly, John Witherspoon brought with him a collection of 300-400 valuable books which he donated to the college to become its first library. Many of the books were from his own collection, but he had also convinced a large number of his colleagues and friends to donate many more to establish the new library in the College of New Jersey. This single act meant that New Jersey College Library started its existence with one of the largest and most modern collections of any of the then eight universities in British North America.

As President of the College (the university would change its name to Princeton University in 1896), the Reverend Dr Witherspoon enjoyed great success. He increased the endowment fund, expanded the range of degrees offered, and healed a rift in the American Presbyterian Church along the way. He remodelled the syllabus on the lines of Edinburgh University, which he considered to be among the most advanced in the English-speaking world.

At first he was careful not to enter into the political debate about the colonies' grievances with Britain, but by 1770 he started siding with the colonists. He saw many similarities between Scotland's often tortuous relationship with England and that of the colonies in America with England. In Witherspoon's mind the same English attitude of arrogance and intolerance was directed to both Scotland and America.

He continued to write, and his thoughtful, compelling arguments drew him to the attention of key decision makers of the revolutionary cause. In 1774–1775 he was elected to represent his county in the New Jersey provincial assembly and there he agitated for the removal of the Royal Governor. For this bold act of defiance he was invited to attend the inaugural meeting of the Continental Congress where for the first time the words rebellion, revolution and independence were being openly spoken. He was fifty-three years old, a much respected churchman and as the head of one of America's few universities had raised it and his own reputation in the colonies. Witherspoon entered the Continental Congress as a learned, respected, senior statesman with much moral authority.

In July 1776, the delegation from Virginia brought a resolution before the Continental Congress to declare independence. Not everyone was in favour of such a dramatic action and some hesitated, not wanting to commit to an armed revolutionary struggle. Indeed, reaction in Witherspoon's own colony of New Jersey was mixed on whether or not they should go to war. There were many settlers from England and some say as much as 15 per cent of the colony was loyal to the Crown.

But Witherspoon had already made up his mind. It was 'liberty or death' as colleague and fellow delegate Patrick Henry from Virginia had reportedly stated in 1775.

There was one more Scottish influence that played a significant role in forming Witherspoon's views on the crucial subject of independence – that was the Declaration of Arbroath. It was little understood outside Scotland, but every thinker in Scotland knew it well, some could even recite the document from memory. In 1320, the noblemen of Scotland sent a plea to Pope John XXII in Rome proclaiming Scottish freedom for the first time in a legal document. The central quote from the Declaration of Arbroath, which has been often repeated over centuries, translated from its original Latin states:

> For as long as one hundred of us remain alive, we will never give consent to subject ourselves to the dominion of the English. For it is not glory, it is not riches, neither is it honours, but it is liberty alone that we fight and contend for, which no honest man will lose but with his life.

Reverend Dr John Witherspoon would have been acutely aware of the Declaration of Arbroath and its legacy as he debated the subject of liberty for the American colonies.

On 4 July 1776, the Declaration of Independence lay on the table of Independence Hall in Philadelphia. It was time for each delegate to sign it, thus committing his life, his fortune, and the future of his family to an armed struggle for independence. If the revolution failed, those who signed the document would be the first to be executed and their families ruined. It was a huge decision to make, made even more remarkable by the fact that Britain was the mightiest military force in the world and America did not even have an army or navy.

Sensing the urgency of the moment, John Witherspoon of New Jersey, the only clergyman present, rose to speak and everyone listened. In a broad Scottish accent that remained with him for his entire life, the black-robed preacher said:

> There is a tide in the affairs of men, a nick of time. We perceive it now before us. To hesitate is to consent to our own slavery. That noble instrument upon your table, which ensures immortality to its author, should be subscribed this very morning by every pen in this house . . . For my own part, of property I have some, of reputation more. That reputation is staked, that property is pledged, on the issue of this contest;

and although these grey hairs must soon descend into the sepulchre, I would infinitely rather that they descend thither by the hand of the executioner than desert at this crisis the sacred cause of my country.

Over the following weeks, the Declaration of Independence was signed by almost all the fifty-six delegates of the congress, including himself, the only clergyman to do so.

In November 1776, he was forced to shut down and evacuate the College of New Jersey at the approach of British forces who were seeking retaliation for his involvement in the revolution. The British troops did much damage to the college, destroying Witherspoon's library in the process. His eldest son, James joined the American revolutionary army and was commissioned Major. He showed great promise, but died fighting the British in the Battle of Germantown in 1777.

Witherspoon served in the Continental Congress from 1776 until 1782, when he resigned to look after his family and his beloved college. He was one of Congress's most influential members with a capacity for work seldom seen in one of his age. He served in over a hundred committees, most notably the standing committees dealing with the conduct of the war, and foreign affairs.

He helped draft the Articles of Confederation in 1781, a temporary measure to govern the country until replaced by the Constitution of the United States in 1789. As well as signing the Declaration of Independence that started the war, he drafted the peace agreement in 1782, which brought it to an end.

Once the war was over, Witherspoon devoted the rest of his life to rebuilding and restoring the College of New Jersey to its former glory before the conflict, but the financial cost almost ruined him as he personally paid for a substantial part of the rebuilding costs himself. Somehow, he also found time to serve in the New Jersey state legislature until 1789.

In 1789, his wife, Elizabeth, passed away. Two years later Witherspoon married a twenty-four-year-old widow. He was almost sixty-nine years old, which of course provoked much comment, and it was thought initially the motive was companionship for an old man, but his second wife would deliver two children to him in as many years. In 1792, Witherspoon lost the sight of both eyes in rapid succession and total blindness led to a marked deterioration in his health. John Witherspoon passed away in 1794 at the age of seventy-three.

During his tenure as President of the College of New Jersey, Witherspoon personally taught the subject of moral philosophy to every student of the college. This way, he shaped the minds of students who went on to become an American president (James Madison) and a vice president (Aaron Burr), as well as thirty-nine United States congressmen, twenty-one US senators, twelve state governors, nine cabinet members and thirty-seven judges, of whom three were Supreme Court justices. Five of the fifty-five members of the Constitutional Convention were his former students. Finally, one third of all the 177 Presbyterian ministers in America in 1777 had been taught by Witherspoon.

John Witherspoon came to a rapidly developing British North American colony as president of an educational facility that would become Princeton University, and he ended up helping to shape the country. His beliefs, ideas and faith helped shape the fundamental principles of the United States – and they all had their origins in Scotland.

NIEL GOW (1727–1807)

FIDDLER, COMPOSER AND CHAMPION OF SCOTTISH FOLK MUSIC

If you have wondered why Scottish folk music is so widespread and so well-regarded around the world – Niel Gow, more than any other individual, is the one you should thank.

Gow was born in Strathbraan, west of Dunkeld, Perthshire. Shortly after, his family moved to Inver (again near Dunkeld) where Niel's father followed his trade as a weaver, as did many in the area. There was a strong tradition of folk music in the countryside at the time, though it was in decline along with the speaking of Gaelic and other customs.

Niel (note the Gaelic spelling) soon showed an aptitude for music, particularly for playing the fiddle. When he was thirteen he was considered a musical prodigy and by the time he was eighteen he was consistently winning competitions for fiddle-playing. Gow gained the patronage of James Murray, 2nd Duke of Atholl, who resided 30 kilometres away at Blair Castle, Dunkeld. The Duke sponsored him to become a full-time musician and lifted his reputation onto the Scottish national stage. It was widely agreed that, as a reel and strathspey player, Gow had no superior, and, indeed, no rival during his lifetime.

He was once visited by another Scottish icon, Robbie Burns (*see* p. 97), who described him as 'a short, stout-built, honest Highlander figure, with greyish hair on his honest social brow; an interesting face, marking strong sense, kind openheartedness, mixed with unmistrusting simplicity' (quoted in John Lockhart et al., *The Life of Robert Burns*).

Many of Niel Gow's compositions – there are over a hundred that are still played today at ceilidhs and country dances – continue to form the backbone of Scottish folk music more than two centuries after his death. In truth it is believed that up to a quarter of Niel's compositions were in fact 'borrowed' from the airs, strathspeys and jigs that were fast losing their popularity and being forgotten in the countryside. But in doing so, Niel Gow saved Scottish folk music from dying, along with the generation of folk players who were being moved off the land. He took folk music, mainly played in the highlands or squalid slums of the big cities and turned it into the national music of Scotland.

However, it is his reputation as a performer that raises him above all others. As a celebrated performer of dance music he inspired and excited dancers with powerfully rhythmical music and regular cries of encouragement; and in non-dance contexts he demonstrated the emotional depth of his art in the performance of deeply moving laments.

At his death, he was survived by three children, one of whom – Nathaniel – went on to produce almost 200 Scottish fiddle tunes on his own, thereby adding to the storehouse of fine Scottish music that remains today.

Niel Gow's continuing high status as a national icon is confirmed by the fact that there is the Niel Gow Fiddle Festival held annually in Dunkeld where the finest performers of Scottish fiddle music compete. One of his portraits had been chosen to adorn a wall in Bute House in Edinburgh, the official residence of the First Minister of Scotland. Gow's original fiddle proudly hangs in the drawing room of Blair Castle along with yet another portrait of him.

Finally, the original painting of Niel Gow by the famous portrait artist Sir Henry Raeburn (*see* p. 91) hangs in the National Gallery of Scotland in Edinburgh where people come to admire not only the painter's work, but the painter's subject – the man who composed and championed Scottish folk music onto the world's stage.

ROBERT ADAM
(1728–1792)

GREAT NEOCLASSICAL ARCHITECT

Born in Kirkaldy, Fife, Robert Adam was one of four sons of the established architect William Adam. Robert studied in Edinburgh until 1745, when he joined the family practice. On their father's death in 1748 he went into partnership with his older brother John, but in 1754 set out on a 'Grand Tour' of Europe, which was quite a common practice at the time for the sons of wealthy families.

Robert Adam spent five years in France and Italy studying architecture, drawing inspiration from the ancient ruins and painted frescoes that would influence his future work. On his return he established his own architectural practice in London with his younger brother James. Initially it was interior design for which he gained a reputation through transforming the interiors of the dwellings of the richer members of British society.

It was after Adam was appointed Architect of the King's Works (along with his main rival William Chambers) in 1761 – thanks mainly to the influence and patronage of fellow Scot John Stuart, the 1st Marquess of Bute – that he moved from focusing on just interiors to designing entire buildings. He then started designing and constructing a number of grand, stately buildings for the King and the British aristocracy.

Although classical architecture was already becoming popular, Adam rejected the Palladian style, as introduced to England by Inigo Jones. Adam continued to be heavily influenced by classic design architecture, but did not follow Roman architectural rules as strictly as Palladianism did. He developed his own style, called naturally enough, the Adam style and in a short period Robert Adam found himself in great demand to build ever grander homes for the wealthy gentry of Britain.

One of Britain's most important architects, he was a main force in the development of a unified style that extended beyond architecture and interiors to include both the fixed and movable objects in a room. He incorporated design ideas from ancient Greece and Rome into his forms and decoration.

Robert Adam was responsible for some of the most beautiful buildings in Britain today. His finest houses are Home House, London; Charlotte Square, Edinburgh; Register House (home of the Scottish National Archives), Edinburgh. Syon House, London. The magnificent Culzean Castle, South Ayrshire, Scotland (built 1777–79) is considered by some to be his finest work and contains a unique and famous double staircase in an oval space.

Adam took on more commissions than he could possibly complete, suffering from chronic fatigue and ill health through overwork. He died of a burst stomach ulcer at his home in 1792, leaving behind almost 9,000 architectural drawings and a legacy that went way beyond the shores of the British Isles.

ROBERT ADAM (1728–1792)

In the United States, the Presidential White house and the Capitol building, both in Washington DC, can trace their design origins back to Robert Adam. In America, Adam's version of neoclassicism became known as the Federal style and has influenced civil and private buildings alike across the USA for the past two hundred years. In Russia, the palaces of the Empress Catherine the Great were also based on the ideas of Robert Adam.

JAMES WATT (1736–1819)

INVENTOR AND MECHANICAL ENGINEER

Watt was born in Greenock, Scotland, then a small but thriving harbour town overlooking the Firth of Clyde. His father was a part-time magistrate and treasurer of the town who ran a successful building business, mainly in ship-building. James Watt was a thin, weakly child who would suffer from poor health for most of his life. His education was a combination of home-schooling from his parents and irregular attendance at the local grammar school. Where he thrived however, was in his father's workshop, where he spent a great deal of time learning engineering skills and becoming fascinated by the navigational aids on ships, such as quadrants, compasses and telescopes.

It was during his youth that an episode in his young life – probably apocryphal – was said to have set him on a course that would change the world and make him famous. When he was six (or twelve in some versions), it is said, he was watching his mother's old-fashioned kettle hanging over the open fireplace when steam started pouring out of its spout. Fascinated, he wondered about the power of steam, which set in train a chain of events that would lead to him being called the 'Father' of the Industrial Revolution.

By his mid-teens James wanted to become an instrument maker and with his father's blessing, he journeyed to Glasgow and then on to London, where he was eventually apprenticed in 1755. He managed to cram a five-year apprenticeship into twelve months by studying diligently and working extra-long hours. It also helped that he was naturally gifted in this field. Watt finished his apprenticeship year successfully, but his health collapsed almost immediately afterwards and he returned to Glasgow to regain his health.

Soon he was well enough to look for work. The University of Glasgow recognised his skills and officially gave him the position of 'Instrument Maker to the University'. It really meant that Watt was brought on as a handyman for the university's elite. Over the next three years he supplemented his university income by taking on the making of musical instruments.

In 1764 he married a distant cousin Margaret Miller, who bore him six children before she died in 1773.

It was only natural that Watt's gift for practical solutions would interest the men of science who surrounded him at the university and when a professor of Chemistry brought him a steam-powered machine to repair in 1764, James Watt seized upon the opportunity to improve the device. At the time, the only steam engines put to any industrial use were the Newcomen engines used to pump water out of mines. The mechanics of these primitive machines were crudely simple and the machine itself grossly inefficient.

While repairing the Newcomen steam engine, Watt realised there was an inherent design flaw in the device: it wasted almost as much steam as it produced. If he could capture the escaping vapour then it could be reused in a continuous cycle.

Over several years he developed what the world now refers to as a 'condenser', because it condensed the steam back into water to be recycled back into steam again. James Watt wanted to continue improvements on the steam engine, but costly experimentation up to that point had earned him a sizeable debt. Thankfully, he patented the concept of the condenser in 1769, which allowed him some collateral to offer potential investors.

Out of all the family and friends he asked to financially support him, it was a wealthy industrialist and amateur inventor by the name of John Roebuck who saw the potential of Watt's device. The two men went into partnership, with Roebuck taking a two-thirds equity on the patent in return for discharging Watt's debts.

However, neither man had enough capital to continue with further developments on the steam engine, so James Watt became a land surveyor and for the next eight years busied himself marking out routes for canals in Scotland, such as the Forth & Clyde Canal and the Caledonian Canal that Thomas Telford (see p. 94) was building at the time. This caused him to be away from Glasgow and his workshop for lengthy periods, during which development of the engine slowed to a trickle.

When, in 1772, Roebuck went bankrupt, a manufacturer from Birmingham took over his two-thirds share in Watt's patent. The man's name was Mathew Boulton and it was this partnership between Watt and Boulton that would eventually turn a crudely improved steam engine into the device that underpinned the Industrial Revolution.

Boulton had a well-established metal manufacturing works in Birmingham that was impossible to move. If Watt wanted to continue to develop his engine he would have to leave Glasgow and relocate to Birmingham. In the event, in 1773, Watt's wife died, leaving him to raise his young children on his own. Without any ties in Glasgow, he moved the family to Birmingham in 1774. Watt and Boulton complemented each other and they got on well. The two immediately set about improving the engine's efficiency and power.

In 1776 the first machines to come out of the Boulton and Watt foundry were almost exclusively used to replace the woefully inefficient Newcomen engines in collieries where they were used to extract water from the mines. Watt's machine was very popular because they were four times more powerful than the Newcomen engines. Other improvements rapidly followed, in particular the 'sun and planet' gearing system that converted vertical movement into rotary. With this single improvement Boulton and Watt were now prepared to open up their market to industries beyond mining.

However, the trouble was that Watt's original patent was about to run out and without legal protection Watt's intellectual property could have been copied by any other manufacturer in Britain. Thankfully, Boulton had well-connected friends who used every ounce of political power they had to extend the patent by an Act of Parliament. The patent gave Boulton and Watt a virtual monopoly over the production of steam engines for the next twenty-five years, allowing Watt to charge his customers a premium for using his steam engines.

In 1776 Watt married again. His second wife, Ann MacGregor, bore him two more children.

In 1782, a local sawmill ordered one of Watt's engines to replace twelve horses. This prompted Watt to use the concept of horsepower as the way to express the power of his engines. Watt used data on lift, weights and distance to determine a unit of horsepower (hp).

From then on all of the steam engines manufactured by Boulton and Watt were horsepower rated. Watt worked out how much each company saved by using his machine rather than a team of horses. The company then had to pay him one third of this figure every year, for the next twenty-five years.

More improvements by Watt followed, including a steam throttle, an engine governor and pressure gauge. With each improvement, more industries joined a growing list of buyers for the engine. Sawmills and mining were soon joined by wool, flour, paper and cotton mills. Even distilleries found a use for the machines. Orders now flooded in.

In 1785 he and Boulton were elected fellows of the Royal Society of London and by 1790 Watt was a wealthy man, having received £76,000 in royalties on his patents in the preceding eleven years. By 1800, it is estimated that there were over 500 Bolton and Watt steam engines installed in Britain's mines and factories.

He gradually withdrew from business, bought an estate at Doldowlod in Staffordshire, which he visited often to escape the hurly-burly of his city house in booming, bustling Birmingham.

Watt continued experimenting after retiring from business in 1800, pursuing a wide variety of interests from improving oil lamps to measuring distances by telescopes. He even advised the great Josiah Wedgwood on aspects of pottery manufacture.

His achievements were amply recognised in his lifetime: he was made doctor of law of the University of Glasgow in 1806 and a foreign associate of the French Academy of Sciences in 1814. He was offered a baronetcy by a grateful government in London, which he politely declined.

He died in 1819 in Birmingham at the age of eighty-three and was buried in St Mary's Church in Hansworth, Birmingham. Matthew

Boulton had died in 1809 and one of James Watt's last requests was that he be buried alongside Boulton in the same churchyard at St Mary's. Subsequently, church extensions covered over the graves and they are now remembered by marble monuments erected inside the church.

The world's oldest Boulton and Watt rotating steam engine is proudly on display at the Powerhouse Museum in Sydney, Australia. This engine was made in Boulton and Watt's factory for Whitbread's London brewery in 1785. There, it was used for over a hundred years, powering equipment for grinding and lifting malt, stirring vats, and pumping water and beer. When it was decommissioned in 1888, a visiting professor from Australia persuaded the brewer to donate it to Sydney Technical College, whose scientific collection became the basis of the Powerhouse museum.

Today, when visitors come to the Powerhouse museum in Sydney, they stand in awe of the Boulton and Watt steam engine before them, as it twirls, spins and hisses, still working perfectly even though its age predates European colonisation of Australia by three years. The same reaction was recorded by observers two centuries before when they too saw their first steam engine. To some back then, it was the 'devil's machine', to others 'a wondrous thing', but to all then and now it represented power, raw industrial power on a scale never witnessed before.

The development of an efficient steam engine transformed industry and society. It helped Great Britain become the world's first industrialised society and led to an era of unprecedented growth. It is not an exaggeration to say that Watt's invention played a crucial role in making Great Britain become the greatest superpower in the world since the Roman Empire.

JOHN PAUL JONES
(1747–1792)

SPIRITUAL FATHER
OF THE US NAVY

John Paul (there was no Jones in the family name), was born in a small whitewashed cottage at Arbigland on the Solway coast south of Dumfries, Scotland in what was then the wonderful sounding county of Kirkcudbrightshire (now Dumfries and Galloway). He was the fourth of seven children. The house he was born in was opened as a museum in 1993, with financial help from American supporters.

His father was a gardener, but this part of Scotland has always been known for producing countless numbers of seamen and John Paul was sent to sea at the age of thirteen as a cabin boy on coastal luggers (trading ships). He spent a number of years sailing out of Whitehaven in neighbouring Cumberland in north-west England, eventually being allowed to sign on with larger vessels. By the mid-1760s, he was now working on the transatlantic trade, transporting goods to and from the new colonies of British North America and the West Indies.

The trade across the Atlantic not only dealt with goods but also human cargo, namely slaves. It was known as the 'Triangular Trade' in that goods such as cloth, copper and guns were shipped from Britain to West Africa where they were exchanged for captured African native slaves. The slaves were taken to the West Indies or America and sold to work the plantations. The traders would then buy the raw products of these plantations, such as sugar, rum, tobacco and cotton, and return to their home ports in Britain. The Scots in particular turned this triangular trade into an art form and two Scottish ports specifically, Glasgow and Greenock (on the Clyde River and Firth of Clyde respectively), boomed under the imports of profitable commodities. It was said that Scotland's first millionaires were tobacco 'barons' who turned Glasgow into the tobacco distribution centre for all of Europe.

The British transatlantic trade was based along the west coast of Africa. There was also a slave trade along the east coast of Africa that had been operating for many years and involved Arab traders. David Livingstone, the famous Scottish explorer (*see* p. 146), would later campaign against this trade and the main slave market at Zanzibar was closed in 1873, a few weeks after Livingstone's death.

By the mid-1700s a small but growing number of people in Scotland were opposed to slavery, but it would be true to say that at the time there were still many more people attracted to it because of the huge profits that could be made. John Paul was one of them. His older brother was working on a tobacco plantation in the Virginia colony of North America and John Paul thought it would be a lucrative venture to ship slaves to him. However, he was so appalled by the shocking reality of how native Africans were treated that he quit being a 'slaver' in disgust after just a few passages.

At the age of twenty-one, John Paul found himself acting skipper of a brig when both the captain and first mate died of yellow fever. He conducted his duties so competently that the ship's Scottish owners promoted him to the rank of captain permanently. But two years later, in 1770, a sailor died after being flogged on the orders of John Paul, leaving him open to charges of manslaughter.

He managed to avoid arrest on this occasion, but in 1773 when he ran another sailor through with his sword during an attempted mutiny on a subsequent trip, people began to have grave concerns about his fiery temper and his ability to handle a ship. Rather than face the prospects of being charged with manslaughter again, John Paul fled to Virginia a few days after the incident. There, he changed his name to John Paul Jones (this name shall be used from this point) and took over the estate of his brother who had recently died.

Jones arrived in America just as the crisis between the American colonies and Britain was coming to a climax. When fighting broke out between British soldiers and colonial militiamen in Massachusetts in 1775 a hastily convened Continental Congress created a Continental Army and Navy and called for volunteers.

John Paul Jones swore his allegiance to the newly declared independent nation of America and offered his services to its navy. His experience was readily accepted and he was commissioned a lieutenant in the fledgling Continental Navy. He served as 1st Lieutenant under Captain Hopkins on the *Alfred*, a 30-gun man-of-war. However, disorganised and ineffectual leadership by Hopkins convinced Jones he should press for his own command.

In 1776, he was given the *Providence*, a 12-gun sloop, with instructions to conduct coastal raids. He was spectacularly successful from the start. During his first voyage off the Grand Banks off Newfoundland, he captured sixteen prizes and destroyed the local fishing fleet. In his second cruise – again to the Grand Banks – he took several more prizes, including the armed transport *Mellish* with its cargo of winter uniforms, which were distributed to the woefully underclad Continental Army.

In 1777, Jones advocated a new naval strategy which was audacious in the extreme. Rather than bravely, but hopelessly, defending America's coast against a vastly superior enemy, why not take the fight to the British by crossing the Atlantic Ocean and raiding their undefended ports throughout the British Isles? In other words, the young navy should hit the British where they least expected it and where they were most vulnerable.

Jones was given command of a newly built 20-gun frigate *Ranger* and told to sail across the Atlantic. In 1778, he caused mayhem in the Irish Sea between Scotland and the British possessions in Ireland, at one time landing in his old port of Whitehaven in England to frighten the town. He concocted a scheme to kidnap the Earl of Selkirk and even landed in nearby Kirkcudbright to affect the capture, but the plan failed because the Earl was away from his home at the time.

Jones managed to capture HMS *Drake* at anchor in the Irish harbour of Carrickfergus near Belfast, and sailed with her as a prize to France. It was the young American Navy's most significant military victory up to this point and caused huge alarm in Britain. Meanwhile, France had recognised America as a sovereign nation, signed a military pact and declared war on Britain. This allowed Jones to raid at will around the British Isles knowing that he could seek shelter and re-provisioning in French coastal ports a short distance away.

On one entry into a French port in 1778, *Ranger* became the first ship to proudly display the 'Stars and Stripes' of the new flag of the

United States of America, the design of which had been approved by Continental Congress only months before.

As a result of his success in *Ranger*, Jones was promoted to Commodore and given command of a small flotilla of ships which he led from his new ship, the much larger 42-gun man-of-war *Bonhomme Richard*. Following his orders, which were to continue his harassment of British ports and shipping, he sailed clockwise around Britain taking prizes wherever possible. Sailing into the Firth of Forth off Scotland, he attempted to capture or destroy any large ships in Edinburgh's seaport of Leith and extort money from the port and perhaps even Edinburgh itself by threatening to bombard the towns. But the weather was against getting close enough to make good his threats and the local garrison, which had seen his arrival, had prepared all available guns to give him a warm reception.

Having lost the element of surprise, Jones decided to move on to other targets, and there were many, for the British ships that had been recalled to deal with this American threat had not yet arrived. As the flotilla moved down the Scottish coast into English waters, many small coastal traders and colliers were captured or sunk. To some in Britain, he was simply an opportunistic pirate preying on weak and defenceless commercial traffic. But to a growing number of British citizens, Jones was becoming a Robin Hood character who, in the fight for American independence, was taking on the might of British sea power and giving it a 'bloodied nose'. To enhance this growing reputation, Jones made sure that the British crews of captured or sunk vessels were dropped ashore further along the coast with enough provisions to safely see them through to the nearest town.

Jones met and engaged a large convoy of transport ships off Flamborough Head, near the Humber Estuary in northern England.

JOHN PAUL JONES (1747–1792)

The convoy of merchant ships was carrying naval stores to England from the Baltic and was being escorted by two naval vessels, the *Serapis* with near to 50 guns, and *Countess of Scarborough* with 20. The fight was not even. Jones' *Bonhomme Richard* took on the superior *Serapis* while a slower and heavier vessel in his flotilla engaged the lighter and faster *Scarborough*. The other two ships in Jones's flotilla were directed to capture or destroy as many of the forty or so transport ships as possible. A task made more difficult by the fact that they scattered in different directions as soon as the Americans were spotted and many of the merchant ships were also armed.

The *Serapis* was captained by Richard Pearson, a forty-eight-year-old naval veteran who had a proven record in combat and had been severely wounded in one prior engagement. He was to prove a worthy adversary on this day. The two ships closed on each other and for the next three and a half hours, most of it in moonlight, shot each other to bits. Towards the end of the conflict, Jones deliberately and expertly brought his ship alongside the British vessel and lashed the two ships together to negate the *Serapis*'s superior firepower, but the two ships continued to pound each other.

Towards the end of the battle, the British ship had more guns in service and was able to fire many times the number of shots into the American vessel as it was receiving. In truth, the American ship was in a terrible shape.

The *Bonhomme Richard*'s hull was holed and she was slowly sinking despite crewmen desperately manning the pumps. All but three of her guns were out of action; her decks were shot away and half her crew of 300 killed or wounded. Fires had started in many places and were fast approaching the magazine. Finally, her rudder and most of her rigging had been shot away. The American frigate was dead in the water, defenceless and in a hopeless position.

But the British ship was almost as badly damaged, though most importantly her hull was still intact and the *Serapis* had more guns firing than the *Bonhomme Richard*. Captain Pearson of the *Serapis* hailed Jones, 'Do you surrender?' he asked over the roar of the battle. Jones instantly shouted back, 'Surrender? I have not yet begun to fight!' With those immortal words, Jones then directed his crewmen to direct musket fire and throw fire bombs (primitive grenades) into the British sailors on the opposite deck. One of the grenades caused a flash fire of stored ammunition and powder on the British ship killing or injuring up to a quarter of the crew in one blast. With this disaster, the big guns of *Serapis* fell silent.

Jones then seized the initiative and with a handful of men boarded the British ship only to find that the fight had gone out of the British. Captain Pearson, seeing the slaughter of his men around him and knowing his crew could not continue the fight, personally made his way to the rear of his warship and hauled down the battle ensign. Jones and his crew had prevailed against all odds, which was fortunate, for the fatally damaged *Bonhomme Richard*, still ablaze, sank from view shortly after the battle.

Jones returned to France where he was treated as a conquering hero. He was presented with a gold-hilted sword by King Louis XVI as well as the Ordre du Mérite Militaire, the highest award that the French could give to a foreigner. He became the darling of Parisian high society, but all this adulation only fed his ego. Jones became absorbed with receiving recognition from the United States Government and wrote many letters to authorities demanding to be promoted to Admiral. At the time the young navy was so small it could not justify the rank of Admiral, but that did not stop Jones from wanting to be recognised as America's first Rear Admiral.

Despite concerns about Jones's self-absorption he was genuinely respected and admired by the people and the government of America. On his return to the United States in 1781, the Congress gave him a vote of thanks – and would later, in 1787, strike a gold medal in his honour. In 1782 he was given the honour of commanding the *America*, the fledgling navy's largest ship and first man-of-war commissioned for the navy. Unfortunately, the ship never sailed under the American flag as it was handed over to the French in payment for outstanding debts.

When peace with Britain was declared in 1783 one of the first things the cash-strapped United States did was to decommission its very expensive navy. Frustrated, Jones returned to Europe, where he travelled for many years.

In 1788 he was appointed by Catherine the Great as a rear-admiral in the Russian navy in charge of a squadron of ships in the Black Sea, though he never relinquished his American citizenship. He returned to Paris in 1790 and was appointed US Consul to Algiers in 1792. However, he died, it is thought of jaundice, before he was able to take up his post. He was only forty-five years old at the time of his death. He was interred in a humble grave in Paris, a neglected hero.

Over the next century his bold strategic ideas and courageous tactics became part of the American Navy's own philosophies, until by the turn of the twentieth century Jones had become revered as a hero who personified the fighting spirit and the never-say-die attitude of the United States Navy. While his personal shortcomings, such as his self-promotion and self-absorption, diminished him, he nonetheless became a symbol for the best that the United States Navy would want to be known for.

Jones's remains were 'rediscovered' in 1905 and in 1912, amid great pomp and ceremony, exhumed and transported to America.

They now reside under permanent military guard in a magnificent marble and bronze tomb, modelled on the tomb of Napoleon, at the United States Naval Academy at Annapolis, Maryland. A far cry from his humble origins in Scotland.

The following inscription was placed in the marble floor in the front of his sarcophagus:

JOHN PAUL JONES, 1747–1792; U.S. NAVY, 1775–1783. HE GAVE OUR NAVY ITS EARLIEST TRADITIONS OF HEROISM AND VICTORY. ERECTED BY THE CONGRESS, A.D. 1912.

SIR HENRY RAEBURN
(1756–1823)

ONE OF SCOTLAND'S MOST SIGNIFICANT PORTRAIT PAINTERS

Raeburn was born in modest surroundings to the son of a manufacturer in Stockbridge, on the Water of Leith; a former village now within the city of Edinburgh. Orphaned at a young age, Henry was raised by his elder brother. He was educated at George Heriot's School in Edinburgh and at the age of fifteen was apprenticed to the goldsmith James Gilliland in Scotland's capital. A number of delightful pieces including beautifully painted minute drawings created by Raeburn during his apprenticeship still exist today.

Soon he started painting watercolour miniatures of his friends and later began painting portraits in oils. At this stage in his development as an artist, he was entirely self-taught. Gilliland watched the progress of his pupil with interest and introduced him to David Martin, who was at that time a noted painter in Edinburgh.

In 1778, when Raeburn was in his early twenties, he was asked to paint the portrait of Countess Leslie, a wealthy widow. There was an instant rapport between them and they married within a month. She encouraged her new husband to devote more time to painting and supported his endeavours financially. Having gained financial independence, Raeburn said farewell to Gilliland and set off to further his study in London accompanied by his wife.

In London, the couple called upon England's most influential painter at the time, Sir Joshua Reynolds. He specialised in portrait painting which was becoming a very lucrative pursuit as London's nouveau riche were clamouring for vanity portraits of themselves and their families. Reynolds's style was neoclassical, with the subjects painted in the poses of ancient gods from Rome and Athens. In many of his paintings the backgrounds were also imagined in the neoclassical style, representing temples and idyllic landscapes from antiquity.

Reynolds urged Raeburn to go to Rome and study the great masters, particularly the renaissance artists such as Michelangelo and Raphael. The Raeburns spent two years in Rome, but there is no evidence in Henry's subsequent work that he was influenced by these great renaissance masters. Instead of grand portraits involving backgrounds of ancient Rome or Greece, Raeburn started placing his subjects in natural surroundings, dressed in the normal attire of the day. What Raeburn had developed while he was away was an altogether new and natural style of portraiture.

He returned to Edinburgh in 1789 and moved into a studio at 32 York Place in the centre of Edinburgh. There, he installed tall windows to allow more light into the room, which can be seen to this day. Raeburn spent the next three decades painting the notable men and women of Scottish society, including Sir Walter Scott, Niel Gow and Thomas Telford (*see* pp. 124, 70 and 94). Perhaps he is best remembered today for his portrait titled *The Reverend Robert Walker Skating on Duddingston Loch*, a lake on the outskirts of Edinburgh.

SIR HENRY RAEBURN (1756–1823)

Raeburn also painted a number of striking portraits of Scottish Highlanders in full tartan attire, such as *The Macnab*, a painting of Francis Macnab, 16th Chief of Clan Macnab. These Highlanders even bore weapons, such as in the painting *Alistair MacDonell of Glengarry*, the last Highland Chief of the MacDonell Clan.

This caused a ripple of comment at the time, as Edinburgh had been briefly occupied by a Jacobite army full of 'wild' Highlanders only half a century earlier. The prohibition against wearing tartan since that Jacobite rebellion of 1745 had only been relaxed shortly before his portraits. Here was Raeburn celebrating the Highlander and his dress as something to be admired, even copied.

After his return from the continent in 1789, Raeburn remained almost exclusively in Scotland over the next thirty-three years. This allowed a Scottish art movement – called Scottish 'Romanticism' – to form and flourish around him. In 1812 he was elected president of the Society of Artists in Edinburgh and in 1815 he became a full member of the Royal Scottish Academy. In 1822 he was knighted by George IV while the King was on a Royal tour of Scotland, the first tour by a reigning British monarch in 172 years.

The following year, in 1823, Sir Henry Raeburn as he was now called, died at his home in Edinburgh and was buried in the nearby churchyard of St Cuthbert's, in the shadow of imposing Edinburgh Castle.

During his lifetime he painted over 700 portraits, leaving the modern world with the most striking record of Scottish life and dress at the beginning of the nineteenth century.

It is remarkable that just at a time when Scotland was beginning to feel national pride, Sir Henry Raeburn perfectly captured the looks of growing confidence and aspiration on the faces of many of its influential and wealthy citizens.

THOMAS TELFORD (1757–1834)

CIVIL ENGINEER AND NOTED BUILDER OF ROADS, BRIDGES, RAIL AND CANALS

Thomas Telford was born at a hill farm near Jamestown, in the parish of Westerkirk, Dumfries. His father, a shepherd, died soon after Thomas was born and for most of his childhood he was raised in abject poverty.

At the age of fourteen, he was apprenticed as a stonemason and after he had qualified, he worked for a time in Edinburgh, before moving to London for more secure employment. There, he came to the attention of a wealthy patron and was offered a position created for him of Surveyor of Public Works in Shropshire. He continued his education and became a qualified architect, though what he was actually teaching himself was the basics of construction and overall project management – the beginning of what would become the discipline of civil engineering.

At this time the Industrial Revolution was beginning to transform Britain and Thomas Telford was at the vanguard of a group of enlightened people who could see that improvements to public infrastructure would directly lead to improvements in the lives of its citizens. He set about developing the road, port, canal and rail system of Britain with an almost religious zeal.

He experimented with iron and designed many new bridges throughout the country utilising this new construction material incorporated along with the more traditional stone. In 1793 Telford won a commission to build his first major project, the Ellesmere Canal in north Shropshire. Shortly after, he designed and constructed the Shrewsbury Canal, then the water supply for Liverpool. He followed these projects with improving London's docklands and finally the rebuilding of London Bridge.

In 1801, Telford devised a master plan for the Highlands of Scotland, involving a network of roads and the construction of the massive 100-kilometre long Caledonian Canal. It would take twenty years to complete and would result in many related infrastructure projects, such as numerous harbour improvements, 1,500 kilometres of roads, 1,000 new bridges and even thirty-two new churches. A phenomenal achievement that earned him the nickname of the 'Colossus of Roads'.

Towards the end of the Highlands project, Telford turned his attention to the Scottish Lowlands and built more bridges and a further 300 kilometres of new roads, including the impressive Cartland Crags Bridge near Lanark in 1822. Perhaps his most aesthetically pleasing achievement during this period of his life was the construction of the Menai Suspension Bridge joining the island of Anglesey to the mainland of Wales. When completed in 1826, it was the longest suspension bridge in the world and would later be considered one of the greatest examples of ironwork ever built.

During this period, Telford's fame had spread overseas. He was consulted by King Karl XIII of Sweden about the building of a great canal to link the Baltic Sea with the North Sea – the Göta Canal. Telford took on the role of consultant and spent considerable time in Sweden between 1808 and 1813, designing and being involved in the initial construction phase of the Göta Canal. When completed in 1832 the canal was longer and wider than Telford's ground-breaking Caledonian Canal which he had finished ten years earlier. Today, the Göta Canal is one of Sweden's best-known tourist attractions, offering long-distance passenger cruises between Stockholm and Gothenburg as well as a wonderful reason to visit a string of charming small towns along its inland route.

Back in Britain, Telford continued to build more roads, bridges and ports. He never stopped improving on methods of roads construction and in later years developed a new system (in collaboration with McAdam, another Scot) that became the international standard for road building. Towards the end of his life, he started to apply his skills to the then emergent transport mode of rail.

He passed away peacefully in his sleep in 1834 at the age of seventy-seven and as a sign of national respect he was buried with honours in Westminster Abbey.

During his very busy lifetime, Telford built over 1,000 bridges, almost 2,000 kilometres of roads, many railways, numerous canals, churches and harbours throughout Britain. But impressive as this list of achievements is, Telford, more importantly, built the infrastructure that dragged the farming countries of Scotland, England and Wales into the industrial age. In fact, Telford should be remembered for developing Britain into a nation that could support an empire.

ROBERT BURNS
(1759–1796)

NATIONAL POET
OF SCOTLAND

Scotland's most celebrated literary figure, Burns was born in a humble cottage built by his father at Alloway (about three kilometres south of Ayr) on the west coast of Scotland. He was the eldest of seven children of a self-educated, though poor, tenant farmer.

When Robert (commonly called Robbie, or Rab for short) was seven, his father moved the family to a larger farm which he rented at Mount Oliphant, south-east of Alloway. It was here that the father hoped their tight financial circumstances would improve, but this venture failed due to the poor condition of the soil.

Burns had little regular schooling being mainly educated at home by his father, supplemented by the occasional year or two at local schools. But his education was thorough and by his mid-teens Burns could read and write in English, French and basic Latin and had absorbed the writings of Shakespeare, Milton, Pope and Dryden. Even at an early age he was fascinated by the tales of

Hannibal who took on the might of Rome, and William Wallace, the Scottish rebel who fought the might of England. By the age of fifteen, Robert had left school to become a full-time labourer on the family farm, where he toiled unceasingly to make the farm a success. Ultimately, his efforts were in vain.

In his spare time he started composing poetry and songs and the first piece he wrote 'O once I lov'd a bonnie lass' (1774) was to a young farm labourer Nelly Kirkpatrick, with whom he had become infatuated. At the time, they were both teenagers. Burns started drawing inspiration from the people and places around him. His observations of a farmer he would call 'Tam' (real name Douglas Graham) who worked on nearby Shanter's farm would surface years later in his most famous poem 'Tam O'Shanter' (1790).

In 1777 the family moved to a farm at Lochlea, not far away near Mauchline, Ayrshire, where the Burns family continued to work the land. Having displayed a flair for poetry and song, the eighteen-year-old Robert was writing constantly. He was also desperate to grow up. He founded a 'Bachelors' Club' (a drinking and debating club) in the nearby town of Tarbolton and in 1780 he was initiated into the Freemasons who met on the same premises.

Burns briefly tried his hand at other pursuits when in 1781 he became a flax-dresser at the coastal town of Irvine in Ayrshire, but was soon back farming again after he and other staff accidentally burnt the factory down during over-exuberant Hogmanay celebrations. By now, grinding poverty had developed a growing rebellious nature within him, which in the near future would cause him to lose friends and admirers by supporting the French Revolution and challenging the status quo on matters such as slavery, which he opposed. Another manifestation of his rebelliousness was in his irresponsible attitude to women. Burns would go on to father thirteen children with five different women, as far as is known. Most of the children died in infancy.

When his father died in 1784, Robert and his brother were glad to move away to what they hoped would be a better farm in Mossgiel near Mauchline, but after two more years this location proved no more successful than any of the previous.

He needed respite from his perpetual lack of finances, so he sent away a small collection of his poems on the off chance they might be published. He also needed to get away from at least one angry father upset that his daughter had succumbed to the young rebel's charm.

Burns seriously considered taking the same course that an increasing number of his fellow Scots citizens were taking at the time, that of emigrating to another country, but just as he was about to leave for Jamaica to become a bookkeeper on a plantation, a small book of his poetry titled *Poems, Chiefly in the Scottish Dialect* (1786) was released to immediate commercial success. It contained some of Burns's best work, including 'To a Mouse', 'The Cotter's Saturday Night', 'Halloween', 'The Twa Dogs' and 'The Holy Fair'.

Buoyed by his sudden reputation as a supposedly unschooled 'ploughman poet', Burns moved to Edinburgh in 1786 to become part of the thriving cultural scene there. He had made promises to one of his lovers, Mary Campbell (the 'Highland Mary' of Burns legend), to take her overseas, but in the event, shortly after he left for Edinburgh, Mary fell ill, possibly with typhus (though there were suggestions that she was pregnant and might have given birth to a stillborn child), and died not much later.

Burn's growing reputation as a poet led to a commission from publisher James Johnson for a collection of Scottish folk songs. There was a renaissance of Scottish culture at the time and Johnson wisely predicted that along with painting, stories and Scottish tartan, there would be a demand for Scottish poetry and songs as well. Burns had already collected a number of folk songs before taking up the commission. Into this collection he added 160 poems of his own. These were published as *The Scots Musical Museum* in five volumes over a period of sixteen years.

This compilation included a reworking of 'Auld Lang Syne' (loosely meaning 'times long past'), which later became a famous song, usually performed on New Year's Eve. It has been translated into many different languages and is sung from Argentina to Zimbabwe, making it one of the most popular tunes in the world.

In 1788, Burns, now twenty-nine, moved back to Ayrshire and married Jean Armour who had already given him two sets of twins. She would go on to have five more children to Robert, the last would be born on the day of his funeral. However, being married did not stop him from continuing to have a string of affairs and lovers.

The following year he took up an appointment as an Excise Officer in Dumfries to supplement the family income. It was a position he would hold until his death. Being an Excise officer was relatively easy work that provided a steady income, which he needed at the time as his writing was not providing sufficient funds to date.

He also rented a farm, but gave that up in 1791, staying on in Dumfries to concentrate on his writing and his Excise duties. The same year he published 'Tam O'Shanter' as an accompaniment to an illustration in a book titled *Antiquities of Scotland*.

He also wrote 'The Slave's Lament' in 1792, to voice his strong opposition to slavery and his equally strong support for the abolitionist movement that was gaining currency in Britain at the time.

Jean Armour would live in the same residence in Dumfries until her death in 1834. In old age she recalled the domestic routine: 'The family breakfasted at nine as [Burns] lay long in bed awake he was always reading. At all his meals he had a book beside him on the table . . . He dined at two o'clock when he dined at home; was fond of plain things, and hated tarts, pies and puddings. When at home in the evening he employed his time in writing and reading, with the children playing about him. Their prattle never disturbed him in the least.'

When not at home, Burns enjoyed the drink and company to be found at the Globe public house or the Hole in the Wall (Queensbury Square). The family worshipped at St Michael's Church, where their pew is marked with a tablet.

A music publisher, George Thomson, enlisted his help in compiling *A Select Collection of Scottish Airs*, which was first published in 1793, with the remaining volumes being published over a period after Burns's death. In total Burns wrote 114 songs for what would eventually be six volumes of songs and he was working on items for this collection right up to his death.

Burns was outspoken in his support for the French Revolution, and in 1795 he sent Thomson a new song he had recently written called 'For a' that and a' that', which echoes the radical ideas (and even in places the words) of Thomas Paine's *The Rights of Man*.

But Burns's three great loves in his life – wine, women and song – were starting to catch up with him. His health declined rapidly during his last years, and his penchant for trying folk remedies only made his condition worse. In 1796, Burns passed away, probably of endocarditis caused by rheumatic fever on the heart. He was only thirty-seven years of age. He was buried in a modest grave in St Michael's churchyard, Dumfries.

Burns did not die wealthy and he left his wife and children

(both legitimate and illegitimate) in fairly desperate financial circumstances, which he had compounded by not making a will. Jean had to take legal action against creditors to secure the small amounts of money owed to Burns.

Subsequently, she arranged to release much of her husband's unpublished material and secured continued payment for the work already in the public domain and was selling well.

Burns gained more fame after his death than he ever did during his lifetime. He achieved the status of an icon of Scottish culture during Jean's lifetime and this afforded his widow and children a degree of comfort he had himself never quite attained.

Jean survived her husband by thirty-eight years, Twenty years after his death, his fame had reached such a point that his coffin was exhumed and reburied in a specially commissioned mausoleum in St Michael's churchyard in Dumfries. Here, Jean Armour and five of their nine children are buried with him.

In 1823, a spectacular monument to Burns constructed by public subscription was erected in the poet's birthplace of Alloway and has become a place of pilgrimage for Burns's admirers and a focus for celebrating his life and work. It was estimated that the opening attracted a crowd of over 100,000 to witness the event.

People ask what it is about Burns that has made him so universally popular for more than two centuries after his death. In part it is his rebelliousness: his risk-taking may be condemned by some, but it is also secretly admired by others. Most of all, though, it is his earthiness and his rustic, rural origins: the 'ploughman poet' may have been a clever slogan dreamed up in Edinburgh to help sell his books, but it is also true in that he did come from humble origins and for many years worked on the family farm ploughing the fields.

But for all his background, attitude and rebelliousness the one matter that has led to his fame and iconic status was the quality and volume of his work. It has stood the test of time and his thoughts, feelings, desires and experiences expressed in his poems and songs are just as relevant today as they were two centuries ago. One of the most popular is his love song 'A Red, Red, Rose'.

Since his death, Burns Clubs have sprung up worldwide to cherish the name of Robert Burns; to foster a love of his writings, and generally to encourage an interest in the Scottish language and literature.

During his short, but productive life, Burns wrote over 600 poems and songs. Many are still favourites today. His birthplace in Alloway is now a public museum and education centre, which attracts more than a half a million visitors to it a year.

As well as monuments and statues across Scotland to Robert Burns (twenty in all), there are commemorations to Burns in many countries around the world, including United States (sixteen), Canada (nine), Australia (eight), New Zealand (four) and England (one).

Thousands gather every year around the globe to celebrate the birthday of Robert Burns, proclaim his 'Address to the Haggis' and then consume the pudding along with fine talk and copious quantities of alcohol. As a result, his birthday celebrations rank up there alongside those of Buddha, Mahatma Ghandi, Martin Luther King and the Emperor of Japan. Now that's fame!

LACHLAN MACQUARIE (1761–1824)

COLONIAL GOVERNOR WHO SET AUSTRALIA ON ITS PATH TO PROSPERITY

Lachlan Macquarie was born on the Hebridean island of Ulva to a cousin of the last Chieftain of the clan MacQuarrie. The family spoke Gaelic, the ancient language of the Hebrides and west coast of Scotland. In 1772, the father moved the family from Ulva to a small farm on the nearby larger island of Mull where they leased 75 acres from the Duke of Argyll. When Lachlan was about fourteen years old his father died and the boy was sent to Edinburgh to receive a rudimentary education and learn to speak and write in English.

But formal schooling did not suit him and the following year he accompanied his uncle to North America where they signed on in the British Army to fight the colonial rebels who had declared their independence. In 1777 he obtained an ensigncy in the 2nd Battalion of the 84th Regiment of Foot (then known as the Royal Highland Emigrants) and performed garrison duty, first in Halifax, Nova

Scotia, and later in New York and Charleston in the closing stages of the American War of Independence. Lachlan was commissioned as a lieutenant in the 71st Highland Regiment in 1781, and subsequently posted to Jamaica.

The spelling of Scottish names has always been a delicate and confusing subject and Lachlan's own family name continues to be spelt several different ways today. It appears that from the early 1780s Lachlan adopted the specific spelling of his surname we still use today – Macquarie.

In 1784 Lachlan returned to Scotland and while on inactive service was reduced to half pay. He took on any work he could until recalled by the army in 1787 when he was re-appointed as a lieutenant and attached to the 77th Regiment of Foot, which was about to sail for India. He would stay in India for fourteen years during which time he distinguished himself through involvement in a number of actions that expanded Britain's control over the rich sub-continent. He was promoted to captain in 1789 and then to major in 1801.

It was also during his service in India that he married Jane Jarvis, the youngest daughter of the Chief Justice of Antigua who was visiting India. But their union proved to be brief and childless as Jane died of tuberculosis after just three years of marriage.

In April 1801, while serving as Military Secretary to Jonathan Duncan, Governor of Bombay, Macquarie was appointed to the post of Deputy Adjutant General to an 8,000-strong army, under the command of Major-General David Baird. This force was sent to Egypt and there it defeated Napoleon, expelling the French from Africa.

Macquarie eventually returned to Britain in 1803 to attend to financial matters after a round of social engagements in London.

When he returned to Scotland and the Isle of Mull on two months' leave he visited family and friends and took possession of a 4,000-hectare farm that he had purchased from a relative. During this brief visit he was advised he was to be promoted to Lieutenant-Colonel and sent back to India to have his own command, the 73rd Regiment of Foot. He had just met and fallen in love with a distant cousin, Elizabeth Campbell. Before his departure, he asked for her hand in marriage, but to keep it a secret until his next return.

However, it was to be three long years before his return, which was only prompted because an impatient Elizabeth wrote Lachlan a letter in which she made it clear that if their wedding was to proceed he needed to return home soon. They married in 1807 in England. She was twenty-nine, he was forty-six.

In April 1809 Macquarie was appointed Governor of New South Wales to replace William Bligh whose governorship had been racked with controversy. Macquarie and his wife sailed with the 73rd Regiment from Portsmouth arriving at Sydney eight months later. He took up his commission as Governor on 1 January 1810 and was made full colonel later that year.

Macquarie's first priority was to restore order. The previous Governor, Captain William Bligh of the HMS *Bounty* mutiny fame, had been arrested by his own soldiers in a rebellion and was effectively under house arrest when Macquarie arrived. Macquarie dismissed the troops responsible for the *coup d'état*, replacing them with his own trusted soldiers from the 73rd Regiment, and then had the ringleaders arrested. At the head of 800 battle-hardened, regular British soldiers – most of them from the Scottish Highlands as well – Macquarie's actions were not challenged by the inferior numbers of the New South Wales Corps, of whom many had become settled in farming, commerce and trade.

LACHLAN MACQUARIE (1761–1824)

Bligh and the accused were dispatched to London on separate ships to be dealt with by British authorities and Lachlan Macquarie turned his attention back to running a colony. Bligh would be declared blameless in the subsequent inquiry while the leader of the rebellion found himself court-martialled and cashiered from the army. For the swift and bloodless way he restored order in the fledgling colony, Macquarie was promoted to brigadier in 1811 and then to major-general in 1813.

When he arrived in New South Wales, the small colony had a population of only 11,600 Europeans, of whom about half were convicts. It was also on the far side of the world and had a tiny foothold on a vast continent that was inhabited by up to 300,000 Aborigines. From the outset, Macquarie could see this outpost's enormous potential, not as a penal colony but as a settlement for free immigrants. Unfortunately, while the numbers of free settlers did increase under his term, so too did the number of convicts transported. Even though the population of New South Wales had more than trebled to almost 37,000 by his departure in 1822, the proportion of convicts still remained stubbornly at about half.

Governor Macquarie's next task was to commence an ambitious programme of public works – new buildings, towns, roads – to help grow the new colony and expand its reach into the unknown continent. He also realised that free men made better citizens than men in chains and under his governorship, Macquarie extensively used the practice of granting convicts tickets-of-leave, whereby criminal sentences were drastically reduced for good behaviour.

This policy of encouraging convicts brought him into conflict with a section of the influential, conservative, elite of the local society. This group, known as the 'exclusives', sought to restrict civil rights and judicial privileges to itself. Many of these free settlers also had influential friends in English political circles.

Convicts whose skills or expertise were regarded by Macquarie as crucial for the future development of the colony often found themselves granted a ticket-of-leave from servitude and placed in relatively senior administrative positions. For example, Francis Greenway arrived in the colony in 1814, sentenced to fourteen years for forgery. In England, he had been a bankrupt architect who had fallen foul of the law by forging a financial document. His original sentence had been death. At the time New South Wales had no architect and Macquarie was desperate to press ahead with his public works programme. The Governor immediately set him the task of designing a number of public buildings, and in 1818, after serving four years of his fourteen-year sentence Greenway was granted a ticket-of-leave (emancipated) and appointed Government Architect on a salary.

The example of Greenway was repeated with others including Dr William Redfern, appointed to colonial surgeon, and Andrew Thompson as a magistrate. Macquarie wrote at the time that 'emancipation, when united with rectitude and long-tried good conduct, should lead a man back to that rank in society which he had forfeited.'

For a number of the colony's wealthy elite, Macquarie's views were seen as far too liberal – even radical – and fed a growing sense of unease in his administration. They also objected to the virtual dictatorial powers he wielded as Governor, for at the time the infant colony did not have a parliament and only a very nascent judiciary to balance Macquarie's executive powers.

His list of opponents continued to grow, as did the letters of complaint against him to influential friends back in England. This caused Macquarie a great deal of frustration and, coupled with recurring bouts of illness, led him to submit his resignation to London authorities on several occasions.

At the same time as Macquarie was dealing with a growing chorus of criticism, he was getting on with the more important task of developing and expanding the colony. In short order he established firm control over Tasmania, New Zealand (then part of his responsibility), and founded new towns in Sydney's west as well as along the coast of New South Wales.

Before Macquarie's arrival the colony did not have money. Up to then the only form of currency was rum. In 1813, Macquarie purchased 40,000 Spanish dollar coins and had a convict punch out the coin's centres thereby doubling the number of coins he could put into circulation. The 'Holy Dollar' as it was known became Australia's first currency and 150 years later would become the corporate logo for a new merchant bank, aptly named the Macquarie Bank.

Also in 1813, he authorised three explorers, Blaxland, Lawson and Wentworth, to find a way through the mountain range to Sydney's west to the land beyond. With the assistance of Aboriginal guides they were successful, which helped open up the enormously productive plains of the interior.

The first European settlement west of the mountains was named Bathurst (in honour of Lord Bathurst, then Secretary for the Colonies). The location was proclaimed by Mr and Mrs Macquarie on an official visit there in 1815. The city of Bathurst prides itself on being the oldest inland settlement in Australia.

Macquarie ordered all traffic on the roads to keep to the left and they still do today. He created the colony's first bank in 1817 and, in the same year, was the first to officially adopt the name 'Australia', after a suggestion by Captain Matthew Flinders who had just returned to Sydney from circumnavigating the continent.

Lachlan Macquarie and his wife Elizabeth both took a keen interest in the welfare of the young people of the colony. In 1813, Governor Macquarie laid the foundation stone to what would become the first public welfare project in Australia – the Female Orphan School in Parramatta. Mrs Macquarie became the school's patroness and ensured that as many young, 'orphaned' females as possible were given a decent education and raised to become productive members of the infant colony. Almost two centuries later the then derelict school buildings were handed over to the University of Western Sydney, responsible for restoring it to its former glory. The building now houses the Whitlam Institute, containing personal papers and physical memorabilia from Gough Whitlam, one of Australia's most beloved prime ministers.

Macquarie's attitude towards the Australian Aborigines could best be described as ambivalent and patronising. He did order punitive expeditions against tribes that resisted European expansion. He also founded a school for the education of Aboriginal children in Parramatta, but it had limited success because it advocated the separation of the children from their parents. He appears to have reflected a fairly common belief held at the time that the natives were inferior to good British stock and the best that could be done for the Aborigines was to assimilate them as quickly as possible into a white society.

A serious illness in 1819 almost proved fatal and when he learned that a commission had been convened to inquire into the state of the colony, he submitted his third resignation to London, which was accepted. In 1822 he and his wife and son (also named Lachlan) departed for England. Elizabeth had given birth to her son after having had six miscarriages over eight previous years.

In 1822–23 Macquarie took Elizabeth and Lachlan, with servants and a tutor, on a grand tour through France, Italy and Switzerland because he was worried about Elizabeth's health. He also vigorously defended his administration of the colony during hearings of the Bigge Commission, named after John Thomas Bigge, the judge appointed to conduct the investigation.

In January 1824 he finally retired with his family to his estate on Mull, but in April that year died from complications (probably septicaemia) from a chronic bowel condition. He was sixty-three years of age and was survived by his wife and son. He is buried in a family mausoleum on Mull that the Australian Government substantially renovated in the year 2000.

Lachlan Macquarie is regarded so fondly in Australia that over a hundred streets, places, rivers, towns and lakes have subsequently been named in his honour. There is also a Macquarie Hospital, a Macquarie University, a Macquarie Bank as previously mentioned and even an entire suburb in Canberra that has been named after him.

Today, he is regarded as the most enlightened and progressive of the early governors of the new settlement. A Scot who sought to change the penal colony of New South Wales into a prosperous country populated by hard-working, free citizens. Some even describe Macquarie as the 'Father of Australia'.

SIR ALEXANDER MACKENZIE
(1762–1820)

FUR TRADER AND EXPLORER WHO COMPLETED THE FIRST EAST–WEST CROSSING OF CANADA

A lexander was born on the Isle of Lewis in the Outer Hebrides to a mercantile family of some prominence. In 1774, Alexander's father took the whole family in search of a better life to the colony of New York. A few years later when the American War of Independence broke out, Alexander was sent to live with relatives in the comparative safety of Montreal, while his father stayed behind and joined the King's Royal Regiment of New York.

Alexander's father died (probably of scurvy) in 1780 at Fort Haldimand on Carleton Island, Lake Ontario, while defending British North America from the revolutionary forces of George Washington. At about the same time, Alexander, now in his teens and determined to carve out a life for himself, signed on with a Montreal-based fur-trading company. The North West Company in Montreal was almost as well-known as the Hudson's Bay Company, which was based at Fort York on Hudson Bay, and the rivalry between these two companies shaped the nation that would soon be known as Canada.

Alexander Mackenzie was physically robust, widely read, determined and had a strong belief in himself. He was a born leader. Eight years later he had become a full partner and was given supervision of the important Athabasca fur district in the Canadian north-west. This was wild country, barely explored by Europeans. In 1789 Mackenzie set out from his headquarters at Fort Chipewyan (now in Alberta) on Lake Athabasca on the first of his two noted trips of exploration.

After reaching Great Slave Lake, he followed the then unknown Mackenzie River to the Arctic Ocean. By the time the expedition returned, they had completed a round trip of 4,800 kilometres in just 102 days. It was a staggering feat for the time, but he was disappointed that the great river which now bears his name did not prove to be a route to the Pacific, which was always his true aspiration.

In 1793 he set out again. He and his small party made their way up the Peace River, across the Rocky Mountains, part way down a mighty river, named years later as the Fraser and eventually made his way overland to the Pacific coast. Thus Mackenzie completed the first east–west journey across North America north of Mexico. Once again Mackenzie brought his crew home safe and uninjured back to the starting point at Fort Chipewyan, after an extraordinary journey of 3,700 kilometres.

In spite of difficulties with indigenous peoples during the second journey, he never needed to fire a shot in anger on either of his great expeditions.

What Mackenzie did not know at the time was that his actions would have a significant impact on Canadian history. Being the first

European to reach the Pacific Ocean overland (twelve years before the Lewis and Clark expedition) he inadvertently strengthened the British Empire's hand decades later when negotiating the disputed boundary between Oregon and British Columbia.

Shortly after this historic exploit, Alexander Mackenzie left the North American west to return to Montreal. He would never venture west again. His memoir *Voyages from Montreal, on the River St Laurence, Through the Continent of North America, to the Frozen and Pacific Oceans; In the Years 1789 and 1793* (published 1801) won him wide recognition and a knighthood from King George III in 1802. Mackenzie was elected to the Legislative Assembly of Lower Canada in 1805, but in 1808 he returned to Scotland, where he lived for the rest of his life.

Mackenzie floated the idea of merging the major fur, fishing and trading companies of the British Empire into one giant trading house to exploit the natural wealth of the empire. Despite there being much merit in his proposal, the plan never got beyond concept as vested interests made sure the idea was stillborn.

In 1812, aged forty-eight, Alexander Mackenzie married his beautiful fourteen-year-old cousin Geddes Margaret Mackenzie. She was the twin daughter of a wealthy, Scottish-born Londoner who had died in 1809, leaving the ample estate of Avoch in the Black Isle, Ross and Cromarty, Scotland. Already extremely well-off from his shares in the fur trade and from book royalties, Alexander purchased for £20,000 the share of the Avoch estate that his young bride had not inherited.

A daughter was born in 1816, and two sons followed in 1818 and 1819. By the time the sons were born Mackenzie's health was failing; Bright's disease (chronic nephritis) appears to have been the most likely cause. In January 1820 he went to Edinburgh to seek medical advice and on the return journey to Avoch, he died unexpectedly in a wayside inn near Dunkeld.

Mackenzie had single-handedly opened up the western half of Canada and in the process helped Britain deny America's dream of forever expanding the borders of the United States of America northwards.

CHARLES MACINTOSH
(1766–1843)

CHEMIST AND INVENTOR OF WATERPROOF FABRICS

Macintosh was born in Glasgow, the son of a wealthy merchant, and educated at a grammar school in Glasgow and then at a school in Yorkshire. His father imported and manufactured chemicals used in dye manufacturing as well as manufacturing dye made from lichen. He wanted Charles to follow him into the business as a manager, but thought his son should learn the ropes of business by starting from the bottom up. So Macintosh began his working life as a clerk, but instead of dealing with other people's chemicals, he wanted to become a chemist himself. While working, he also studied chemistry at the University of Glasgow and then went on to study at Edinburgh.

On his return to Glasgow, Macintosh resigned his clerkship to open a small workshop, manufacturing chemicals on his own. He was highly successful from the start, inventing various new processes and introducing new chemicals from overseas that he replicated in his own workshop, which grew into a factory. Macintosh started making aluminium acetate, which was used widely in treating skin ailments, wounds and burns. He then imported lead acetate from Holland that was used as a fixative in the colour and dye industry, particular in large-scale calico printing.

In 1790, Macintosh married Mary Fisher, daughter of Alexander Fisher, a merchant of Glasgow.

In 1795, Macintosh started the first alum works (aluminium sulphate) in Scotland at Hurlet about 10 kilometres from Glasgow, having found that the waste shale from old exhausted coal mines contained the raw material. Alum was used extensively in the paper, cloth and tanning processes, but its prohibitive cost up to then had limited the growth of these industries. But Macintosh was soon producing over 2,000 tons of alum a year, which lowered its price from £25 per ton to £12 per ton and led to a mini-boom in dependent industries using this product in Scotland.

In 1808, he commenced manufacturing Prussian blue pigment, a very expensive ingredient in painting, ceramics and the dye industry. While a very complex manufacturing process, the raw ingredients were actually quite plentiful, being the horns and hooves of animals. Macintosh managed to simplify the production process and started flooding the market with an inexpensive, quality product. This led to yet another boost in the dye industry, which was beginning to concentrate around Glasgow and Macintosh's supply of essential chemicals.

Also living in Glasgow was Charles Tennant, who had a large chemical plant at St Rollox, where he made a bleaching liquor. Macintosh and Tennant worked together to produce a bleach in powdered form, called chloride of lime, and became partners in the new product, which they patented. Bleaching powder replaced bleaching liquid overnight and was used extensively in the cloth and paper manufacturing processes. The large-scale manufacture of chloride of lime proved to be a source of considerable wealth for both men and Macintosh remained associated with the St Rollox chemical works until 1814. The success of the plant made it, for a while, the largest chemical works in Europe.

In 1818, while analysing by-products of a factory making coal gas, Macintosh produced naphtha – a volatile, oily liquid hydrocarbon mixture. Macintosh believed he could find new ways to utilise this substance. It was already known that naphtha could dissolve indiarubber (natural latex from the rubber tree), yet the liquid remained sticky and pliable, even at room temperature. Macintosh, joined two sheets of fabric together with this solution, allowed them to dry, and discovered that the new material could not be penetrated by water. He had invented the first waterproof cloth.

He patented his discovery in 1823 and when the fabric was later used to make a raincoat, it was called a macintosh after him. Before long, it had acquired the extra letter, 'k', possibly introduced by the English, and 'mackintosh' seems to have been quickly accepted by the general public, while 'macintosh' – for the garment – was relegated to 'variant spelling'.

The Duke of York (son of King George II) made the raincoat popular from the start, when a stylish waterproof military cloak of blue cloth, lined with crimson silk, was made for him in the 1820s. Many young officers from the Guards regiments started wearing the garment and soon all of London, then Britain, wanted one.

With the invention of the raincoat, Macintosh went from being a chemist to a clothing manufacturer. In 1825, he set up in Manchester with several partners. New buildings were constructed and the entire plant was driven by one of the new steam engines produced at the Boulton and Watt iron works in Birmingham. With the discovery of vulcanised rubber in 1839, Macintosh was able to incorporate the new material into his fabrics, thereby avoiding the stiffness or stickiness experienced in the early models. Macintosh's business continued to grow and expanded into the manufacture of other India rubber goods, including rubber shoes and cushions. The factory he started is now owned by the Dunlop Rubber Company.

In 1823, Macintosh was elected a fellow of the Royal Society in recognition of his superb achievements in chemistry. Even so, his inventiveness was not yet exhausted. Macintosh devised a short-cut way of using carbon gases to convert malleable iron to steel and invented a hot-blast process to produce high-quality cast iron.

He died in 1843 still living close to his native hometown at Dunchattan, near Glasgow and was buried in the churchyard of Glasgow Cathedral. He was seventy-seven years old.

Macintosh will be forever remembered for his invention of the raincoat and subsequent waterproof apparel, but it is his lifelong association with advances in chemistry that should receive the greater recognition. His outstanding contributions to the cloth, paper, coal, dyeing and chemical industries which grew up in Scotland and around Glasgow in particular, created employment for many thousands of people over a century. Macintosh helped Glasgow earn the deserved reputation for being the 'workshop of the Empire'.

CAROLINA OLIPHANT, LADY NAIRNE (1766–1845)

COLLECTOR AND WRITER OF SCOTTISH SONGS AND BALLADS

Carolina was born near Dunning in Perthshire into an aristocratic family who had lived in the area since the 1200s. Carolina's parents both strongly supported the Jacobite cause and had had their lands confiscated by the government for it. For a while Carolina's father, Laurence Oliphant, had to go into exile to avoid arrest. Even Carolina's name was chosen because it was the female equivalent of Charles (after Bonnie Prince Charlie) who was still living in exile in Europe when Carolina was born.

From an early age she was taught to read and write both prose and poetry and she started recording the traditional country songs she heard being sung in the nearby villages and farms. Many of the refrains were written down verbatim, but some had fairly ribald lyrics, which Carolina discreetly replaced with her own compositions. She also produced material with a strong Jacobite flavour for the benefit of her family who never lost heart in the fruitless cause to have a Stewart monarch returned to the throne. Her best-known pieces today are perhaps 'Charlie is my darling' and 'The Hundred Pipers'. Without knowing it, she was recording a rich tradition of Scottish folk music at the very time it was rapidly disappearing.

On a personal note, Carolina was considered so beautiful that she became known as the 'Flower of Strathearn' (the name for the river and surrounds near her home in Dunning). But despite a number of suitors, she chose not to marry until 1808 when she was forty-one years of age. Her husband was a relative, Major William Nairne, and they moved to Edinburgh when he was appointed Inspector-General of Edinburgh Castle. In 1808, Carolina gave birth to her one and only child who was sickly from birth.

Carolina who had been collecting and writing poetry all her life had amassed a sizeable portfolio of material by the time she was married. A close friend persuaded her to publish the material and arranged for a publisher she knew to take on the work. At that time it was considered improper for upper-class women like Carolina to tarnish their good name and status by working. Carolina had kept her poetry and song-writing secret from her new husband, so she adopted a pseudonym, like several other Scottish women writing at the time. Her first book of poetry was published in 1824 in six volumes under the title *Scottish Minstrel*.

Coincidentally, in 1824, titles forfeited by Jacobites after the 1745 uprising were restored and William became Baron Nairne, with Carolina becoming Lady Nairne. After William died in 1830, Carolina lived in Ireland for three years, but then decided to travel through Europe with her invalid son. Unfortunately the rigors of travel proved too great for the twenty-nine-year-old son and he died in Brussels in 1837. Carolina returned to the old familiar family house in Dunning in 1843, dying there in 1845 at the age of seventy-nine.

The year after her death, Carolina's sister published a posthumous collection of Carolina's verse and song, entitled *Lays of Strathearn*, and for the first time she was publicly identified as the true author of many popular songs and poems.

Her most loved piece of writing is a song and lyrics that she originally wrote about a Bonnie Prince Charlie. It has since become known around the world as a song of farewell. It is called 'Will ye no come back again?'.

After her death Carolina's words continued to move people. In 1881 there was a great storm out on the North Sea that took the lives of 189 Scottish fishermen. It was the worst Scottish fishing disaster ever recorded. Many of the men were from the east-coast fishing village of Eyemouth, on the coast of the Scottish Borders. A stone monument was erected shortly after the event displaying a symbolic broken mast. More recently a series of evocative bronze statues standing on a stone plinth have been unveiled depicting lifelike images of wives and children looking out to sea searching in vain for their missing men.

Words from one of Carolina Oliphant's poems accompany the statue:

Wha'll buy my fresh herrin'?
They're no' brought here without brave darin',
Buy my caller herrin',
Haul'd through wind and rain.

Buy my caller herrin'!
Though ye may ca' them vulgar farin'.

Wives and mithers, maist despairin',
Ca' them lives o' men.

Her body of work is considered second only to that of Robert Burns, Scotland's National Poet (*see* p. 97). Altogether, she wrote or adapted nearly a hundred songs and poems in her lifelong endeavour and without her, much of the Scottish musical heritage would have been lost.

SIR WALTER SCOTT
(1771–1832)

WRITER, LAWYER, POET
AND HISTORIAN

Scott was born in Edinburgh, the ninth child in a family of twelve, of whom the first six died in infancy. His father was a well-known lawyer and his mother was the eldest daughter of a Professor of Medicine at Edinburgh University. Both parents were descended from well-regarded and influential families in the Scottish Borders. The twin influences of academic excellence and the history of the Scottish Borders would go on to shape young Walter's life.

Scott contracted an illness (probably polio) as a child which left him with a permanent limp. At the age of about two he was sent to his grandparents' farm in the hope that the country air would strengthen his health. While he was there his aunt spent much time reading to him, and teaching him to read. Although his lameness remained, Scott's health improved and he returned to Edinburgh, eventually to begin his full-time education at Edinburgh High School and then, in 1783, Edinburgh University, where he trained as a lawyer. Practising law may have paid the bills, but devouring books, learning foreign languages and absorbing history became his passion.

The first books he wrote were translations of German Romantic ballads and were published anonymously in the mid-1790s. He did not write under his own name until 1827. The German translations were followed by several collections of Border ballads that first drew his writing to the public.

In 1797, Scott married Charlotte Carpenter, of a French royalist family, who bore him three sons and two daughters. They lived a very happy life together, until her death in 1826.

He continued to practise law and was appointed Sheriff-Depute of Selkirkshire in 1799. His legal duties paid well, but were not that onerous, allowing him to produce a prolific number of poems. One of the better-known poems from this period is *Marmion* (1808).

Other long narrative poems followed, including *The Lady of the Lake* in 1810 and *Rokeby* in 1813. But about this time, Scott felt that he was being eclipsed in popularity by the poet Byron and determined he should try his hand at creating a new form of writing in which stories are set in the past and characters and events can be real or imagined. His first novel in this genre, *Waverley* (1814), was about Scotland during the Jacobite Rebellion of 1745. It was an instant triumph.

About this time he purchased an estate on the banks of the Tweed River at Galashiels in the Scottish Borders, which he renamed 'Abbotsford', and which he continued to build on to for many years. It was to be his residence for the rest of his life and one of two causes of his financial ruin in the future. The other was his book-publishing and printing business.

Encouraged by the spectacular success of his first novel, Scott penned off a string of novels in quick succession, including *Guy Mannering* (1815), *The Antiquary* (1816), *The Black Dwarf* (1816), *Old Mortality* (1816), *Roby Roy* (1817), *The Heart of Midlothian* (1818), *The Bride of Lammermoor* (1818), *A legend of Montrose* (1819) and *Ivanhoe* (1819), which is considered by many as his finest work.

More historical novels followed over the next dozen years or so, now mainly set in England to appeal to a wider audience. Scott also found time to write volumes, essays, reviews and critiques on a wide range of subjects, though many of them were focused on history.

Scott's interest in all things Scottish led him to explore the dungeons of Edinburgh Castle, with permission, where he unearthed the Scottish crown and sceptre that had lain forgotten in a wooden chest for centuries. A grateful King George IV granted Scott the title of baronet in 1820.

Two years later the King insisted Scott stage-manage the Royal tour of Scotland, the first for a reigning British monarch since 1650. With only three weeks for planning and execution, Scott created an outstanding and comprehensive pageant designed not only to impress the King, but also the Scottish people. He practically re-invented Highland society and clan tartans, and even managed to dress the enthusiastic King in a false tartan outfit. In one stroke, Scott managed to rehabilitate the wearing of tartan that had been banned since the Jacobite rebellion of 1745. In the process, he also allowed the people of Scotland to feel good about themselves and their history (even though much of it had been romanticised by Scott himself).

In 1825, a banking crisis resulted in the collapse of Scott's printing business. He had also been extravagant in expanding his baronial mansion at Abbotsford in the Borders. In total he found himself owing the then staggering sum of £120,000. Rather than declare himself bankrupt or accept help from friends (including a financial offer from the King), he was determined to write his way out of debt. He kept up his prodigious output of fiction, until his health started failing him in 1831. He died in his beloved home at Abbotsford in 1832. Within two years of his death, continuing royalty payments had discharged all of his debt.

Although he published biographies of Swift and Dryden and some history, as well as poems and novels, his chief claim to distinction was his invention of a new genre in literature, the historical novel. Many other great writers have since emulated his narrative style of historical novels, including Alexandre Dumas, Honoré de Balzac, Charles Dickens, Victor Hugo, Washington Irving and Leo Tolstoy.

His popularity, both with the people and as a writer, was almost unparalleled and in 1840, a grateful nation erected a magnificent monument to him in Princes Street Gardens, Edinburgh, next to what would become Waverley Station (after Scott's most famous novel).

In 2013, Queen Elizabeth II officially re-opened Abbottsford to the general public after the completion of a two-year, multimillion-pound restoration project. Today, it is a spectacular place to visit or stay. The magnificent library room contains one of the largest private collections of antiquarian books in Britain, some so rare they may be the only remaining copies in the world. All were accumulated by Sir Walter Scott himself.

Every year one of the richest prizes in British literature is awarded in Scotland for historical novels. It is, naturally enough, called the Sir Walter Scott Prize.

ROBERT STEVENSON
(1772–1850)

CIVIL ENGINEER AND FAMED
BUILDER OF LIGHTHOUSES

Stevenson was born in Glasgow and when he was still an infant, his father and uncle, who were partners in a West Indian trading house, both died of fever in the Caribbean. The loss of both partners in the same business caused great financial hardship to the remaining family members and forced the family to move to Edinburgh, where Robert could be educated in a charity school.

His mother intended him to become a minister of religion, but when he was fifteen, she married Thomas Smith, an engineer of the newly formed Northern Lighthouse Board, and this changed the direction of Stevenson's life completely.

Lighthouses had been around since ancient times, but were exceedingly rare and mainly constructed to signal the whereabouts of a port to the weary sailor. With an exponential rise in ocean-going travel from the early eighteenth century, there was a crucial need to warn shipping of hazards such as reefs or rocks. Thus the

Northern Lighthouse Board was formed in 1786 as the lighthouse authority for Scotland and the Isle of Man.

The young Robert Stevenson started as assistant to his stepfather in the supervision of the few and primitive lighthouses that existed on the coasts of Scotland at the time. But as the main purpose of the Northern Lighthouse Board was to construct urgently needed modern navigation warnings it was only a matter of time before he was allowed to turn his hand to construction. In 1791, after four years of diligent apprenticeship, Stevenson was entrusted with the erection of a new lighthouse on the island of Little Cumbrae on the Firth of Clyde.

Interspersed with his apprentice duties, Stevenson studied at university to receive a qualified education in civil engineering. He attended lectures at the Andersonian Institute in Glasgow (now renamed the University of Strathclyde) as well as the University of Edinburgh alongside a very demanding schedule at work. Despite his conscientious application to higher education, his Latin and ancient Greek language skills – which were prerequisites to an engineering degree at the time – were insufficient for him to receive a formal qualification.

Nevertheless, his practical knowledge and demonstrated skill in the design and construction of lighthouses was so outstanding, that Stevenson was appointed engineer to the Lighthouse Board after his stepfather Smith's retirement in 1797.

Stevenson experienced first-hand the perils that faced sailors every day at sea. In 1794, while supervising the construction of a lighthouse on the Orkney Islands the sloop returning him to the shore became becalmed. The captain kindly arranged for Stevenson to be rowed the short distance to land, but he and the crew stayed behind on the sloop. A violent gale suddenly came upon them and drove them on to the very rocks on which Stevenson was erecting his lighthouse. Everyone on board the sloop perished.

In the early 1800s Stevenson embarked upon a project that would become the most important work of his life, the Bell Rock Lighthouse. It was urgently needed yet would prove extremely difficult to construct.

The rock was mostly a submerged reef covered with water in all but the lowest tide and located about 22 kilometres due east of the east coast of Scotland opposite the town of St. Andrews. It was directly in the path of shipping wishing to enter Dundee on the Firth of Tay, or Leith (the port for Edinburgh) on the Firth of Forth.

Several ships a year were being lost on the rock during heavy winter storms, causing the loss of many sailors' lives. In 1799, without warning a violent storm struck shipping in the North Sea and over seventy vessels were lost and hundreds of sailors perished in Scotland alone. Many of these vessels broke up on the Scottish coast trying to avoid Bell Rock. But worse was to come in 1804, when the 74-gun *York* from the Royal Navy, unable to detect its presence in the storm, foundered on Bell Rock itself, with the loss of all her crew.

Bell Rock Lighthouse was so difficult to erect it required Stevenson to invent new techniques of construction, new designs and even the use of new materials. Being almost submerged, Stevenson had only one-to-two hours a day available to actually work on the rock. He constructed each part of the structure separately on land and transported it to the rock for installation. Some days he was able to fit one stone only, other days the seas were too rough even to allow access to the rock. Of course, in winter, when the weather was at its wildest and seas at its most unpredictable it was too dangerous to work at all.

ROBERT STEVENSON (1772–1850)

He insisted the tower be built out of Aberdeen granite to withstand the destructive forces of nature and meticulously designed each block so that they slotted into the others with the precision of a jigsaw puzzle. Masonry was held in place with dovetail joints reinforced by steel rods.

In fits and starts over a three-year period (1807_1810), the lighthouse tower slowly rose to its required height of 35 metres above the rock. When all the lights, reflectors and lamps were installed, the resultant beam shone out into the North Sea for an unprecedented 50 kilometres in every direction. Before the lighthouse was built, literally hundreds of ships had been lost on Bell Rock. In the two hundred years since its construction, only two ships have been known to have struck the rock; one in 1908 in a very thick fog and the other in 1915 when First World War restrictions caused the light to be switched off.

Today Bell Rock lighthouse remains the oldest working lighthouse in the world. Its masonry has remained unchanged in 200 years, despite being pounded by some of the most ferocious storms in recorded history. Bell Rock Lighthouse was considered by many to be the most notable engineering achievement in the world at that time and its design by Stevenson became the template for all lighthouses built afterwards.

The period after Napoleon's defeat at Waterloo in 1815 was a time of much improvement of the fabric of Britain, and engineering skills were much in demand. Besides his work for the Northern Lighthouse Board, Stevenson acted as a consulting engineer on many other projects such as roads, bridges, harbours, canals, railways and river navigations. He was responsible for the design of London Road and Regent Road in Edinburgh and oversaw the construction of the Hutcheson Bridge in Glasgow.

He was made a Fellow of the Royal Society of Edinburgh in 1815. He published an *Account of the Bell Rock Lighthouse* in 1824; and also a paper on the North Sea, establishing by evidence that it was eroding the eastern coastline of the United Kingdom and that the great sandbanks were the resultant spoil taken by the sea.

Stevenson worked for the Northern Lighthouse Board for fifty-five years (1787–1842) during which time he designed and oversaw the construction of at least fifteen major new lighthouses in Scotland and the improvement of many more. He made innovations in the choice of light sources, mountings, reflector design and the use of Fresnel lenses to extend the reach of life-saving beams of light. Further, Stevenson also invented the movable jib and the balance crane as a necessary part of lighthouse construction.

Many lighthouses in Ireland and the colonies of the British Empire were fitted with apparatus prepared under the superintendence of Robert Stevenson. He was also an inventor of intermittent and flashing lights, which gave each lighthouse an individual light 'signature' for shipping to easily recognise. For this breakthrough in maritime safety Stevenson received a gold medal from the King of the Netherlands as a mark of appreciation.

In 1799, when Stevenson was twenty-three years of age, he married Jean Smith (the daughter of his stepfather by an earlier marriage). They had a large family of whom three sons followed their father into the lighthouse-building business. Robert retired in 1843, and his eldest son Alan became Engineer to the Northern Lighthouse Board. Robert died in 1850 aged seventy-nine. His wife predeceased him in 1846 and both lie in the Stevenson family plot in New Calton Cemetery in Edinburgh, together with their children, many of whom died in infancy.

For over one hundred years Robert Stevenson and his

Above left: Hazel Aronson, Lady Cosgrove.
© David Reid – www.davidreidart.com. The portrait is currently owned by The Faculty of Advocates, Edinburgh, and hangs in the Advocates' Reading Room, Parliament House.

Above right: John Logie Baird.   *© Mary Evans Picture Library*

Below left: Alexander Graham Bell.   *© Illustrated London News/Mary Evans*

Below right: Susan Boyle.   *© Getty Images*

Above left: Robert the Bruce.

Above right: Robert Burns.

Below left: Calgacus.

Below right: Andrew Carnegie.

Above left: Sir Alexander Fleming.   © *Mary Evans Picture Library*

Above right: Sir Patrick Geddes.   © *Mary Evans Picture Library*

Below left: Niel Gow.   © *Mary Evans Picture Library*

Below right: Field Marshal Lord Haig.

© *David Cohen Fine Art/Mary Evans Picture Library*

Above left: David Hume. © *Mary Evans Picture Library*

Above right: Dr Elsie Inglis. © *Wellcome Library*

Below left: James VI and I. © *Mary Evans Picture Library*

Below right: John Paul Jones. © *Mary Evans Picture Library*

Above left: John Knox. © *Mary Evans Picture Library*

Above right: Piper Daniel Laidlaw, VC. © *Illustrated London News/Mary Evans*

Below left: Dr David Livingstone. © *Mary Evans Picture Library*

Below right: Flora Macdonald. © *Ashmolean Museum/Mary Evans*

Above left: Major-General Lachlan Macquarie. © *Mary Evans Picture Library*

Above right: John Muir. © *Photo Researchers/Mary Evans Picture Library*

Below left: John Napier. © *Mary Evans/BeBa/Iberfoto*

Below right: Margaret Oliphant. © *Mary Evans Picture Library*

Above left: Mary, Queen of Scots.

Above right: Sir Henry Raeburn.

Below left: Joanne (J.K.) Rowling.

Below right: Sir Walter Scott.

© *Mary Evans/BeBa/Iberfoto*

© *Mary Evans Picture Library*

© *Getty Images*

© *Mary Evans Picture Library*

Above left: Adam Smith.   © *Mary Evans/Fonollosa/Iberfoto*

Above right: Robert Louis Stevenson.   © *Epic/Mary Evans*

Below left: Sir Jackie Stewart.   © *Mary Evans/Marx Memorial Library*

Below right: James Watt.   © *Mary Evans Picture Library*

descendants designed most of Scotland's Lighthouses. Battling against the odds and the elements, Robert Stevenson constructed wonders of engineering that have withstood the test of time, an amazing historical achievement. No one has conducted a study of the number of ships and crew saved by Stevenson's involvement in lighthouse design and construction, but in the two centuries before his arrival on the scene, deaths of sailors at sea were so common memorials were everywhere and many people simply refused to travel over water. In the two centuries since, maritime deaths have become a very rare occurrence indeed.

Many of Stevenson's designs and improvements in lighthouse construction were implemented around the world and it is probably no exaggeration to say that Robert Stevenson's lighthouses have saved countless number of sailor's lives globally.

Inspired by the life-saving legacy Robert Stevenson left the world, Sir Walter Scott (*see* p. 124) on a visit to Bell Rock Lighthouse wrote the following poem 'Pharos Loquitur' in the visitors' book:

> Far in the bosom of the deep,
> O'er these wild shelves my watch I keep;
> A ruddy gem of changeful light,
> Bound on the dusky brow of Night,
> The Seaman bids my lustre hail,
> And scorns to strike his timorous sail.

THOMAS COCHRANE, 10TH EARL OF DUNDONALD (1775–1860)

NAVAL HERO AND FOUNDER OF THE NAVIES OF THREE COUNTRIES

Born near Hamilton, in South Lanarkshire to the eccentric 9th Earl of Dundonald, he spent the majority of his early years at the family's estate in Culross, beside the Forth of Firth.

While his father secured him a commission in the British Army, his uncle, an officer in the Royal Navy, had his name entered on the books of navy vessels from the age of five. This practice reduced the amount of time the young Thomas would need to serve before becoming an officer, if he elected to pursue a naval career.

At the outbreak of the French Revolutionary Wars in 1793, the eighteen-year-old Thomas Cochrane chose to become a midshipman in the Royal Navy. He sensed correctly that more adventures and rewards awaited him in the Navy than in the Army. Thanks to his name being placed earlier on the rolls of ships he never served on, he was promoted to Lieutenant within three years.

But his service was not without problems. In 1798, during his time aboard HMS *Barfleur* in the Mediterranean as 8th Lieutenant, Cochrane was court-martialled for showing disrespect towards the ship's First Lieutenant. He was reprimanded for flippancy. This inability to get on with people around him was a trait that would repeat itself throughout his life.

In February 1800, Cochrane acted courageously in successfully bringing a French prize ship into port after being almost lost in a storm. As a reward, he was promoted to Commander and given control of the small 14-gun HMS *Speedy*. Later that year, a Spanish warship disguised as a merchant ship almost captured him. He confused the Spanish momentarily by flying the Danish flag and this allowed him to escape, but a chase ensued. It seemed like only a matter of time before the more heavily armed Spanish frigate would slowly overtake HMS *Speedy*.

As the pursuit continued into the night Cochrane ingeniously placed a lantern on a raft and let it float away. At the same time he doused all the lights on the *Speedy*. The Spanish vessel, which had been following the faint glow of *Speedy*'s lights changed direction and followed the decoy, allowing Cochrane to escape. When he returned to port, it was to the rapturous applause of the Admiralty and the British public.

The following year (1801) he took on and captured a Spanish frigate which was armed with twice as many guns and almost six times as many men. Cochrane deceived the Spanish captain by ordering the American flag to be flown. This allowed him to approach so closely, the bigger ship could not fire down on to HMS *Speedy*. The Spanish then tried to board and take over the ship, but every time they were about to board Cochrane pulled away briefly and fired on the concentrated boarding parties waiting on the enemy frigate's decks. Eventually, the number of enemy crewmen became so depleted that Cochrane could turn the tables on the Spanish by boarding the enemy frigate, which he easily captured.

HMS *Speedy* had spent thirteen months on station in the Mediterranean and during this time had captured, burned, or driven ashore a total of fifty-three enemy naval and merchant ships. So annoyed were the French that in July 1801 they sent a squadron of three ships of the line (large, heavily armed ships carrying on average 74 guns) under an admiral to find Cochrane and destroy his 14-gun ship. When they caught up with Cochrane he did everything he could to outrun the French, but it was a hopeless task against a faster and more powerful foe. Commander Cochrane reluctantly struck his flag (surrendered) and was taken into captivity. Surprisingly, a few days later he was exchanged for a captured French captain and once again, he returned to Britain to an enthusiastic reception. Cochrane was promoted once more, to the rank of Captain.

There was a brief period of peace, but when war resumed between the French and the British in 1803, Cochrane was given charge of the 22-gun HMS *Arab*. A ship with poor handling, Cochrane would describe it later in his autobiography as more a collier than a frigate. For the next year HMS *Arab* patrolled the backwater of the North Sea beyond the Orkney Islands, while Cochrane bided his time waiting for something better to come along.

In December 1804, his prospects brightened considerably when he was appointed to command the newly-built 32-gun frigate HMS *Pallas*. Over the next eighteen months he cruised the Azores and French coast capturing and destroying several Spanish and French vessels, which again drew favourable attention from the Admiralty. Meritocracy ruled the Royal Navy at the time, not seniority and the more daring the adventures that Cochrane undertook, the more rewards he was given when they succeeded.

In 1806, he was given command of the 38-gun frigate HMS *Imperieuse* and set about raiding the French Mediterranean coast. Not only did he attack shore installations, but he captured enemy ships in harbour by leading his men in 'cutting out' operations. He was a meticulous planner of every operation, which limited casualties among his men and maximised the chances of success.

In 1809, Cochrane led a successful attack by a flotilla of fire ships on a powerful French squadron anchored off Rochefort on the French coast along the Bay of Biscay. In the confusion all but two of the French ships of the line were driven hard on shore. For this action he was created a Knight of the Order of the Bath by a grateful Parliament. Exploits, such as the attack on Rochefort and many other raids along the French coast, earned Cochrane the nickname 'Le Loup des Mers' ('The Sea Wolf') from the enemy. In the course of six years aboard *Pallas* and *Imperieuse*, Cochrane made over £75,000 in prize money from captured shipping. He was now a very wealthy man.

Even though his reputation with sections of the British and French public continued to grow, so did the number of his opponents within the Admiralty. After the Rochefort attack, Cochrane abrasively criticised his Admiral for not seizing the opportunity to destroy the weakened French fleet completely. Cochrane wanted the Admiral court-martialled for not following up the initial attack. There was no doubt that Cochrane was his own worst enemy. He had few equals as a man of action but he seriously lacked tact and diplomacy. As far as the Admiralty was concerned, Cochrane's reputation was in tatters for falsely accusing a superior officer. All that he achieved was to create more enemies.

Elected to Westminster Parliament for the seat of Honiton in 1806, Cochrane sided with the Radicals, championing reform and standing against corruption in the Royal Navy. These efforts further lengthened his list of enemies and even though he could still technically continue his career in the Navy, he had alienated so many senior members of the Admiralty that Cochrane was not given another command. His parliamentary career was no happier, his peers, exasperated by his blunt views and lack of political tact, turning their backs on him.

Cochrane's downfall came two years later during the Great Stock Exchange Fraud of 1814, two years after he had married Katherine Barnes. In early 1814, Cochrane was accused and convicted of being a conspirator in defrauding the Stock Exchange. Though subsequent examinations of the records show he should have been found innocent, he was expelled from Parliament and the Royal Navy, as well as stripped of his knighthood. Promptly re-elected to Parliament that July, Cochrane relentlessly campaigned that he was innocent and that his conviction was the work of his political enemies.

All that Thomas Cochrane wanted was to return to sea and feeling that he was making no headway with his campaign for reinstatement, decided that he would pursue his career elsewhere in the world where his skills and reputation as a man of action would be appreciated.

In 1817, at the age of forty-two, Cochrane accepted an invitation from Chilean leader Bernardo O'Higgins to take command of the fledgling Chilean Navy in its war of independence from Spain. Named vice admiral and commander-in-chief, Cochrane arrived in South America in November 1818. Immediately re-structuring the fleet along British lines, Cochrane commanded from the frigate *O'Higgins*. Quickly showing the daring that had made him famous in Europe, Cochrane raided the coast of Peru and captured the town of Valdivia in February 1820. He was also made a Chilean citizen by O'Higgins. After convoying General José de San Martin's army to Peru (the Freedom expedition to Peru), Cochrane blockaded the coast and later cut out the Spanish frigate *Esmeralda*. With Chilean independence secured, Cochrane soon fell out with his superiors over financial matters and claims that he was treated with disrespect.

However, the country was always grateful for Cochrane's contribution to their freedom. In 1842 they built a museum in his name, the Museo del Mar Lord Cochrane, for the dashing Scottish naval hero, overlooking Valparaiso harbour. Housed in a beautiful tile-roofed, colonial-style building above the Plazo Sotomayor, visitors get a splendid view of the harbour and the sea beyond. A bronze statue of him was also erected in the main street.

Departing Chile, he was invited by the first independent ruler of Brazil, Emperor Pedro I in 1823 to create the Brazilian Navy. Quickly taking over what ships were available, Cochrane conducted a successful campaign against the Portuguese who were trying to retake power over their former colony. Emperor Pedro I was so impressed he conferred the title Marquess of Maranhão on Cochrane (a north-eastern state of Brazil).

After putting down a rebellion the following year, Cochrane made claims that a large amount of prize money was owed to him and the fleet. When this was not forthcoming, he and his men seized the public funds in São Luís do Maranhão and looted the ships in the harbour before hastily leaving for Europe in one of the naval vessels he had commandeered (stolen). Despite such an unpleasant end to his time in South America, Cochrane's name continues to be revered in Brazil's history.

In Europe, where he was still widely regarded as a naval hero, Cochrane briefly led Greek naval forces in 1827–28 during their struggle for independence from the Turkish Empire under the Ottomans. His actions leading the Greek navy were not as successful as they had been with other navies, but even so a small skirmish against the Ottoman forces at the Gulf of Lepanto indirectly drew in the navies of Great Britain, France and Russia on the side of the Greeks against the Turks. These three powers destroyed the Ottoman fleet at the Battle of Navarino (1827) which forced the Turks to agree to Greek independence.

Returning to Britain, Cochrane was finally pardoned in May 1832 at a meeting of the Privy Council. By this time, he had succeeded his father as 10th Earl of Dundonald and took the title Lord Cochrane. Although restored to the Navy List with a promotion to rear admiral, he refused to accept a command until his knighthood was returned. This did not occur until Queen Victoria reinstated him as a Knight of the Order of the Bath in 1847. Now a vice admiral, Cochrane served as commander-in-chief of the North American and West Indies station from 1848 to 1851. Promoted to admiral in 1851, he was given the honorary title of Rear Admiral of the United Kingdom three years later. In 1854, at the age of eighty, he was deeply disappointed not to have been given a command in the Crimean War.

Troubled by kidney stones, he died during a surgical operation in 1860 in his eighty-fifth year.

During his career Cochrane continued to improve the efficiency and effectiveness of the Royal Navy. He invented improvements to gas lighting, convoy lanterns and, later, tubular boilers, steam turbines and screw propellers for ships. He also pioneered the use of compressed air which would be used for the construction of the Blackwall Tunnel under the River Thames in London some twenty years after his death.

THOMAS COCHRANE, 10TH EARL OF DUNDONALD (1775–1860)

Cochrane was one of Britain's most extraordinary naval heroes. He wrote two books about his life. The first, *Narrative of Services in the Liberation of Chili, Peru and Brazil from Spanish and Portuguese Domination* (1859) was followed by *Autobiography of a Seaman* which was published in the year of his death. Both books were widely read at the time, leading to a further enhancement of his reputation. They have since become classics of naval literature.

Such were his exploits that he went on to inspire notable fictional characters in literature as C. S. Forester's Horatio Hornblower and Patrick O'Brian's protagonist Jack Aubrey.

It is a shame that Forester and O'Brian chose to turn their heroes into Englishmen, because Cochrane spoke with a distinctive, Lowlands Scottish accent all his life and constantly reminded people that he was always intensely proud of his Scottish roots.

SIR DAVID BREWSTER
(1781–1868)

INVENTOR, MATHEMATICIAN, PHYSICIST AND SCIENCE WRITER

David Brewster was born in Jedburgh in the Scottish Borders. His father was rector of the local grammar school and a teacher of considerable reputation. The entire family was gifted intellectually, though David, who was the third of six children, was recognised as a child prodigy. He was sent to Edinburgh University at the age of twelve to study divinity like his three brothers, who all became ministers.

Although he graduated in divinity and in fact preached at least one sermon, his preference was inclined towards unravelling the mysteries of the natural world. He altered his pursuits from religion to science, with a special interest in optics and mathematics.

His early work concentrated on the diffraction of light, then a little-known field of science, and to his surprise, his energetic, intelligent, scholarly approach led to several discoveries that were published in a number of scientific journals. This resulted in Brewster becoming noticed by the international scientific community. He then confirmed his growing reputation by defining a set of laws that govern how light behaves.

In 1811, after years spent investigating light refraction and reflection through glass, minerals and crystals, seeking a general law of light polarisation, Brewster made a discovery that would ultimately have life-saving implications. He constructed a series of stepped lenses of then unequalled quality for power and brilliance. The polyzonal lenses, as they were called, magnified rays of light so powerfully they would lead to the birth of the modern lighthouse as we know it today. The lens is now known as a Fresnel lens, after the French inventor who – unknown to Brewster – developed the same kind of lens at about the same time. Although Augustin Fresnel was slightly behind Brewster, the French authorities were quick to use the lenses in their lighthouses, while the British Lighthouse Boards were slow to adopt them.

Brewster was admitted to the Royal Society in 1815; he was awarded a prize in 1816 by the French Institute for his work on light polarisation; and he was elected to the premier scientific societies of a number of European countries.

He went on to discover a simple way to calculate the optimum angle for light polarisation: Brewster's Angle is useful in all kinds of practical applications, from adjusting radio signals to building microscopes capable of examining objects on a molecular scale.. Further, the phenomenon of light diffraction he pioneered gave birth to the commercially valuable field of optical mineralogy – the study of minerals and rocks by measuring their optical properties.

Brewster's contributions to the field of optics led him to be dubbed the 'Father of modern experimental optics'. Two of his more light-hearted inventions have brought much joy to adults and children alike for almost two centuries – the kaleidoscope and the stereoscope (where two images of the same object became one three-dimensional object when viewed through the device). Both these inventions caused a sensation when released commercially. However, he did not receive any financial reward for these devices which have sold in the millions, through tardiness and some naivety with the lodgement of patents.

Brewster continued to quietly satisfy his unquestionable thirst for scientific knowledge and made further discoveries concerning the optical properties of crystals and binocular camera. He had a restless, inquiring mind that would not remain idle. The more he leant about the universe, the more he realised there was so much more to discover. During his lifetime he published an astonishingly 2,000 or so scientific papers, articles, reviews and books, including a highly thought-of biography of Isaac Newton.

With his great intellect and haste to pursue further scientific research came a degree of abruptness with those less fortunate and less driven than himself. One of his daughters would later describe him as a man of 'strong personality, strong constitution and possessed of great personal charm' who could be 'impatient, irritable, litigious and verbally aggressive' to others. A strong Christian belief was central to Sir David Brewster's life and it caused him to publicly oppose Charles Darwin's Theory of Evolution, which Brewster described as 'a dangerous and degrading speculation'.

More honours followed with him being knighted in 1832 and becoming Principal of St Andrews University. He received a number of other scientific honours, including the Prussian order of merit in 1847, while in 1855 Napoleon III awarded him the cross of the Légion d'honneur. Later, Brewster was also made Principal and Vice Chancellor of his alma mater Edinburgh University from

1859 until his death in 1868. He was survived by his second wife and their daughter, and three children from his first marriage.

His research and inventions have changed the world – from improved lighthouse mirrors saving lives of countless seafarers, to producing superior methods of detecting and exploiting the world's mineral riches, to photographic lenses and Polaroid sunglasses. It is an understatement to say Sir David Brewster improved the lives of everyone on the planet.

DAVID LIVINGSTONE (1813–1872)

MISSIONARY, EXPLORER OF AFRICA, CRUSADER AGAINST THE SLAVE TRADE

David Livingstone was born in Blantyre, Lanarkshire, at the time a small mill town some twelve kilometres from Glasgow on the banks of the River Clyde. He was part of a large, impoverished family who all worked in the town's cotton mill and lived crammed with two dozen other families into a fetid tenement block that the mill owned. The family were strict evangelical Protestants who believed in the literal interpretation of the Bible and going out into the world to do God's work. He was also taught by his father to read and write, and from an early age became a voracious reader. The young David grew up with an aspiration to become a missionary himself.

At the age of ten, David Livingstone also started working in the mill, fourteen hours each day for six days a week for the next thirteen years. Yet despite the long work hours, he was able to educate himself sufficiently after hours to enter Anderson's College in Glasgow (now the University of Strathclyde) in 1836 to become a medical missionary. There he read Classics, Medicine, Theology and Greek, and in 1840 he joined the London Missionary Society to be trained in overseas mission work.

His first choice of an overseas posting was China, but due to the outbreak of war (Britain had started the First Opium War against China in 1840) he was sent, at his insistence, to Africa instead. Livingstone wanted to go to a pioneer mission, one where no Europeans had been. If the interior of China was no longer accessible, then the interior of Africa was where he wanted to be.

When Reverend Dr Livingstone arrived in the Cape colony of southern Africa, he insisted on being sent as far into the interior as possible. He ended up in Bechuanaland (now Botswana), where his attempts to convert native Africans to Christianity were unsuccessful. It had been recognised for some time that Livingstone was not a good speaker, but it was hoped his enthusiasm and missionary zeal would be enough to win the native Africans over. It was not.

In 1844 he was at a settlement where the villagers were lamenting that lions were attacking their sheep and cattle, day and night. He took up his gun and managed to shoot and fatally wound a lion, which then turned and attacked him, badly injuring his left arm, before some villagers managed to distract it and were themselves attacked. Fortunately for all, Livingstone's shot took effect and the lion dropped dead. For this act of bravery the local natives began to respect him, but still they would not become Christians, preferring to retain the traditional beliefs that had served them well for thousands of years.

While recovering from the lion attack, he was nursed back to health by Mary Moffat, the eldest daughter of a fellow missionary.

They married in 1845 and set up home in a new mission station beside the Kalahari Desert. It was about this time that Livingstone started making trips into Africa's vast unknown interior, which was largely unexplored by Westerners. Having a keen eye for observation and skills in navigation, Livingstone started recording and mapping his journeys into what was then called the 'dark continent'.

In 1849 and again in 1851, he travelled across the Kalahari, on the second trip sighting the upper Zambezi River. In 1852, he began a four-year expedition to find a route from the upper Zambezi to the coast. This filled huge gaps in Western knowledge of central and southern Africa. In 1855, Livingstone discovered a spectacular waterfall which the natives called 'Mosi-oa-tunya' (meaning 'the smoke that thunders'). He named it 'Victoria Falls' in honour of the young British Queen. He reached the mouth of the Zambezi on the Indian Ocean in May 1856, becoming the first European to cross the width of southern Africa.

It was during these long treks that Livingstone encountered slavery for the first time, a practice outlawed in Britain twenty years earlier. Arabs traders were however, not under British control and they continued their incursions into the interior from their bases on the east coast, trapping and abducting Africans. He was horrified at the brutality and inhumanity of slavery and became convinced that if he could bring Christianity and civilisation to the interior, he could do away with slavery. From these beginnings grew a life-long opposition to the slave trade.

In 1856, he returned to Britain to a rapturous reception as his reputation of a seasoned explorer had gone before him. He became a national hero, spoke at meetings crammed with people fascinated by his journeys, and wrote a bestselling book about his adventures, titled *Missionary Travels and Researches in South Africa* (1857). At the end of the 1850s, he resigned from the London Missionary Society to devote more time to exploration.

He was now convinced that opening up the interior of Africa and bringing Christianity, Commerce and Civilisation to its peoples would stop the practice of slavery by making the Africans healthier, wealthier and more spiritually enlightened.

He received a gold medal from the Royal Geographic Society and a government position to continue his journeys of discovery throughout the interior. He left for Africa again in 1858, and for the next five years carried out official explorations of eastern and central Africa for the British government. His wife died of malaria in 1862, which was a bitter blow for him and may have affected his performance, because in 1864, he was ordered home by a government unimpressed with the results of his travels.

At home, Livingstone ignored the criticisms and campaigned against the horrors of the slavery. This was during the American Civil War which was being fought over a number of issues, especially slavery. For David Livingstone the issue of slavery had become personal. His eldest son, Robert had died in a Confederate prison camp fighting to rid America of the scourge of slavery. The British public were enthralled by Livingstone and chose to focus on his anti-slavery crusade rather than any failure to please government bureaucrats.

He also fired the public with his desire to lead another expedition to solve one of the last great mysteries of modern geography: the whereabouts of the source of the mighty Nile River. The public were captivated by this mission and Livingstone soon secured more than enough private funding to launch another expedition into the heart of Africa.

Livingstone returned to Africa in 1866 and with a relatively small party of native 'helpers' he set off for the interior one last time. After nothing was heard from him for over almost two years the fretful British public demanded to know what had happened to their intrepid explorer.

There were even persistent rumours that he had died from malaria. Henry Stanley, an American explorer and journalist, working for the New York *Herald*, set out to find Livingstone. This resulted in their meeting near Lake Tanganyika in October 1871 during which Stanley uttered the famous phrase 'Dr Livingstone, I presume?'

Stanley noticed that Livingstone was weary, fatigued and suffering from disease. He stayed with Livingstone for the next three months repeatedly urging him to return to the coast for rest, but Livingstone had become obsessed with finding the source of the Nile and declined all Stanley's offers. In the end Stanley returned to civilisation with letters and papers proving that Livingstone was still alive. But that was the last time any white person saw him alive.

In 1872, still wandering the interior of the African continent on his search to find the source of the Nile, Dr Livingstone succumbed to the ravages of prolonged malaria and dysentery. He was fifty-nine years of age when he died in the company of three trusted African helpers.

One of the last sentences he ever penned in his journal was this: 'I would forget all my cold, hunger, suffering, and trials, if I could be the means of putting a stop to this cursed traffic.' (Quoted in Mrs J. H. Worcester's *Life of David Livingstone*, 1888.) He was, of course, referring to slavery.

A myth developed that his faithful servants so loved Livingstone that they cut out his heart and gave back his body saying, 'You can have his body, but his heart belongs in Africa!'. The truth however may be more prosaic. The attendants knew that Livingstone's body was going to be conveyed back to England, a trip that would ultimately take almost ten months. It was customary in tropical Africa to remove the internal organs to slow down decomposition, a practice that extended back in time to the Pharaohs of Ancient Egypt, and beyond. Not only would they have cut out his heart, but also lungs, intestines and other organs in Livingstone's body cavity, though this is by no means confirmed by historical records. It would not have been a sign of disrespect either, but of loyal attendants anxious to ensure their friend's body arrived back in England relatively intact.

His body was taken back to England and in 1874 buried in Westminster Abbey, with a long inscription on his headstone, beginning: 'Brought by faithful hands over sea and land, here rests David Livingstone, missionary, traveller, philanthropist . . .'

He may not have been successful finding the source of the Nile, or even preaching Christianity to Africans, but Livingstone made a difference when it came to the slave trade. Spurred by Livingstone's death the British public demanded an end to slavery everywhere the British Empire could reach. In the year following Livingstone's death, the Royal Navy enforced a ban on slavery throughout Africa and the Middle East, shutting down the infamous slave market at Zanzibar from which hundreds of thousands of slaves had been shipped, and stopping the Indian Ocean slave traffic.

While Livingstone's original aim had been to bring Christianity to Africa, it was his Christian beliefs that drove him to try to stop the slave trade: a goal to which he gave his own life fighting to achieve.

MARGARET OLIPHANT
(1828–1897)

PROLIFIC SCOTTISH
NOVELIST AND WRITER

Born Margaret Wilson at Wallyford, East Lothian, just outside Edinburgh to a clerk in the Customs office, Margaret spent her childhood in Glasgow and then, from the age of ten in Liverpool, England. She would live in England for the rest of her life, but always identified with Scotland being her homeland, visiting it for extended summer holidays every year when an adult. Much of her writing is set in Scotland or shows a concern with Scottish themes and her writing displays strong connections with the Scots oral tradition.

In 1849, when only twenty-one years old, Margaret had her first novel published, *Passages in the Life of Mrs Margaret Maitland*, which dealt with the Scottish Free Church movement. It was followed by *Caleb Field* in 1851, the year in which she met the publisher William Blackwood in Edinburgh and was invited to contribute to the then famous *Blackwood's Magazine*. The connection was to last for her whole lifetime, during which she contributed well over 100 articles and short stories.

In 1852, she married her cousin, Frank Oliphant, an artist, and settled at Harrington Square in London. A few years later, Frank developed tuberculosis and was advised to relocate to a warmer climate for the sake of his health. The young family (now including two children, three others having died in infancy) moved to Italy, but it was a futile venture as Frank died in Rome in 1859.

Margaret and the children returned to England where she set about supporting her family through writing, an unusual occupation for women in Victorian Britain, but in her case a necessary one. She had now become a popular writer, and worked with amazing industry to sustain her position. Unfortunately, her home life was full of sorrow and disappointment. In January 1864, she went with her children and some friends to Rome, and there her only remaining daughter, ten-year-old Maggie, died and was buried in her father's grave. Her brother, who had emigrated to Canada, was shortly afterwards enmeshed in financial ruin and Mrs Oliphant offered a home to him and his children, which added to her already heavy responsibilities.

In 1866 she settled at Windsor to be near her two remaining sons who were being educated at Eton. This would be her home for the rest of her life and for the next ten years at least would be her most productive too. The ambitions she cherished for her sons were unfulfilled with both sons dying in the early 1890s within four years of each other. With the death of the last of her children, she lost interest in life. Margaret's health steadily declined and she died at Wimbledon, London in 1897.

Margaret had outlived her husband and all of her children. She supported one alcoholic brother (Willie), which led to her writing that alcoholism was, 'one of the worst vices possible', and looked after a second brother Frank after his bankruptcy in 1868, which was swiftly followed in 1870 by the death of his wife, and, when he unexpectedly died, his three children.

Over the course of her career, Oliphant wrote over two hundred novels and short stories, plus a number of well-researched critical pieces, such as *A Literary History of Scotland* (1882), studies on *Francis of Assisi* (1868), *Thomas Chalmers, preacher, philosopher, and statesman* (1893), as well as travel writing on Florence and Jerusalem.

Oliphant was constantly under financial pressure to produce more material for publication. As a result, her prolific output was criticised for its variable quality. Some books were regarded as masterpieces, such as the five-novel series titled *Chronicles of Carlingford* (1863–1866) and *Kirsteen* (1890). Other works, unfortunately, were hurriedly produced and show it.

The close relationship that Oliphant formed with the Blackwood family in 1851 helped her to stay financially solvent. In additions to loans given on the security of future works, the Blackwoods gave Oliphant various commissions for their publishing house and magazine, including a biography of Edward Irving, translations of Count de Montalbert's work, and the history of the publishing house itself.

Late in life, Oliphant wrote a series of supernatural short stories called *Tales of the Seen and Unseen*. Most notable among these shorter works is the novella *A Beleaguered City* (1879). These stories feature ruptures of the supernatural into the real world, often as a result of tragedy and grief.

She was Queen Victoria's favourite novelist and although she fell out of fashion later, it must be remembered that during the Victorian era, Margaret Oliphant was considered the main rival of the Brontë sisters and was compared favourably to Jane Austen. In the early twenty-first century, Oliphant is enjoying a resurgence in popularity and academic interest. Her books are being read again. One of the main themes of her novels was women's issues and in particular how women overcame the struggles and crises that befell them through their own ingenuity and determination, not dependency on males.

As a Scottish writer of a prodigious quantity of material, Margaret Oliphant's reputation is undergoing a deserved renaissance as a skilful story teller who created memorable portraits of strong, capable women. For mid-Victorian society this was radical literature indeed and makes her one of the first 'feminist' writers. In the 1880s she declared, 'I think it is absurd that I should not have the vote, if I want one'. She advocated a married women's property act, a mother's right to custody of her children, women doctors and university education for women.

ISABELLA ELDER (1828–1905)

PHILANTHROPIST, PROMOTER OF WOMEN'S EDUCATION AND BENEFACTOR OF THE POOR OF GLASGOW

Isabella Ure was born in the Gorbals area of Glasgow, the daughter of a solicitor. She had an older brother, John, who would figure prominently later in her life. Although the details of her education are unknown, it is clear that she was literate and numerate by the time she became an adult. This was not an unusual circumstance in Scotland as free education was offered universally to both males and females from the 1600s and differentiated Scotland from almost all other countries in Europe at the time.

In 1857 Isabella married thirty-three-year-old John Elder, a marine engineer who was a full partner in Randolph, Elder & Co, a thriving marine engineering firm based along the Clyde River near the centre of Glasgow city. John Elder was a very inventive engineer who held a number of patents that significantly improved marine steam engines to the point that steamships were now more efficient and more powerful than sailing ships. John Elder took the engineering company into the direction of shipbuilding and it acquired the old Govan shipyard, further along the Clyde River in 1860. Orders started flooding in from all over the world for Elder's patented steamships.

In 1868 the now thriving business changed its name to John Elder & Co., and moved to the even larger Fairfield shipyards, still in Govan. John Elder & Co was employing 5,000 men in the new shipyards and turning out up to fourteen ships a year. It was regarded as one of the leading shipbuilders and marine engineering companies in the world. Mr and Mrs Elder were now very influential people in the city of Glasgow and Isabella was known as a gracious hostess, especially among the growing numbers of the city's new commercial elite.

But in 1869, John Elder succumbed to a liver disease and died after a painful illness that lasted seven months. He was only forty-five years old at the time of his death and both the company and he were in their prime. When he died most businesses in Govan closed for the day as an expression of esteem and respect at the news of his death. As sole owner of the company following her husband's death, Isabella Elder took over the shipyard and successfully managed it for nine months. She then arranged for her brother, John Ure, a harbour engineer working in Newcastle, to take over day-to-day management of the company.

As a wealthy widow with no children, she now had time on her hands and began touring the continent for extended periods and from the 1870s she increasingly became a major philanthropist in her home city. While her husband had been alive, husband and wife had encouraged workers to attend evening classes and even paid the fees of those who could not afford them. She and John had also discussed other ways to improve the squalid lives of the shipyard workers and now with profits mounting from the exceedingly successful shipbuilding firm, Isabella Elder concluded that education, women and the physical environment should be the main directions of her philanthropy.

At the time and for the next three decades, the widow Elder lived in a beautiful Georgian house, No. 6 Claremont Terrace, which bordered Kelvingrove Park and was just across from the University of Glasgow.

In 1873, she gave the university the then significant sum of £5,000 to support the Chair of Civil Engineering. In 1883, she went further and provided £12,500 to endow the John Elder Chair of Naval Architecture at the same university.

In the same year Isabella made two very significant purchases. The first was 15 hectares of ground, near her late husband's Fairfield Shipyards, which she converted into a public park for the enjoyment of the people. Elder Park, named after her husband, John, was gifted to Glasgow in perpetuity for the 'healthy recreation by music and amusement' of the people. It was opened to great fanfare in 1885. Today, there is a bronze statute to Isabella Elder in the park that was erected in 1906. For the following half-century, Isabella Elder and Queen Victoria were the only statues of women in Glasgow, though lately several more statues of women have joined them.

The second significant purchase made by Elder in 1883, was North Park House in the city's West End. She donated the house, rent free and with sufficient funds to maintain the rambling home, to the Association for Higher Education of Women on what was then Hamilton Drive (now Queen Margaret Drive) overlooking the Botanic Gardens opposite. The Association had started Queen Margaret College, named after Scotland's eleventh-century canonised queen. Queen Margaret College was the first higher education institution for women in Glasgow and only the second in Scotland, after Edinburgh. Isabella Elder invited the Association to move the college into the premises at North House, which immediately elevated the status and reputation of women's education in Glasgow and Scotland.

In 1890, Mrs Elder then agreed to fund the second all-women medical school in Scotland, which was also housed in the Queen Margaret College building. Two years later, in 1892, after much agitation by Elder and others, the then four universities of Scotland (St Andrews, Edinburgh, Glasgow and Aberdeen) were forced to open their doors to women, leading to Queen Margaret College effectively becoming part of the University of Glasgow. In 1895, a purpose-built medical school was constructed adjoining North House that contained lecture halls, laboratories, classrooms, a dissection room and a museum. It was designed by architect John Keppie, in association with a young and up-and-coming architect named Charles Rennie Mackintosh (*see* p. 204).

Throughout these developments Isabella insisted that women should receive the same quality of education as men and in 1899 she refused to allocate more money to the college when she felt standards of instruction were dropping. The building continued to be used by the university until sold to the BBC for its Scottish Head Office in 1934.

In 1885, Isabella established a School for Domestic Economy where girls and women from the poorer suburbs of Glasgow learned how to cook and perform other household tasks on a limited budget. Classes included lessons on the influence of food, clothing, cleanliness, ventilation, care of children and prevention of the spread of infectious diseases. In 1901, she also provided £27,000 to meet the cost of building the Elder Free Library and the purchase of books for the citizens of Glasgow.

In recognition of her unstinting support for women and the poor of Glasgow, Mrs Isabella Elder was awarded an Honorary Doctorate from the University of Glasgow in 1901, which it is believed may have been a first for a woman in Britain.

Finally, in 1903 she built and paid the running expenses for the Elder Cottage Hospital which she financed until her death. This hospital was originally intended to be for maternity services only, but at Mrs Elder's insistence she increased her funding so that it could turn into a general hospital.

Isabella died at her home in Glasgow in 1905 of heart failure, gout and bronchitis. Her death certificate was signed by Dr Marion Gilchrist, the first woman to graduate from the medical school that Isabella Elder had established.

In her will she left the then staggering sum of more than £125,000 for the good of the women and people of Govan and Glasgow. The trust set up in accordance to her will still operates more than a century later. In 2010, the Scottish Parliament passed an Act modernising the conditions of the original fund in order to keep up with inflation and to cover a greater range of activities than specified in the original deed. But, as Isabella Elder intended, the trust she created is still handing out thousands of pounds to assist women's education and the poor of Glasgow.

ANDREW CARNEGIE
(1835–1919)

INDUSTRIALIST AND
PRODIGIOUS PHILANTHROPIST

It is hard to imagine how a small boy born in a weaver's hovel in Dunfermline, Fife could grow to become one of the richest men in the world, but this is exactly what happened to Andrew Carnegie.

Andrew's father was a handloom weaver, a laborious job that earned very little money. In the early 1840s, Scotland was hit by an economic recession, forced evictions from the Highlands, crop failures and finally the collapse of the cottage-based weaving industry. Andrew's father borrowed money from friends and moved the family to the United States in 1848 for a better life.

Upon their arrival in America, all members of the Carnegie family immediately started working in the cloth manufacturing industry around Pittsburgh, but in 1850 Andrew saw an opportunity to earn more money as a telegraph boy and took it. Telegraphy was an emerging industry and the fifteen-year-old Andrew was determined to learn as much as he could about it. Within a year, his efforts were rewarded by being promoted to operator. It was then that Andrew realised railroad companies were operating their own telegraph lines alongside the rail tracks and this provided greater opportunities to advance himself.

Starting in 1853, he joined the Pennsylvania Railway Company as a telegraph operator and by the age of eighteen had become the superintendent of the Pittsburgh Division, the largest telegraph operation in America at the time. Carnegie was now earning enough money to make his first investments in railroad-related companies, such as rail carriage manufacturers, iron producers for railway tracks and bridge construction companies. He even organised a merger of rival companies supplying sleeping cars, taking a percentage of his fees in shares, which turned out to be highly lucrative. As the railway industry expanded, so did the amount of capital from Carnegie's investments.

During the American Civil War, transportation (railways) and communication (telegraph) became vitally important for both sides in the conflict. Andrew Carnegie aligned himself with the Unionist North and rapidly found himself at the centre of activity. He was put in charge of all railways and telegraph lines in Union-controlled territory throughout the eastern United States. He opened rail lines into Washington DC, personally organised troop movements and ensured that the telegraph system was secure enough to swiftly relay vital military messages across vast distances.

Carnegie's eye for opportunities also continued during the war. He invested heavily in the growing iron and steel industry in North America and took a stake in an oil company. After the war he left railways to concentrate on his steel investments. Rather than invest in other people's companies he created his own and started building steel plants himself. In the process, he turned Pittsburgh into the iron and steel manufacturing centre of the United States.

Over the next forty years Carnegie made an enormous fortune in the steel industry constantly buying out rivals and introducing new improvements, such as the Bessemer process for steel manufacturing. By 1890 the output of steel in the United States exceeded that of the UK and Carnegie owned most of it.

In 1901, Carnegie, at the age of sixty-six, was considering retirement when he was approached by another major industrialist J. P. Morgan who wanted to buy him out. It took months of negotiations but in March 1901 Carnegie agreed to sell his steel-making businesses to Morgan for $480 million, out of which he would personally receive the then unheard-of sum of US $225 million (in today's terms worth in excess of $9 billion!).

During his life he had always been an avid reader and where possible had given donations to many good causes, but liberated from the grind of corporate work and blessed with being one of the richest men in the world, he turned his attention fully to philanthropy. He paid to have built and equipped more than 3,000 public libraries throughout the English-speaking world, started a university that would eventually be known as the Carnegie-Mellon University in Pennsylvania that is consistently ranked as one of the top universities in the world. He loved music and therefore funded the construction of 7,000 church organs throughout the world. He also built and owned Carnegie Hall in New York as a venue to present the best musical artists in the world to the American people.

Carnegie never lost his love of Scotland and would sometimes encourage American artists to picture or draw him as a highlander in full tartan regalia. In 1898, he purchased Skibo Castle, near Dornoch in the Scottish Highlands and used it as a base to conduct much charitable work throughout the country. In 1901 he established a $10-million endowment fund for the then four universities in Scotland, a staggering amount that was over thirteen times the total government assistance to these universities at the time. He also donated large sums of money to Dunfermline, the place of his birth. In addition to a library he had built there earlier, he created a public park for the town. Then, in 1903, he established the Carnegie Dunfermline Trust to add value to the lives of the people of his place of his birth. It is still enriching lives today, supporting a wide range of activities and projects in the arts, sport, education, recreation, welfare, and so on.

He was a pacifist and as the beat of militarism grew louder leading up to the First World War, he funded several peace organisations in an effort to stem the rising tide of national bellicosity. He was personally shocked when war broke out in Europe in 1914 and his considerable and expensive efforts proved fruitless. By the time of his death in 1919 from bronchial pneumonia at eighty-four years of age, Carnegie had given away more than US$350 million to various causes. His fortune had actually grown over the years, despite his best efforts to reduce it. At his death, he still had another $30 million remaining in his estate.

According to his own words Andrew Carnegie lived by following three basic principles all his life. They were:

To spend the first third of one's life getting all the education one can.

To spend the next third making all the money one can.

To spend the last third giving it all away to worthwhile causes.

JOHN MUIR (1838–1914)

NATURALIST AND FOUNDER
OF NATIONAL PARKS

John Muir's birthplace was in a four-storey tenement house in the East Lothian coastal town of Dunbar. Born to parents Daniel and Ann Muir, he was the third of eight children. His father was a religious zealot who taught John to memorise and then recite passages from the Bible. His birthplace is now a museum celebrating his life and work.

John Muir's boyhood was fairly typical for a Scottish lad at the time and when not spent at the local school or indoors reciting the Bible, it involved scrapping with other boys, re-enacting romantic battles from Scotland's Wars of Independence and scouring the countryside hunting for birds' eggs or rabbits. In his autobiography, Muir says that it was during these long walks through the Scottish landscape that his love of nature and the environment was born.

John's father, Daniel Muir, had become dissatisfied with the Church of Scotland, based on Scotland's sixteenth-century John

Knox's preaching of Presbyterianism (*see* p. 20). Specifically, he felt the church was not strict enough in its faith and practice. Daniel knew of a Scottish-born Minister (Alexander Campbell) who had started several fundamental Christian churches in America and in 1849, he moved his family to a farm in Wisconsin, USA to be near one of these congregations. John Muir was eleven at the time.

The regime in the Muir household was harsh, not cruel. Each family member worked long hours on jobs around the farm, but in his spare time John and his younger brother would roam the fields and woods of the rich Wisconsin countryside. The more John observed of the world around him, the more he fell in love with it.

He also became somewhat of a noted inventor of labour-saving devices, such as a machine to automate the sawing of logs, a gadget to get him out of bed in the morning, and accurate wooden clocks. With the encouragement of a neighbour, John Muir displayed some of his products at the state fair in the Wisconsin capital of Madison in 1860 where they were well received, but he did not keep any of the newspaper clippings for fear that his father might accuse him of the sin of vanity.

In that same year, and without parental support, he entered the University of Wisconsin-Madison where he signed up to study an eclectic mix of five scientific subjects plus Greek and Latin, rather than a normal degree course. He paid for this wide-ranging education by taking on whatever jobs he could find during term time as well as during holidays, and left the university after three years of good grades.

John Muir was a committed pacifist opposed to the American Civil War. In 1864 he left the United States to avoid the draft and spent a period of time making broom handles and rakes in Ontario. After the Civil War was over, Muir returned to the United

States and was working in Indianapolis, Indiana, when he had an accident: a tool slipped and pierced an eye; he became blind in both eyes but fully recovered his sight in the uninjured eye after a few weeks. During his recuperation he became obsessed with the idea of emulating the journeys of Prussian explorer Alexander von Humboldt through South America. He cashed in his savings and walked the first part of the trip, which was the 1,600 kilometres from Indianapolis to Florida. He kept a journal as he went, which was published as a book called *A Thousand-Mile Walk to the Gulf* released in 1916, after his death.

Muir then caught a boat to Cuba, but the heat, humidity and a bout of malaria prevented him from going further towards the equator (as a Scotsman, this was his first experience of life in the tropics). Instead, he purchased a ticket on a boat to Panama, crossed the Isthmus and sailed up the west coast of America, landing in San Francisco, California in 1868. From this point on, even though he would go on to travel the world, California would always be his home.

Later that same year, Muir made his first trip to Yosemite and he was in raptures. He would later write about his experiences, saying 'No temple made with hands can compare with Yosemite . . . it is the grandest of all special temples of Nature.' He was so entranced with the majesty and beauty of the area that he took a series of local jobs to allow him to roam and study the valley of Yosemite and the mountain range that surrounded it, the Sierra Nevada. During these first years of travel, John Muir replaced a rigid adherence to fundamental religion, with a deep-seated sense of spiritualism based on the natural world around him. He was becoming a naturalist and passionate about it.

In 1871, the Smithsonian Institution asked Muir to send reports on his observations while exploring California's high peaks, and his first letters caused a sensation. Muir had discovered hidden glaciers high up in the Sierra Nevada and conjectured that many of the valleys flowing down from the mountain range might have been caused by past activity of glaciers long melted away. Geology was a science in its infancy and his theory (now proven correct) was met with much scepticism. Despite the controversy, the New York *Tribune* went ahead and published, in December 1871, an article Muir wrote based on these letters, 'Yosemite Glaciers'. He wrote two more pieces on Yosemite that were published in the *Tribune* over the next few months, and soon he was being asked to supply material for other journals, such as *Overland Monthly* and *Harper's New Monthly Magazine*. It was during the writing of articles for these publications that Muir began to form the idea that Yellowstone and other places of such beauty should somehow be preserved from the effect of man's encroachment.

In 1880, Muir married Louie Strentzel, daughter of a prominent physician and horticulturist with a 1,000-hectare fruit orchard in northern California. He settled down to look after his young family and to run his father-in-law's fruit farm. All was fairly quiet for the next ten years as he applied himself fully to family life, but during a camping trip in 1889 with a friend, Robert Underwood Johnson, influential writer and publisher, he was persuaded to start campaigning to save Yellowstone. Underwood believed that the timing was right for the still-infant conservation movement to be taken seriously and promised that if Muir argued his case for national park status he would make sure the right people would hear about it.

Muir's arguments were simple, direct and compelling. He wrote, 'Unless reserved or protected, the whole region will soon be devastated by lumbermen and sheepmen, and of course be made unfit for use as a pleasure ground.' (Gifford (ed.) *John Muir: His Life and*

Letters and Other Writings.) He achieved partial success immediately when the area was placed under the control of the California State Government. Next, the US Congress expanded the size of Yosemite, without having legislative power to actually protect it. Finally, in October 1890, US President Harrison used his 'reserve powers' to create the world's first National Park and Yellowstone valley was protected in perpetuity. For good measure, Sequoia National Park, also in California, was established at the same time.

Muir had found his purpose in life in protecting nature. The relative ease of achieving national park status for Yellowstone and Sequoia convinced him he could continue to achieve success with other well-deserving geographical features of the country. The spiritual quality and enthusiasm towards nature expressed in his writings inspired readers, including presidents and congressmen, to take action to help preserve large nature areas. However, future victories would prove more difficult to realise, especially over the philosophical difference of whether national parks could be sustainably used or preserved in their entirety.

To help in his cause, in 1892, he founded the environmental lobby group, the Sierra Club, and served as its president until his death in 1914. The Sierra Club Bulletin for which Muir wrote prolifically, provided a vital and growing outlet to raise awareness of environmental issues. Mount Rainier National Park was subsequently created in 1899.

In 1903 Muir accompanied President Theodore Roosevelt on a visit to Yosemite. On the journey there, Muir was able to convince the president of the value and future of national parks. At one point the President and Muir set off to explore the vast wilderness of Yosemite by themselves. They camped in the back country and talked during the cold, clear, star bright night. They slept in the open and when they awoke the next morning they were covered in a light dusting of powdery snow. It was a night Roosevelt never forgot and Muir Woods National Monument in California just north of San Francisco was established by President Roosevelt in 1908. It contains some of the best examples of Redwood forest left in America.

Although he had won early battles, Muir felt he was beginning to lose the fight against the interests of loggers and big business. He was unable to prevent the government from approving a dam project in the Californian high country and allowing logging through pristine but unprotected forests.

Muir found himself to be the lightning rod for many worthwhile causes, including the plight of Native Americans. For many citizens, the Native American was seen as lazy, dissolute and probably heading for extinction. Muir's attitude grew more respectful the more he understood about their lifestyle before European contact and he wrote passionately to change other people's perceptions of them.

Towards the end of his life, he was always in demand. He was a friend of three US presidents. He gave speeches and lectures to audiences throughout America and also in Australia, South America, Africa, Europe, China and Japan, In his life, Muir published six volumes of writings, 300 articles and eight books all describing explorations of natural settings. Four additional books were published posthumously.

John Muir died in a Los Angeles hospital on Christmas Eve 1914 from pneumonia, at the age of seventy-six, his bed covered with manuscript pages from a book he was preparing. He was survived by two daughters.

Muir's personal activism helped save Yosemite Valley, Sequoia National Park and other wilderness areas from man's greed. In the process, he started a global movement that has developed from naturalism to environmentalism. Towards the end of his life he wrote in *The Yosemite* (1912) the following prophetic words for humanity to heed: 'Everybody needs beauty as well as bread, places to play in and pray in, where nature may heal and give strength to body and soul alike.'

After his death, Grand Canyon National Park was established in 1919. Yellowstone and Sequoia Parks were the first of their kind in the world, but the concept was quickly adopted in Australia (Royal National Park, Sydney in 1879) and Canada (Banff National Park in 1885). Since then, according to the latest figures by the World Bank (2012), over one hundred and ninety countries have set aside land as national parks, totalling a staggering 15 per cent of the world's land area, or about 21 million square kilometres. To put this into perspective, collectively the area set aside for national parks globally is larger than the continents of Europe and Australia, combined!

On the 100th anniversary of his death, Scottish authorities dedicated a 200-kilometre walking trail in his name. The John Muir Way links his birthplace in Dunbar on the eastern coast of Scotland to Helensburgh on the west coast from which the Muir family departed for America. On the way the route passes through Scotland's capital of Edinburgh and its first national park, Loch Lomond and the Trossachs.

In 1983, the American writer Wallace Stegner published an article in *Wilderness* magazine entitled 'The Best Idea We Ever Had', writing, 'Absolutely American, absolutely democratic, they reflect us at our best rather than our worst.' He was alluding to a comment that the British Ambassador, Lord Bryce, had made in 1912 that the national park was the best idea America had ever had. Trouble is the idea was not American, it was the creation of a man born in Scotland. John Muir, humble Scots-born lad, managed to feed our soul at the same time as allowing our planet to breathe. He just may have saved the future of earth too.

SIR JAMES DEWAR
(1842–1923)

CHEMIST AND PHYSICIST

James Dewar was born in Kincardine, Fife, Scotland, the son of an innkeeper and the youngest of six boys. He attended local schools until he was ten when he suffered a serious case of rheumatic fever lasting two years. During this period he built a violin, and music remained a lifelong interest of his. He lost both parents when he was fifteen, but still managed to enter the University of Edinburgh the following year, where he studied physics and chemistry.

He studied under Lord Playfair and impressed him enough to be made his assistant. After graduating he stayed on at Edinburgh University holding various appointments, until he secured a professorship at the University of Cambridge in natural experimental philosophy (precursor of modern physics) in 1875. At the age of thirty-five, Dewar was also appointed as Fullerian Professor at the Royal Institution in London. Both positons he retained for the rest of his life.

From all accounts, his experimental prowess rivalled that of other great physicists of his day and from the start of his stellar career, his contribution to chemistry and physics was prodigious. His early work concerned organic chemistry, atomic spectroscopy, the effect of light upon the retina, electricity, and the measurement of high temperatures.

In 1867 Dewar described several chemical formulae for benzene. Then he experimented with producing liquefied gases at extremely low temperatures and it is for this field of research (known as cryogenics) that he is best remembered. In 1885 he produced large quantities of liquid oxygen and then in 1898, he was the first to produce commercial quantities of liquid hydrogen which had an immediate application across a range of industries from oil refining to welding. . In collaboration with Sir Frederick Abel, another renowned chemist, he developed a smokeless gunpowder, which they called cordite; it was later adopted by the British Army.

To further his research in cryogenics Dewar invented a double-walled vacuum flask in 1892, which he omitted to patent. When the bottle was subsequently commercialised it became known as the Thermos bottle.

In 1905 he began to investigate the gas-absorbing powers of charcoal when cooled to low temperatures, and his discoveries led in time to future experiments in atomic physics Dewar continued his research work into the properties of elements at low temperatures, specifically low-temperature calorimetry (rate of energy transfer) until interrupted by the outbreak of the First World War.

Manpower shortage during and after the war meant that Dewar never again had the right quality and quantity of researchers to further his work. But that did not stop him from trying. At the time of his death in 1923, the eighty-year-old Dewar was still experimenting, using a charcoal-gas thermoscope to measure infrared radiation from the sky.

Throughout his illustrious career he received numerous awards and prizes from British and foreign governments. He was also knighted by the King in 1904, but the coveted Nobel Prize eluded him. Dewar was nominated nine times for this prestigious award and it was thought his somewhat abrasive personality may have worked against him, as he could be brusque, argumentative and self-centred at times.

Described as a remarkable, brilliant and gifted scientist, Sir James Dewar advanced our understanding of science significantly in the field of cryogenics. Along the way he gave us commercial quantities of liquid oxygen and hydrogen, the Thermos and cordite.

ALEXANDER GRAHAM BELL
(1847–1922)

EMINENT SCIENTIST
AND INVENTOR

Born in Edinburgh, Alexander Graham Bell was the second of the three sons of Alexander Melville Bell and his wife Eliza Grace Bell. His father and grandfather were authorities on elocution, his father specialising in teaching deaf people to speak, using his system of 'Visible Speech'. His mother, who painted miniatures, had become profoundly deaf by the time he was twelve. These circumstances go some way to explaining Bell's early fascination with the mechanics of speech.

At school he did not do particularly well and he did not finish his course at University College London as he left the United Kingdom. After the tragic loss of both his brothers to tuberculosis, and with his health giving cause for concern, the family emigrated to Canada in 1870.

The following year Bell, now twenty-four, moved to the United States to teach. For a while he trained teachers of the deaf in his father's 'Visible Speech', and in 1872, he founded his School of Vocal Physiology and Mechanics of Speech in Boston to teach deaf people; among his pupils was Helen Keller, who was to dedicate her auto biography to him. Another pupil was Mabel Hubbard, a daughter of one of his backers, who'd been deaf since she was five. He married her in 1877. The school subsequently became part of Boston University, where Bell was appointed Professor in 1873. He became a naturalised American citizen in 1882.

Bell had long been fascinated by the idea of transmitting speech, and by 1875 had come up with a simple receiver that could turn electricity into sound. Other people were independently working along the same lines, including Italian-American Antonio Meucci and the electrical engineer and inventor Elisha Gray, and debate continues today as to who should be credited with inventing the telephone.

On 10 March 1876, Bell was working on some finishing touches to his telephone device when he unwittingly called down the line to his assistant in the adjoining room, 'Mr Watson, come here – I want to see you'. Watson heard the words clearly and came running. It is believed this was the first successful test of a telephone transmission in the world.

Alexander Graham Bell was granted a patent for the telephone in the same year and his invention became an instant sensation. Within a year the first telephone exchange was built in Connecticut and the Bell Telephone Company was created in 1877, with Bell the owner of a third of the shares, quickly making him a wealthy man.

Driven by a genuine and rare intellectual curiosity, Bell continued to seek to learn more and create new things. His other inventions were as diverse as ground-breaking work in optical communications, sheep-breeding, hydrofoils and aeronautics. In 1880, with his assistant Charles Sumner Tainter, he invented a wireless telephone, which could carry voices on a beam of light. Now recognised as the precursor to fibre-optic communications, this 'photophone', he believed, was his greatest achievement; he had to be dissuaded from naming his newborn daughter Photophone.

He also started the prestigious journal *Science* in 1883 and then went on to become one of the founding members of the National Geographic Society in 1888. In 1885 he acquired land in Nova Scotia and established a summer home there where he continued experiments, particularly in the field of aviation.

Alexander Graham Bell died of diabetes in his home in Nova Scotia in 1922, at the age of seventy-five, leaving behind a wife and two daughters. During his funeral every phone in North America was briefly silenced in honour of the great inventor.

Few men have had such a profound impact on the world. The fact that almost everyone on the planet is now able to communicate with each other was Alexander Graham Bell's immeasurable legacy and gift to the world.

KATE CRANSTON (1849–1934)

BUSINESSWOMAN AND PATRON OF THE ARTS

Catherine Cranston, more widely known as Kate Cranston or simply Miss Cranston, was born in a Glasgow pub in George Square operated by her father, which would later be renamed Cranston's Hotel and Dining Rooms. The Cranston family was noted for its innovative approach to hotel management and would eventually run a chain of temperance hotels in Glasgow, Edinburgh and London, which provided guests with high-class accommodation in an alcohol-free environment.

Tea had once been very expensive and thus a luxury of the rich, but, from the 1830s, with greater supply it became more affordable to the masses. It was also promoted as a healthy alternative to alcohol by the growing Temperance movement. Nevertheless, it was not until the 1850s that tea rooms and tea shops had become fashionable in England, whereas they were still unfamiliar in Scotland, even up to the 1870s.

Kate Cranston's older brother had become a tea merchant and Kate could see an opportunity to offer the people of Glasgow something they had not experienced before. In 1878 she opened her first tea room and immediately set herself apart by combining elegant, sophisticated service with the latest styles of decor, chosen from among the leading architects of the day in Glasgow. A second tea room followed in 1888.

In 1892 she became happily married to John Cochrane, but continued to trade under the name of Miss Cranston's Tea Rooms. Cochrane was a wealthy businessman who would provide much of the finances to underpin her most celebrated projects. She opened her third tea room in 1897 (designed by yet another architect) and finally completed her chain of four establishments in Glasgow with the now famous Willow Tea Rooms in Sauchiehall Street in 1903.

For this establishment, she chose to employ a young, up-and-coming architect who was advocating a new trend of design, blending Scottish Baronial style with Japanese influences and Art Nouveau into what was being called the 'Glasgow Style'. His name was Charles Rennie Mackintosh (*see* p. 204).

The opening of the new tea room and particularly the use of his new design style on everything from the lighting, furniture, lead-light windows, and even the menu, caused a sensation in Glasgow and beyond. It assured that both architect and proprietor would become household names and started a professional partnership that would last almost twenty years.

Kate Cranston would eventually commission Mackintosh to renovate her other tea rooms and such now was the exclusiveness and uniqueness of her premises, that it cost more for a cup of tea in Miss Cranston's Tea Rooms than anywhere else in Glasgow. Miss

Cranston's Tea Rooms became fashionable social centres for all and a place where everyone had to be seen.

In 1904, Kate Cranston commissioned Mackintosh to carry out the redecoration and design of new furniture for the house she and her husband lived in. She also encouraged Mackintosh and his wife Margaret, a designer, to exhibit their work. Thanks to Kate Cranston's patronage, the reputation of Mackintosh, his wife and two other fellow artists (known collectively as the 'Glasgow Four') spread beyond Scotland.

In 1917, her husband John Cochrane died quite suddenly and Kate was greatly distressed. She sold off all her tea rooms and other businesses and withdrew from public life. She had no children and when she in turn passed away in 1934, she left two-thirds of her sizeable estate to the poor of Glasgow.

Operated by a succession of owners, the tea rooms continued trading under the name of Miss Cranston's Tea Rooms for several decades until by the 1950s they had all closed. The story of Kate Cranston's life could have ended here, but the memory of Glasgow's once famous tea rooms would not go away.

In 1983, Anne Mulhern, another Scottish female entrepreneur recreated the Willow Tea Rooms in its original setting in Sauchiehall Street, Glasgow. Over 150,000 tourists now visit the establishment each year to partake of tea and food in the grand, opulent ambience of Edwardian Britain. Visitor numbers were boosted further during the Glasgow Commonwealth Games in the summer of 2014.

The reopening of Miss Cranston's Tea Room in Glasgow has led to a resurgence of interest in the Glasgow style of design, Mackintosh, the Glasgow Four and of course Kate Cranston herself. It is as if her spirit and her patronage continue to live on many decades after the original people have passed away.

ROBERT LOUIS STEVENSON
(1850–1894)

NOVELIST, TRAVEL WRITER
AND ANTHROPOLOGIST

Robert Lewis (later 'Louis') Balfour Stevenson was born in Edinburgh into a family of well-respected lighthouse engineers (his grandfather was Robert Stevenson, responsible for building lighthouses; *see* p. 128). His upbringing was comfortable and middle-class. From the beginning he was sickly, and through much of his childhood was attended by a faithful nanny, Alison Cunningham, the daughter of a Fife fisherman, who filled his head with wild stories of Scotland's religious and secular past. At the age of seventeen, Robert enrolled at Edinburgh University ostensibly to follow in the family's footsteps of engineering. However, he really wanted to be an author and as a compromise, he studied law while he waited for an opportunity to write.

In his last years at university, he travelled to France during the summer holidays and published a number of travel pieces. He was beginning to use his keen sense of observation to write about the physical world around him, but also the characters and personalities of the people he met along the way.

In 1876, he met his future wife, Fanny Osbourne in France. He was twenty-five and she was thirty-six, separated from her husband and travelling with her two young children. He was completely besotted with her and within two years had followed her to California. Penniless and in very poor health from a cold winter in the high California mountains, Stevenson wrote another travelogue about his journey titled *The Amateur Emigrant*, which was published in 1895, a year after his death. Some consider this book to be his finest work. After Fanny obtained a divorce, she and Stevenson married in San Francisco in 1880. They would remain together until his death.

Stevenson developed the ability to visit a place and then weave an appealing story about it. Such was the case when the newly married Stevensons stayed two months at Mount Saint Helena in Napa Valley, California for their honeymoon. Their lodging was a rundown cabin near an abandoned mine site which Stevenson wrote about at length in a travelogue titled *The Silverado Squatters* (1883).

It was during the 1880s that Stevenson produced a large number of short stories, travel books and also a few novels that would propel him onto the world stage as an international bestseller. It is also the decade that Stevenson's health, which was never robust, deteriorated significantly. He suffered from bleeding of the lungs that might have been from undiagnosed tuberculosis.

While in a bedridden state, which frequently occurred during the 1880s, Stevenson wrote some of his most popular fiction, most notably *Treasure Island* (1883), *Kidnapped* (1886), *Strange Case of Dr Jekyll and Mr Hyde* (1886), and *The Black Arrow* (1888). *Dr Jekyll and Mr Hyde* was a spectacular success, selling over 40,000 copies in the first six months after release. The idea for *Treasure Island* came from a map that Stevenson had drawn to keep his twelve-year-old stepson amused on holidays in Braemar, Aberdeenshire, Scotland. Stevenson conjured up a pirate adventure story from his imagination to accompany the map and soon realised he had more than enough material for a novel.

In 1888, on the advice of his doctor, Stevenson and his family journeyed to the warm South Pacific where he hoped to recuperate before eventually returning to Scotland. While in Hawaii, Stevenson visited a leper colony long enough to finish his novel *The Master of Ballantrae* (1889).

By the time the family arrived in Samoa, Stevenson realised his health would never stand a return trip to Scotland. Despite his homesickness, he decided the family would stay permanently in Samoa. The location stimulated his imagination and several more books were set in the exotic South Seas.

He also took a genuine liking for the native people of Polynesia and felt duty bound to write their stories and their histories from their point of view rather than from a paternalistic European perspective. For this refreshing and enlightened attitude for the time, the people of Samoa respected and admired him greatly. Towards the end of his life he wrote increasingly of his longing for Scotland. In one letter, to a fellow novelist, S. R. Crockett, he said, 'I shall never see Auld Reekie [affectionate name for Edinburgh]. I shall never set my foot again upon the heather. Here I am until I die, and here I will be buried.'

Robert Louis Stevenson died of either a cerebral haemorrhage or a stroke in 1894 at his home in Vailima, Samoa near the capital Apia. He left unfinished another epic novel that many consider had the makings of yet another masterpiece. The *Weir of Hermiston* was a novel set in Edinburgh and the Lothians at the time of the Napoleonic wars. The incomplete novel was published in 1896 to honour the dead writer.

Stevenson was buried at the top of Mount Vaea, which overlooked his Polynesian home. It was said he was placed looking out to sea in the direction of his beloved Scotland. Fanny returned to the United States and then, infected by Stevenson's love of journeying, spent many years travelling around America and Europe. She died twenty-five years after her husband. Her daughter took her ashes back to Samoa and placed them in his grave.

Stevenson has a very important place in the literary history of Scotland. He may be best remembered for his children's adventure books, but he also wrote travelogues, poems, essays, plays, short stories, anthropologies and histories. His output was prodigious. He produced forty-one separate pieces of work during his short twenty-year career as a writer.

Some of his material, such as *Kidnapped* and *The Master of Ballantrae* capture forever the culture of Scotland during the late eighteenth and early nineteenth centuries. In his day he was considered to be the direct literary successor of Sir Walter Scott.

SIR PATRICK GEDDES (1854–1932)

PHILOSOPHER AND PIONEER OF TOWN PLANNING

Geddes was born in Ballater in Aberdeenshire but grew up in Perth. He started work in the National Bank of Scotland but three years later he went to study botany at Edinburgh University. He hated the formal study in Edinburgh and left after a week, going instead to London, where he enrolled at the Royal School of Mines (later incorporated into Imperial College). It was while he was in London between 1877 and 1878 that he was influenced by the radical thinker, Thomas Huxley.

He never finished any degree, but nevertheless in 1880 Geddes returned to Edinburgh, where he secured employment as a lecturer in zoology at Edinburgh University. In 1886, he married Anna Morton who was the daughter of a wealthy merchant and she bore him three children.

Geddes initially considered himself primarily a sociologist, but in reality he had an eclectic field of interests covering areas such as biology, botany, social thinking, town planning, politics and literature. His mind was always restless and he was constantly seeking ways to apply his considerable and wide-ranging talent. There was one area that offered him the opportunity of applying practical solutions – town planning – and in time it would earn him a revered place as one of the 'founding fathers' of this profession.

Geddes was successful in creating the first student hall at the university and started advocating a revolutionary concept of urban design for his day. He believed that people prospered and were healthier and happier if they lived in a healthy, friendlier and more attractive environment. Specifically he could see a direct connection between fresh air, gardens and decent housing and the well-being of the general population.

Very early in his career Geddes and his new wife demonstrated the practicality of his approach to town design. In 1886, they purchased a row of slum tenements in Edinburgh turning them into one building with wide, open spaces surrounding it. Sunlight and airflow were improved as did the health of the tenants.

His ideas on town planning were influenced by social theorists such as Herbert Spencer and Frederic Le Play, but they were considered radical and Geddes was passed over for promotion at Edinburgh University. However, that did not mean every university in Scotland rejected his ideas. He was offered and accepted the Chair of Botany at University College, Dundee, a position he retained from 1888 to 1919.

Throughout his life he would continue to develop his theories of social engineering, drawing upon and going beyond the early theorists to create his own unique beliefs. He would constantly draw inspiration from many fields of interest, seeing unifying principles or common interlocking patterns lying just underneath the seemingly disparate and unconnected disciplines.

Geddes championed a model for town planning that placed human needs at the centre of its thinking, rather than grand buildings and other inanimate structures.

He advocated the use of the 'scientific method' in testing ideas and theories. He believed that close observation and study would eventually reveal the relationships between the physical environment, people and their activities. Over the next decade or so, he initiated a number of projects that improved the living conditions of many people in Edinburgh, especially in the Old Town, which was impoverished by poor housing and primitive sanitation. He obtained a building at the top of the Royal Mile near Edinburgh Castle, which he converted into a 'sociological observatory' to allow the general public to see for themselves these relationships. He called it the 'Outlook Tower' and its famous camera obscura is still on display in the building today.

In 1909, Geddes assisted in the planning for Edinburgh's Zoological Gardens, which gave him the opportunity of demonstrating his 'holistic' approach to designing the built environment. Between the 1890s and 1913, Geddes created and toured the widely acclaimed 'Cities Exhibition' in Edinburgh, London, Dublin, Belfast and Ghent in Belgium. The exhibition set out his philosophy and theories about town planning, and helped to make his name in this field.

As his reputation grew so did the offers to conduct work outside the United Kingdom. In 1919, Geddes was commissioned to draw up a master plan for Jerusalem which he followed up in 1925 with a master plan for the centre of Tel Aviv.

Geddes's work in improving the slums of Edinburgh led to an invitation from the Governor of Madras to travel to India in 1915 and advise on planning issues for that city. From there, he travelled throughout India advising other cities on their planning matters. He held a position in Sociology and Civics at Bombay University from 1919 to 1925. While in India, his wife died of typhoid fever in 1917.

He surprised many Indians by his sympathy for and understanding of Buddhism, Hinduism and Islam, and how these religions could be accommodated into the planning decisions of the rapidly expanding cities on the Indian sub-continent. But he also infuriated the same people when he wrote that poverty could only be alleviated by embracing progress, not stubbornly adhering to the social customs of the past.

In 1924, Geddes's health began to deteriorate and he was advised to leave India. He settled in Montpellier in the South of France as the warm Mediterranean climate seemed to agree with him. Patrick Geddes accepted a knighthood in 1931, shortly before his death in Montpellier in 1932.

The ideas and philosophy of Sir Patrick Geddes influenced a generation of town planners on several continents. His approach was wholly or partially adopted in Europe, North America, Australia and parts of Asia. It is estimated that Geddes created the plans for fifty cities in India alone.

DOUGLAS HAIG, 1ST EARL HAIG
(1861–1928)

SUPREME COMMANDER OF THE BRITISH IMPERIAL FORCES ON THE WESTERN FRONT DURING THE FIRST WORLD WAR

Douglas Haig was born in Edinburgh, the eleventh child of John Haig, who was the head of the successful Haig whisky distilling company. He was educated at Clifton College in Bristol and then at Oxford University where he led an active sporting and social life, but left without attaining a degree. An expert horseman, he once represented England at polo.

Haig entered the Royal Military College at Sandhurst in 1884 for a one-year officer's course and graduated first in his class. He already loved horses, but it was at Sandhurst that Haig developed a deep and abiding love of what horses in the military – the cavalry – could achieve. He was commissioned into a cavalry regiment and sent to India where he was promoted to captain after three years and became the aide to the Superintendent of cavalry in India.

In 1897 he joined Lord Kitchener's expedition to reconquer Sudan and learned first-hand the effectiveness of fast-moving cavalry in open terrain. After another promotion to brigade major, Haig was sent to South Africa to serve in the Boer War. In charge of a cavalry division, he acquitted himself well enough to argue that in any future conflict it would be the cavalry that would play the most important role in victory, whereas artillery and infantry should be relegated to mopping up operations.

Lord Kitchener was impressed by Haig and promoted him to major-general, responsible for training the Indian cavalry.

In 1905, he married Dorothy Vivian, the daughter of Lord Vivian, who had connections to the British crown. Over the next several years Dorothy gave birth to three daughters and one son. The royal connections led to him being appointed director of training for the new Territorial Army in Britain in 1906. It was off to India again in 1909 as Chief of Staff with another promotion to lieutenant-general. Then back to England to take control of the 1st Army Corps in the lead-up to what was to become the First World War.

Haig commanded his troops well during the first difficult days of the war in which the small British Expeditionary Force along with the French successfully staunched the German advance towards Paris. Later in 1914, he was promoted to full general and given command of the entire British Expeditionary Force under the supreme command of General John French. It was about this time that Haig concluded the war would be won on the Western Front and only the Western Front. Other theatres of war, such as Russia, the Balkans, Italy and Gallipoli were merely diversions. In this belief, Haig would be proved correct, but it did not explain the tactics he stubbornly employed for the rest of the conflict.

Haig's actions at the Battle of Mons and the First Battle of Ypres earned him praise while, conversely, John French's fortunes plummeted as the British failed to make any headway on the

Western Front. French's fate was sealed by his disastrous handling of the Battle of Loos in late 1915, following which Prime Minister Asquith removed French and appointed Haig as his replacement in December 1915. Haig was now Supreme Commander of all British Imperial troops on the Western Front, consisting of more than two million men from the United Kingdom, Australia, New Zealand, South Africa, India, Canada and sundry other British colonies.

The first challenge facing Haig was to prepare his rapidly increasing army to go on the offensive against the Germans. The enemy was consolidating its occupation over large parts of Belgium and France and pressure was mounting to remove them as quickly as possible. The British and French agreed that in the summer (August) of 1916 their two armies should launch coordinated attacks against the Germans across a wide front in order to break the enemy lines. But in February 1916, at Verdun, the Germans attacked first in a strategy that was designed to 'bleed France white'. The French absorbed appalling and escalating losses for months and it was clear by May that if the British did not launch an attack soon to alleviate German pressure on Verdun, France itself might fall.

Haig was reluctant to go ahead with his planned offensive until he received all the men and materiel he wanted, but he was forced by Prime Minister Asquith to launch an all-out attack at the earliest. Even though the timing of this offence at the Somme was earlier than Haig would have preferred, he was nevertheless satisfied with its strategy.

Haig envisaged a number of continuous set-piece battles rolled out over several months that would eventually wear down the Germans. A breakthrough would occur at some point that would be exploited by divisions of cavalry waiting in the rear for just this opportunity to rush forward.

DOUGLAS HAIG, 1ST EARL HAIG (1861–1928)

On 1 July 1916, Haig threw 300,000 men (24 divisions) against the German line at the Somme held by 220,000 battle-hardened German soldiers (12 divisions) who were in well-entrenched defensive positions. He felt confident of victory, but everything went wrong. The preparatory seven-day bombardment had not destroyed the German defences as expected because of defective manufacture with the artillery shells. Notwithstanding a critical lack of damage to the German fortifications, Haig still ordered his men to attack and to march across no-man's-land in neat rows shoulder-to-shoulder. The British infantry went to their slaughter.

On the first day of the battle, the British Expeditionary Force suffered almost 60,000 casualties, of which over a third were killed. It remains the single greatest loss of lives ever, in British military history.

But Haig was undeterred. He pressed on with his plan of further battles that were matched with further appalling losses, in the unshakeable belief that the Germans would crack, *must* crack.

Over the next four months Haig used a total of almost 750,000 men against the Germans who poured in almost 900,000 reinforcements. Haig believed the predicted breakthrough would occur at any moment and on several occasions brought up his cavalry in anticipation of the breakout that never eventuated. The tactics that had failed on the first day were repeated for the next 142 days.

When the horrific ordeal of the Somme was finally over in November 1916, the British had suffered over 400,000 killed, wounded, missing or captured. It is estimated that German casualties were in the order of 500,000.

Allied forces did gain some ground, but had advanced only 12 kilometres at its deepest point. The closest German border was still 300 kilometres further away to the east.

By the summer of 1917, new offensives involving repeated frontal assaults had also failed disastrously up and down the Western Front. After its last attempt at piercing the German line during the Neville Offensive of April 1917, the French army had broken and mutinied. Haig had no new tactics to offer, but that did not dent his unwavering belief that if he tried one more time the Germans would surely crack.

The next offensive he planned is technically called the Third Battle of Ypres, but it is now more popularly known for the ruined, little Belgium village that so many men died at, Passchendaele. In preparation for this battle Haig received everything he asked for; more men, more tanks, aeroplanes, ammunition and a massive number of heavy artillery pieces. His plan was to blast the Germans out of their defensive positions and overwhelm them with infantry. Then the cavalry would ride through the breach and outflank the retreating Germans.

It did not go to plan. Haig ordered his troops forward into a wet and sodden battlefront that his artillery had conveniently, for the Germans, turned into a quagmire. Men and machines could not move in the mud and horses collapsed from exhaustion. So many men died unable to extricate themselves from shell-holes filled with vile liquid that drowning became the one of the major causes of death in this battle.

The offensive lasted four months and cost more than 250,000 casualties. From the outset it was a doomed and hopeless attack, but Haig insisted it continue as he clung to his belief that the Germans were on the verge of collapse again. But there was no breakthrough. The predicted collapse of the German front did not happen. In November 1917, when the weather became too cold to continue, Haig reluctantly called off the offensive. It was a good thing too, because it was actually the British army that was on the verge of collapse.

Haig was now becoming unpopular with his political masters in London and in particular with the new Prime Minister Lloyd George, who had come to power only a year earlier. The Prime Minister began to contemplate Haig's dismissal, but before any action could be taken the Germans launched a massive all-out attack on the British lines in early 1918 in a last-ditch attempt to win the war before the Americans arrived in numbers.

When the German offensive broke like a huge wave on 21 March 1918, the British army lost more ground than it had gained in any of Haig's great offensives. For days the outcome of the battle was in doubt, but in the end the British held, just barely.

By May 1918, with the arrival of half a million Americans to the front, the tide of the Great War had now turned in favour of the Allies. Haig still commanded the forces of the British Empire. Together, the combined armies of Belgium, America and troops from the British and French Empires pushed the Germans back to the point where the enemy agreed to an armistice in November 1918.

After the war, Haig was posted as Commander-in-Chief of Home Forces until his retirement in 1921. He was popularly portrayed as a hero and granted £100,000 by the British government, which was a colossal sum then.

It was Haig who did much to help the war veterans. In 1921, Haig became one of the founders of Royal British Legion and helped introduce the poppy of remembrance into Britain. He championed the rights of ex-servicemen, refusing all titles until the government improved their pensions, which duly came in August 1919. Haig was then made Earl Haig in 1919 (and at the same time received in addition the subsidiary titles of Viscount Dawick and Baron Haig of Bemersyde).

When Haig died in 1928, 200,000 veterans filed past his coffin and a million others paid their respects. Haig died from a heart attack brought on, according to his widow, by the strain of wartime command. He was sixty-six. He was buried at Dryburgh Abbey, near Bemersyde in the Scottish Borders.

Early biographies were laudatory, but over time the attitude towards Haig went from praise to condemnation.

Lloyd George was never one of Haig's supporters. In his *War Memoirs*, published in 1936, he accused Haig of being 'second rate'. Indeed, Lloyd George confided to his biographer that if the war had continued into 1919 he would have had Haig replaced with either General Currie, a Canadian on the Western Front, or General Monash, the commander of Australian troops in France. In Lloyd George's opinion, both these generals had amply demonstrated a better grasp of modern warfare than Haig.

Haig remains one of the most controversial figures associated with Britain's efforts in the Great War. To some he was the man who 'won the War'; to others he was the 'butcher of the Somme'. Perhaps there is a third perspective between these two extreme viewpoints. It might be more accurate to see Haig as a product of the ideas and army structure of late Victorian Britain where class, a mediocre education and a stultifying government bureaucracy crushed any sense of innovation in him. Yet outside the restrictive confines of his khaki world, inventions were transforming society through rapid technological advances.

In the generation preceding the First World War, submarines, planes, telephone, electrical lighting, machine guns, high-explosive artillery, torpedoes, motor vehicles and the radio had been invented.

These devices and others like them were altering the way warfare would be waged, yet very few in the British military – including Haig – recognised this.

Haig certainly did care for his men and he was concerned about casualties and the slaughter, but he just could not think of another way to progress the war. His thinking was unimaginative, conservative and predictable. Every offence was always the same. First the enemy positions would be 'softened up' by intense artillery bombardment. This was followed up by a massive frontal infantry assault to achieve a breakthrough, which would then be exploited by cavalry. But these tactics did not work, no matter how many times he tried.

The trouble was that Haig was fighting a twentieth-century war using nineteenth-century tactics.

In June 1925 Haig gave a speech that was reported in *The Times* of London. It has been quoted many times since (often in the first person), to show that seven years after the Great War he was still clinging stubbornly to outmoded ideas. According to *The Times*, Douglas Haig, now Earl Haig, said, speaking about what he thought the future of horses in warfare would be like, that:

> . . . he believed that the value of the horse and the opportunity for the horse in the future are likely to be as great as ever . . . aeroplanes and tanks . . . were only accessories to the man and his horse, and he felt sure that as time went on they [the military] would find just as much use for the horse – the well-bred horse – as they had ever done in the past.

DR ELSIE INGLIS
(1864–1917)

SURGEON AND SUFFRAGIST

Elsie Inglis was born, at a beautiful hill station in India, where her Scottish father, John David Forbes Inglis, was employed in the Indian Civil Service. Her mother had had to take their first six children back to Britain at the time of the Indian Mutiny and had reluctantly left them there when she returned to her husband in India. There she bore him three more children, Elise being the eldest. In 1878, Inglis retired as the Chief Commissioner of Oudh and took his wife and youngest children – fourteen-year-old Elsie, her sister Eva, and her little brother – back to their former home in Edinburgh taking in a two-year stay in Tasmania visiting their oldest sons who had settled there.

Elsie's parents were enlightened people who believed that the education was equally important for children of both genders. They also supported her in realising her ambition to become involved in medicine.

DR ELSIE INGLIS (1864–1917)

She started her medical training at the revolutionary Edinburgh School of Medicine for Women, which had been established only two years previously by Dr Sophia Jex-Blake. After three years there, she then studied under Sir William McEwen at Glasgow Royal Infirmary (now part of Glasgow University). By 1892 she was fully qualified as a surgeon and physician and went to work in London. She was appalled by the poor standard of care and lack of specialisation in the care of female patients, and returned to Edinburgh determined to do something about it.

In 1894, Inglis set up a medical practice with another woman doctor and opened a maternity hospital and midwifery resource centre for the poor in Edinburgh High Street. This later became the Elsie Inglis Memorial Hospital. Elsie often waived the fees for medical services and paid for patients to convalesce at the seaside.

Elsie Inglis was particularly concerned about repealing a law that prevented women from having any surgical operation without her husband's consent. As she struggled against this inequity, Elsie came to realise that improving the medical care of women also required political backing, but the early signs of political activism in favour of women were scattered in pockets over Scotland. To co-ordinate all the disparate activities, Elsie Inglis was at the forefront in forming one consolidated organisation. In 1906 she founded the Scottish Women's Suffragette Federation and became its first Secretary. She organised meetings all over the country and delivered hundreds of lectures on the suffrage question. From then on her life was completely occupied with her practice, her suffrage work, and the founding of a nursing home and maternity centre.

Even though she was at the vanguard of the suffragette movement, she still knew who had set her on the course of campaigning for women's equality. At one of the biggest meetings she addressed in

London years later, her sister Eva later wrote in *Elsie Inglis: The Woman with the Torch*, Elsie said, 'If I have been able to do anything, I owe it all to my father.'

By 1914, Dr Inglis had established herself as a well-respected surgeon and lecturer. But it was Elsie's efforts during the First World War which really brought her fame.

Up to August 1914, Dr Inglis and her fellow suffragists had been part of a growing movement of social change that at times involved civil disobedience, even civil unrest through demonstrations. But as soon as war broke out everything changed overnight. In a unanimous decision, the women advocates for social change agreed to a moratorium on their campaign for the vote and instantly offered their services to the government in support of the war effort. There was however an implicit agreement in this change.

If women showed their support and loyalty during the war, then government would grant them the right to the vote after the war. As it turned out, women over thirty years of age in Britain were indeed given the vote in 1918, although Elsie never lived to exercise that right herself.

At the outbreak of war, Inglis suggested the creation of medical units staffed by women to serve at the front. The British authorities were opposed, with one senior War Office clerk telling Inglis, 'My good lady, go home and sit still.' Despite this setback and the insult, she set up the Scottish Women's Hospitals for Foreign Service, funded entirely by the women's suffrage movement. She found that the French were not so discriminatory and in December 1914 the first all-female medical unit dispatched by Inglis was operating a 200-bed hospital in France.

Over time her Suffragette Federation would organise and fund medical teams to go to Serbia and Salonica (now Thessaloniki) as well as Russia. Sir Thomas Lipton, a fellow Scot and self-made millionaire from the growing and distribution of tea, placed his ships at Dr Inglis's disposal to assist in the transportation of personnel and equipment to Serbia.

In early 1915 Inglis accompanied a women's medical unit to Serbia that was urgently needed to combat the dreaded disease of typhus sweeping through the country at the time. Serbia was an ally of Britain, France and Russia and was being badly crushed by the much larger Austro-Hungarian army that was destroying great swathes of the land, leaving the civilians without fresh water or sanitation.

Dr Inglis opened two hospitals and insisted the Serbian authorities institute basic hygienic practices across the parts of the devastated country they controlled. With a combination of steely determination, logic and impressive results she won the Serbians over to her way of thinking. The authorities implemented the measures she demanded, such as boiling drinking water and reducing the overcrowding in the treatment centres, and gradually Inglis and her team triumphed in a long-drawn-out battle against the disease.

Later that year, just as the health crisis was stabilised, Germans poured over the border of Serbia in a co-ordinated attack with Austrian and Bulgarian forces. The quarter-of-a-million-strong Serbian army had no chance against a three-pronged attack by over half a million enemy troops. The front line collapsed and the Serbians were soon retreating towards Albania. Dr Inglis and some of her staff in the hospitals refused to leave their patients behind and stayed on to be captured by the advancing Germans.

The Germans did not know what to do with Dr Inglis. Quite frankly they had never seen anyone quite like her. She remained treating patients for several months, though now technically a

German prisoner, but was finally released when the United States Government (then still a neutral power in the war) intervened on her behalf.

After being returned to Britain in early 1916, Inglis threw herself into new plans for hospitals in Russia, where many Serbians had managed to escape. She managed to raise the necessary finances in just a few months and, supported by eighty qualified women, she headed the team that went to Russia later in 1916.

After forty days' continuous travelling, some of it through U-boat infested waters, Dr Inglis and her group of highly dedicated staff arrived at Odessa and made their way straight to the stretchers of the wounded who had been defending the city against an advancing German army.

For the next fifteen months Dr Inglis worked tirelessly treating the wounds of the sick and the dying, conducting surgery for many long hours, and all the while slowly losing her own strength as she was now dying from cancer.

In all her short communications back to Britain, she was full of unstinting praise for the work of her team. She told no one of her condition until the news came that the hospital was to be relieved and she felt able to go home for a well-earned rest. Even then, she barely mentioned it, writing 'Have not been well – nothing to worry about.'

On the journey home she had a relapse, violent pain set in, and she was forced to take to her bed. Still, her courage did not fail her. She insisted on checking the hospital accounts, she interviewed personally each member of her unit, and invited them to volunteer for service in a new hospital which she was planning in her head for Salonica in Greece.

As the ship docked at Newcastle in England in November

1917, she insisted on walking unaided down the gangway wearing her worn uniform and hat with the now famous Scottish tartan headband. Once she got down on to the dock she collapsed and was rushed to hospital in a state of complete exhaustion. Elsie Inglis died the next day. The cancer had eaten her insides away, but she would tell no one.

Dr Inglis was buried in Edinburgh, her funeral attended by a huge number of friends and supporters who were still shocked at her sudden passing. The flags of Great Britain and Serbia were draped over her coffin and the lilies of France were placed around her, while over her head hung the Saltire of Scotland. She was fifty-three years old.

By the end of the war, four Scottish Women's Hospitals had been established together with another fourteen smaller medical clinics in areas as diverse as France, Serbia, Corsica, Salonika, Romania, Russia and Malta. In all, 1,000 women doctors, nurses, orderlies and drivers served. As well as the Scottish contingents, women from various parts of Britain, Ireland, Canada, Australia and New Zealand served in Scottish Women's Hospital units. Every single one of them was proud to wear the distinctive tartan headband as part of her uniform.

Elsie Inglis's greatest achievement was saving the lives of countless thousands in the Great War and blazing a trail for innumerable women of Britain and elsewhere who wanted to contribute more to making society a better place.

CHARLES RENNIE MACKINTOSH
(1868–1928)

ARCHITECT WHO PIONEERED
THE 'GLASGOW STYLE' OF
DESIGN IN SCOTLAND

Mackintosh was born in Parson Street, Glasgow, the oldest and one of the roughest parts of the city. He was the second of eleven children of a strict Presbyterian Highlander who was a Superintendent in the Glasgow Police force. His early education was difficult as he had learning problems that would probably be identified today as dyslexia. However, in the 1870s he was simply regarded as slow. To add to his disadvantages, he suffered from a pronounced limp from a deformed foot and these two afflictions made him an outsider to his classmates.

At sixteen, and against his father's wishes, he became apprenticed to the local architect John Hutchinson. Just as crucially, to complement his training during the day, Mackintosh attended evening classes at the Glasgow School of Art. At the time, the educational institution was under the directorship of the visionary Francis Newbery who quickly identified in Mackintosh a talented, intelligent young man, whom he nurtured. It was through the School of Art that in 1888 Mackintosh gained his first commission as a professional, and won a prize from the Glasgow Institute of Fine Art (a separate organisation) for his design for a terraced house.

It was also at the School of Art that Mackintosh was befriended by a group of three people who together with Mackintosh would go on to influence Glasgow and the world. Women had been allowed to enter the School of Art since the late 1870s, but it was under the enlightened leadership of Newbery, that, from the mid-1880s, women participated on equal terms with the male students. Alongside Francis Newbery was his wife Jessie Newbery who was instrumental in bringing about a revolution in textiles and embroidery to the School. As head of the Embroidery Department she achieved international recognition for her designs, patterns and motifs, particularly in Germany and Austria.

Two sisters, Margaret and Frances MacDonald, who were exposed to the best and latest in design funded by their wealthy engineer father, enrolled at the School of Art in 1890. They had an immediate impact on Mackintosh and another student, James Herbert MacNair. Within a short time, the four were inseparable. MacNair worked for architects Honeyman and Keppie, a larger, more successful city practice than John Hutchinson, where Mackintosh still worked. Whether influenced by MacNair or not, Mackintosh transferred to Honeyman and Keppie in 1899, where he was employed initially as a draughtsman, then as a partner from 1904.

Together, Mackintosh, MacNair and the MacDonald sisters became known as the 'Glasgow Four' and leaders in a new innovative style of design that had its origins in Art Nouveau, but would go beyond it. Eventually the four would go on to display their artworks at international exhibitions in Glasgow (1895), London

(1899), Vienna (1900), Turin (1902), Dresden (1903), Glasgow and Berlin (1905). The style they promoted went on to strongly influence the Viennese Art Nouveau movement. In 1899, James MacNair married Frances Macdonald, and in 1900 Mackintosh married Margaret MacDonald.

While Mackintosh's style may have started as Art Nouveau, he did not stop developing and expanding it over his career. Into Art Nouveau he blended the Scottish Baronial style, to which he later added Japanese design influences. It is therefore difficult to pigeon-hole Mackintosh's design style into one single category. It is more appropriate to say that Mackintosh developed his own unique style of architecture and design that incorporated elements of the above three categories. A style that has been named the 'Glasgow Style'.

Back in Glasgow, matters were progressing well for the young architect and designer, Charles Mackintosh. In 1890, he won a £60 prize for his design of a public meeting hall. It was enough to pay the rent on his flat and fund a four-month working holiday to Italy sketching ancient Roman buildings. By 1906 Mackintosh had become a member of the Royal Institute of British Architects.

It was over a twenty-year period from 1890–1910 that Mackintosh would produce what is regarded as his most memorable work, although at the time, reactions were somewhat mixed. Today, however, his work is universally admired for its style, innovation, and its aesthetic appeal which, if anything, continues to grow over the decades.

Mackintosh's first major commission (as designer for Honeyman and Keppie) was in 1895 for the design of the Medical Hall for Queen Margaret College adjoining North Park House, located opposite Glasgow University's Botanic Gardens. Queen Margaret College was Scotland's first college for women in 1884 and part of Glasgow University in 1892. The building showcased his Glasgow style of architecture and interior design to the city of Glasgow that had never witnessed anything like it before. It instantly polarised people, with some thinking it looked ugly and stark, while others welcomed the refreshing change from heavy, ornate late-Victorian architecture.

Thankfully, Mackintosh continued to receive commissions for more work. His design for the Glasgow Herald Building (1894) incorporated some cutting-edge technology including a hydro-pneumatic lift and fire-resistant concrete flooring. Later at Martyr's Public School (1895), he was able to experiment with elaborate detailing on the central roof trusses, which drew much comment.

In 1896, Mackintosh received what would become his most important and substantial commission; the design of a new building for the Glasgow School of Art. This was to be his masterpiece. The building was constructed in two distinct phases, 1897–99 and 1907–9, due to funding limitations. While the exterior was impressive, it was the interiors that attracted most attention. The library in particular was outstanding, being a complex space of timber posts and beams fusing Japanese, Art Nouveau and Scottish Baronial styles in a way never quite seen before or since. In honour of his design genius, the Glasgow School of Arts building was renamed the Mackintosh building after his death.

Further commissions followed. Ruchill Free Church Halls were completed in 1899. Queens Cross Church opened for worship in 1899. Hill House in Helensburgh, 50 kilometres north of Glasgow along the River Clyde, one of the few private residences he was asked to design was completed in late 1903. It was built as the new home for wealthy publisher William Blackie and was such a striking example of Mackintosh's brilliance that it was placed into the hands of the National Trust of Scotland in 1982 and has remained one of Scotland's major tourist attractions ever since.

The Daily Record Building was finished in 1905 and the Scotland Street School was built in 1909.

Mackintosh had an eye for detail that was both his strength and his weakness. The strength was that when a client asked him to design the interiors, Mackintosh would do so, down to the very last detail, including cutlery, window fixtures, lamps and in the case of Miss Cranston's Tea Rooms, the actual menu itself. It was also his weakness, because he would often spend time obsessing about these fine details to the frustration of his clients and ultimately the profitability of the commission. Some people have speculated he may have suffered from a mild form of Asperger's syndrome.

Throughout his career, Mackintosh enjoyed only a handful of patrons and supporters, as the general public did not understand, nor care for his individualistic style of architecture and design. Apart from the publisher Blackie, the other most devoted patron was Glasgow businesswomen Catherine 'Kate' Cranston (*see* p. 179).

Kate Cranston showed a remarkable flair for business and was a pioneer of the tea room movement which featured greatly in Glasgow's social life at the turn of the century. The luncheon rooms and tea rooms which carried her name were well known to most Glasgow citizens, demonstrating her refined taste in the fixtures and fittings as well as the decor. Between 1896 and 1917, Kate Cranston commissioned Mackintosh to build or renovate almost all of her growing number of tearooms. He had total freedom of design for both building and interiors down to the smallest detail, even including the menus which he designed personally. The completed rooms were among the most stunning pieces of original and innovative commercial architecture anywhere in the world.

Despite success in Europe and the support of clients such as Blackie and Cranston, work declined considerably for Mackintosh from about 1910. People were still not sure what to make of his so-called 'Glasgow style'. Despairing of ever receiving another commission in Scotland (after trying several times), Mackintosh took to drink and resigned his partnership with Honeyman and Keppie in 1913. He and his wife moved to the south of England to begin again.

The timing could not have been worse. Shortly before their move to Suffolk, what would become known as the Great War had started and their arrival was treated with deep suspicion. Their home was even searched by MI5 convinced they had found German spies! The war years and beyond were a lean period for Charles and Margaret Mackintosh with only a few residential renovations and redecorations from which to eke out a living.

By 1923, the Mackintosh couple were nearly bankrupt, so they moved to the south of France where the climate was warmer and the cost of living much cheaper. There, he turned his considerable artistic skill to painting watercolours. He intended to mount an exhibition of his work in London to relaunch his career as a painter and had completed forty examples of his work when his mouth became very painful to the touch and he had difficulty swallowing.

Mackintosh journeyed to London for a medical check-up, where he was told the disastrous news that he was suffering from tongue cancer. Mackintosh had been a tobacco smoker most of his adult life. He had radium treatment followed by surgery, but it was too late, Charles Rennie Mackintosh died in December 1928 at the age of sixty. Margaret Mackintosh died five years later in 1933.

Glasgow at the turn of the twentieth century defined itself as the 'workshop' of the British Empire; a location where foundries and factories were to be preferred over fine art. Further, Glasgow was also a threatening, masculine, alcoholic place where the slums of Govan (along the Clyde River) were said to have become the worst in Europe. Never as successful or as recognised in his day as he should have been, Mackintosh was viewed as a bit of a 'dandy' who merely produced drawings on paper, whereas the 'real' men of Glasgow worked with iron and steel, went to the pub and were not afraid to get involved in a fight.

A century later and Mackintosh has since gone on to become a hugely influential icon in the world of international architecture and design. He is now celebrated and even loved by Glasgow, the city which he left in despair in 1914. Recently, four chairs he designed, that were among his estate when he died, were sold at auction for more than £100,000 each. Their recorded valuation at the time of his death was 'worthless'.

In May 2014, an electrical fire in the basement of the iconic and world-renowned School of Arts building caused a major fire throughout its four floors. As an example of how much Glaswegians have come to venerate Mackintosh, fire crews risked their lives for days to not only save the building but also its priceless contents. When the last of the fire crew departed, students, teachers and Glasgow residents lined the narrow street outside the burned-out building to give them a heroes' send-off, accompanied by loud cheers and a piper.

Thanks to the efforts of the fire officers it is believed that 90 per cent of the structure was saved as were as much as 70 per cent of its priceless contents. A multimillion-pound fund was launched to fully restore the building, which will take years to complete. But Glasgow will wait patiently for the Mackintosh building to become whole again, for as the city has matured and gentrified over the last century, so has its appreciation of the genius of Charles Rennie Mackintosh and the legacy of the Glasgow style of architecture he left the world.

JOHN BUCHAN, 1ST BARON TWEEDSMUIR (1875–1940)

NOVELIST, HISTORIAN AND GOVERNOR GENERAL OF CANADA

Buchan was born in Perth, Scotland, the first-born son of a Free Kirk minister, and brought up in Kircaldy in Fife. Summer holidays with his grandparents in the Scottish Borders imbued in him a love of the outdoors, walking, bird watching, fishing and the wonderful views of the Scottish countryside.

He attended Hutcheson's Grammar School in Glasgow and then secured a scholarship to attend the University of Glasgow where he studied classics, wrote poetry and became a published author. Oxford University followed, after which he read for the bar.

After a spell as barrister, during which he continued to write – he had by now published a number of books, including three novels – he was sent to South Africa for a couple of years, where he became familiar with its culture, politics and especially its landscape. John Buchan was already developing his gift of accurately describing the world around him that he would apply to great effect in his future novels. His 1910 adventure novel *Prester John* drew on his observations of South Africa.

He returned to Britain in 1903, returned to the bar, but continued to write and publish privately. In 1907, he married Susan Grosvenor, a distant cousin of the Duke of Westminster; they were to have four children. At this point, he started working for the Edinburgh publishing company, Nelsons.

With the outbreak of the Great War in 1914, Buchan wrote communiqués for the British War Office. In his own time, he produced two brilliant novels for which he enjoyed great commercial success – *The Thirty-Nine Steps* (1915) and *Greenmantle* (1916). In 1916, he enlisted in the Army and was commissioned Lieutenant in the Intelligence Corps, where he wrote speeches for Sir Douglas Haig (*see* p. 190). In 1917, he was appointed Director of Information and wrote a monthly serialisation of *History of the War*, which would be reissued later in 24 volumes.

After the war, he moved his growing family to village of Elsfield in Oxfordshire, where walking in the countryside became one of his favourite pastimes. Three more novels followed in swift succession and after his massive *History of the War* was published in 1923 he took a break by being elected to parliament in 1927 and then becoming High Commissioner to the General Assembly of the Church of Scotland in 1933 and 1934.

But writing was never far away and during this time he wrote more thrillers, branched out into historical novels and wrote biographies of Sir Walter Scott and the Marquess of Montrose.

In 1935 Alfred Hitchcock turned *The Thirty-Nine Steps* into a film which became a box-office success. That same year King George V created Buchan Baron Tweedsmuir, of Elsfield (his home in Oxfordshire) – a considerable honour that was swiftly followed by his appointment as Governor General of Canada.

John Buchan (now Lord Tweedsmuir) continued writing during his time in Canada, but he also took his position as viceroy seriously. From the outset he made it his goal to travel the length and breadth of Canada and meet as many Canadians as he could. He worked tirelessly for Canadian unity and conducted himself with great distinction. Encouraged by his wife, who was also an accomplished writer, Lord Tweedsmuir created the Governor General's Literary Awards, which are still Canada's primary awards for literary achievement.

The Tweedsmuirs built the first proper library at Rideau Hall, Ottawa, the official residence of the Governor General. President Roosevelt was the first American President to officially visit Canada in 1936 and was well received by Lord Tweedsmuir as the King's representative.

In 1938, a huge 13,000-square-kilometre park was created and named in Lord Tweedsmuir's honour. In the foreword to a booklet published to commemorate his visit, he wrote, 'I have now travelled over most of Canada and have seen many wonderful things, but I have seen nothing more beautiful and more wonderful than the great park which British Columbia has done me the honour to call by my name. '

On 9 September 1939 he had the solemn duty as Governor General of signing Canada's declaration of war, an act that would lead to the deaths of over 45,000 Canadian soldiers. Lord Tweedsmuir had worked tirelessly since his appointment as Governor General to help draw Canada, Britain, and the United States closer together. Now that war had come, these countries and the rest of the world fighting aggression from the combined might of Germany, Italy and Japan would need each other even more.

In 1940, Lord Tweedsmuir suffered a severe head injury from a fall he suffered during a stroke and died five days later in hospital. There was an outpouring of grief throughout Canada the likes of which had never been seen previously. He was cremated and his ashes returned to his family estate in Oxfordshire.

Throughout his sixty-five years, Lord Tweedsmuir wrote over a hundred books, including nearly thirty novels, several collections of short stories, a massive history of the Great War and four extensively researched biographies on major historical figures such as Sir Walter Scott (*see* p. 124), Julius Caesar, the Roman Emperor Augustus, Oliver Cromwell and the Marquess of Montrose. But his most famous books were his spy thrillers, of which he wrote several; all of them are still in print today. His novel, *The Thirty-Nine Steps* continues to be regarded as one of the top one hundred books of the twentieth century, but it is his biographies and historical studies that are still regarded as classics of scholarship.

DANIEL LAIDLAW (1875–1950)

PIPER WHO WON A VC AT
THE BATTLE OF LOOS, 1915

Laidlaw was born in Little Swinton, in the Scottish Borders, and joined the army in 1896 as an infantryman. He served on the Indian frontier for two years and returned to Britain where, in 1912, he was transferred to the King's Own Scottish Borderers (KOSB) as a piper. Having served sixteen years in the regular army he was placed on the reserve list. Upon the outbreak of war in Europe, Laidlaw re-enlisted, at the age of forty, with the KOSB in September 1914. He was attached as a piper to the 7th Battalion of the KOSB when they, along with 100,000 British soldiers, were called upon to attack the Germans across a 30-kilometre front centred on the French mining town of Loos.

The Battle of Loos was one of the major British offensives launched on the Western Front during the First World War. However, the first day of engagement, 25 September 1915, was a disorganised mess: the wrong gas cylinders had been sent, and what gas could be released blew back onto the British trenches. Then the Germans started pouring heavy artillery down on the soldiers before the attack had started.

The 7th Kings Own Scottish Borderers had the specific objective of capturing a small hill named Hill 70 on the first day of the battle. While they waited in their trench before the scheduled start of the attack, matters deteriorated rapidly. Men succumbed to their own poison gas and the intense German shelling caused even more distress. Seeing the collapsing morale around him, the commanding officer caught sight of Laidlaw standing nearby with his pipes waiting orders to go 'over the top'.

'Pipe them together, Laidlaw, for God's sake, pipe them together,' cried the commanding officer.

Scottish pipers played their regiments into battle – a very dangerous role. Being unarmed and drawing attention to themselves with their playing, pipers were always an easy target for the enemy. The death rate among pipers was extremely high: it is estimated that around 1000 pipers died in the First World War.

None of that mattered to Piper Laidlaw. He immediately climbed onto the parapet and began marching up and down the length of the trench. While his fellow soldiers were still coughing and spluttering from the effects of gas, or wearing their gas masks to prevent being affected, Laidlaw took off his mask and stayed blowing into his bagpipes.

Bullets whizzed past him, shells burst near him, but oblivious to the danger he played 'All the Blue Bonnets over the Border', the stirring regimental march of the KOSB. Men watched in awe as their piper stood above them seemingly impervious to everything the Germans were throwing at him.

The effect it had on the battalion was immediate. The men took courage and the commanding officer gave the order to advance and shouted, 'Come on, Borderers, who'll be the first to reach the German trenches?'

Those not overcome by the gas swarmed up out of the trenches with bayonets bristling and followed Laidlaw into the assault. Men began falling all around him, but Laidlaw continued piping. Then just as he was getting closer to the barbed wire entanglements near the German lines, he was hit by shrapnel from an exploding German shell. Shrapnel and wire cut off the heel of his boot and a strand of barbed wire lodged deeply into his foot. Laidlaw was badly wounded in the ankle and leg while the officer moving with him was killed outright. Laidlaw continued to play and tried to hobble after the regiment.

Exposed and unarmed in no-man's-land, Laidlaw could no longer stand. The loss of blood and the pain forced him to kneel, then lie down, but all the while he continued to play the pipes. He was still playing famous Scottish martial tunes when his battalion managed to secure the heavily defended objective of Hill 70. Afterwards, he was escorted from the battlefield by returning soldiers.

By the end of the three-day battle the battalion of approximately 750 officers and men had suffered an incredible 80 per cent casualty rate, of which almost a quarter had died securing and trying to hold Hill 70. Across the entire front the British suffered similar appalling casualty rates and in the end were forced to pull back to their original trenches. In total some 60,000 British soldiers were killed, wounded, captured or missing – for no gain in territory whatsoever.

For his efforts, Piper Laidlaw received the highest bravery award possible, the Victoria Cross, which was pinned on him by King George V at Buckingham Palace.

The official entry in the *London Gazette* reads:

During the worst of the bombardment, Piper Laidlaw, seeing that his company was badly shaken from the effects of gas, with absolute coolness and disregard of danger, mounted the parapet, marched up and down and played the company out of the trench. The effect of his splendid example was immediate and the company dashed out to the assault. Piper Laidlaw continued playing his pipes even after he was wounded.

Laidlaw also received the French Croix de Guerre and was afterwards promoted to sergeant-piper. He was demobilised after the war in 1919 having served a total of twenty years in the British Army. Laidlaw died peacefully in 1950, aged seventy-four, near Norham on the Scottish border with England and is buried in the local St Cuthbert's cemetery. His medals, including his Victoria Cross, are on display at the National Museum of Scotland in Edinburgh.

SIR ALEXANDER FLEMING
(1881–1955)

BIOLOGIST AND DISCOVERER
OF PENICILLIN

There are very few individuals ever in the history of man who have truly saved the lives of hundreds of millions of people – Sir Alexander Fleming is one of them.

Alexander Fleming was born on a remote farm near Darvel, Ayrshire, Scotland. He was the third of four children his father had with his second wife, the daughter of a nearby farmer. There were another four surviving children from the first marriage. The Fleming children spent much of their time ranging through the streams, valleys and moors of the countryside.

Fleming went to school in Darvel earning a scholarship to Kilmarnock Academy. When Alexander (called Alec) was seven his father died. One older brother took over the running of the farm and another studied medicine and set up a practice in London. Soon, four Fleming brothers and a sister were living in London and Alec joined them when he was fourteen, where he continued his education at the Royal Polytechnic Institution (now the University of Westminster).

In 1900, when the Boer War broke out between the United Kingdom and its former colonies in southern Africa, Alec and two brothers joined the London Scottish Regiment (part-time reserve). This turned out to be as much a sporting club as anything; they honed their shooting, swimming, and even water polo skills, but were never called upon to fight in the Boer War. After working in a shipping office for four years, the twenty-year-old Fleming inherited some money from an uncle. His older brother Tom, the physician, suggested Alec should follow the same career, and in 1903, Alec enrolled at St Mary's Hospital Medical School in Paddington, London. Alec was a brilliant student and in 1906, he passed with distinction from the medical school.

The Medical School had a rifle club and Fleming was a crack shot. The captain of the club, wishing to retain him in the team after his graduation suggested that Fleming join the research department at St Mary's, where he worked under the supervision of Almroth Wright, a noted scientist in the relatively new fields of bacteriology and immunology. In 1908, Fleming gained a Bachelor of Science degree in Bacteriology and became a lecturer at St Mary's until 1914.

During the First World War, Fleming enlisted as a captain in the medical corps and served with many of his colleagues in the battlefield hospitals at the Western Front in France. Fleming saw at first hand the failure of the antiseptics that were in use at the time to treat infected wounds and when he returned to London in 1918 he was determined to find a solution to the problem.

Initially, he experimented with vaccines and enzymes all with limited success, though in November 1921 he managed to isolate a substance he named 'lysozyme'; naturally occurring in secretions such as tears, saliva, milk, it has mild antibacterial qualities, and has subsequently been used as a food preservative, and in some medical treatments.

In 1927, Fleming was investigating the properties of staphylococci (a strain of bacteria). He was already well-known from his earlier work, and had developed a reputation as a brilliant researcher, and in 1928 he was promoted to Professor of Bacteriology at the University of London.

Still working in his untidy research laboratory at St Mary's Hospital, Fleming made his greatest breakthrough later that year when he discovered an effective antibacterial agent. And it was an accident.

He had left his work unattended while away on a summer holiday. On returning to work on 3 September, he saw that a greenish mould had grown in a petri dish containing one of his cultures of staphylococcus bacteria, and observed that in a rough ring surrounding the patch of mould the staphylococci had been destroyed, while the bacteria colonies further from the mould were normal.

This was Fleming's 'eureka' moment – he quickly deduced that some antibacterial agent had crept in and killed the bacteria. By the end of the month he had identified this antibacterial agent as a rare form of the fungus *Penicillium notatum*, which had drifted in from a mycology lab nearby. He much later remarked about that day: 'When I woke up just after dawn on September 28, 1928, I certainly didn't plan to revolutionise all medicine by discovering the world's first antibiotic, or bacteria killer . . . but I guess that was exactly what I did.'

Nearer the time, though, he wrote in the *British Journal of*

Experimental Pathology, explaining how he identified the mould and investigated its properties:

> While working with staphylococcus variants, a number of culture-plates were set aside on the laboratory bench and examined from time to time. In the examinations these plates were necessarily exposed to the air and they became contaminated with various micro-organisms. It was noticed that around a large colony of a contaminating mould the staphylococcus colonies became transparent and were obviously undergoing lysis [breaking down].
>
> Subcultures of this mould were made and experiments conducted with a view to ascertaining something of the properties of the substance which had evidently been formed in the mould culture and which had diffused into the surrounding medium. It was found that the broth in which the mould had been grown at room temperature for one or two weeks had acquired marked inhibitory [bacteria-killing] properties to many of the more common pathogenic bacteria.

The full article published in the *British Journal of Experimental Pathology* roused little interest. The major drawback was refining and growing sufficient quantities of penicillin to be useful outside the laboratory. This would take another decade of experimentation to achieve. Fleming in the meantime ascertained that penicillin did not affect the pathogens that caused typhoid fever and paratyphoid fever, and diverted his attention to finding a way to combat these.

In 1939, a team of scientists at Oxford University began work on trying to make a large quantity of Fleming's penicillin. The team was led by Professor Howard Florey and Dr Ernst Chain.

Eventually, they were able to extract the penicillin in sufficient quantities to start producing it on a commercial scale, just in time for the start of the Second World War.

Initial supplies were used exclusively by the armed forces and when the world realised this new substance was saving the lives of thousands of soldiers, Fleming and the others became famous overnight. Fleming was knighted in 1944 and Fleming, Florey and Chain received the Nobel Prize for Physiology and Medicine in 1945.

After being awarded the world's most prestigious prize in science, Fleming, with characteristic humility, said, 'One sometimes finds what one is not looking for.' He deliberately avoided patenting penicillin, wanting the world to have unrestricted access to a substance that would save millions of lives.

Fleming's accidental discovery and isolation of penicillin in September 1928 marked the start of modern antibiotics.

There is a popular story that in the 1890s Winston Churchill was saved from drowning in a Scottish loch by a young farm boy called Alec. In gratitude, Churchill's father paid for the education of this young boy, who then went on to become a brilliant scientist and the discoverer of penicillin. The story continues that in 1943, the now mature Winston Churchill was struck down by pneumonia in the Middle East and in a wonderful twist of fate it is Alec Fleming who saves Churchill's life for a second time with a dose of his precious penicillin.

It is a good tale, but unfortunately none of it is true. It is only mentioned in this biography to acknowledge its persistence and to refute it. Winston Churchill was not rescued from drowning in Scotland by Alec Fleming or anyone else. Churchill did, however, contract pneumonia while in the Middle East in 1943, but he was treated with another drug entirely. It was a sulfadiazine produced by May and Baker Pharmaceuticals and called 'M&B' for short.

In 1915, Fleming married a trained nurse, Sarah Marion McElroy of County Mayo, Ireland. Their only child, Robert Fleming (b.1924) became a general medical practitioner. After Sarah's death in 1949, Fleming married, in 1953, Dr Amalia Koutsouri-Vourekas, a colleague at St Mary's Hospital.

After being knighted and receiving the Nobel Prize, Sir Alexander Fleming (as he was now called) continued to write, teach and lecture in the field of bacteriology and on the accidental discovery he made that changed medicine. Honours and plaudits kept coming and he was in constant demand at international science conferences and seminars.

In 1955, Fleming died at his home in London of a heart attack. He was seventy-four years of age. He was buried in St. Paul's Cathedral following a State funeral. He was survived by his wife Amalia, who died in 1986, and by his son.

The laboratory at St Mary's Hospital where Fleming discovered penicillin has been preserved and is home to the Fleming Museum that still remains a popular London attraction today. St Mary's Hospital Medical School merged with Imperial College London in 1988. The main teaching building of the Imperial College School of Medicine, opened in 1998, was named the Sir Alexander Fleming Building.

In 1999, *Time* magazine named Fleming one of the '100 Most Important People of the 20th Century'.

Fleming's accidental discovery has conquered some of mankind's most dangerous diseases and in the process has literally saved the lives of hundreds of millions of people on the planet.

HUGH DOWDING, 1ST BARON DOWDING (1882–1970)

THE MASTERMIND BEHIND VICTORY IN THE BATTLE OF BRITAIN IN THE SECOND WORLD WAR

B orn in Moffat, Dumfries and Galloway, Scotland, Hugh Dowding was the son of a schoolmaster. He attended St Ninian's Preparatory School as boy and continued his education at Winchester College until the age of fifteen. But having failed to achieve academically, he enrolled in the Royal Military Academy, Woolwich to become an officer in the British Army. He avoided alcohol, was decidedly uncomfortable in the company of women and was considered so aloof that he was nicknamed 'Stuffy', a name that stuck with him the rest of his life.

In the Army, he gained the rank of Second Lieutenant and became a much-travelled individual, being posted to many locations around the world including Ceylon (now Sri Lanka), Hong Kong and Gibraltar. In 1904 he was assigned to the No.7 Mountain Artillery Battery in India.

On his return to Britain, he was accepted for the Royal Staff

College and began classes in January 1912 to gain higher rank. In his spare time, he quickly became fascinated by flying and aircraft, and when he visited the newly opened Aero Club at Brooklands on the outskirts of London, he was able to persuade them to give him flying lessons on credit. A quick learner, he soon received his flying certificate. With this in hand, he applied to the Royal Flying Corps (RFC) to become a pilot. They were desperate for qualified pilots and Dowding's request was approved immediately. He joined the RFC in December 1913, which was less than a year before war broke out.

In the four years of the Great War, Dowding's rise up the promotional ladder was fast. After just one year of serving with the RFC in France, he commanded his own squadron. By the end of the war in 1918, he was the equivalent of a brigadier-general. However, during the Battle of the Somme in 1916, in which the RFC was to provide close air support for the infantry, Dowding clashed with the Chief of the RFC, Major General Hugh Trenchard over the need to rest pilots at the front. Trenchard was forceful and demanded his pilots adopt a more aggressive stance, but Dowding disagreed. Trenchard thought Dowding was a lacklustre leader who was far too negative and timid. He described Dowding as 'dismal'.

Trenchard ensured that Dowding played no active role at the front again and transferred him to a series of desk jobs back in Britain for the remainder of the war. In 1918, Dowding moved to the newly created Royal Air Force (RAF) and in the years after the war led first No. 16 Group and then No.1 Group as Group Captain.

After the unexpected death in 1920 of his young wife Clarice, after a short illness, Dowding's introverted nature worsened. Perhaps it was a form of depression, but he became more reclusive and distant from friends and colleagues. They had been married only two years and had one son, Derek, who went on to become a fine RAF pilot, rising to the rank of Wing Commander.

In the early twenties, Dowding's career seemed to be stagnating, but then in 1926 he was unexpectedly appointed the position of RAF's Director of Training, where he proved he was a successful technical thinker. Throughout the thirties, while Germany was rearming itself, the orthodox thinking among the chiefs of the RAF was that bombers would win any future war. Dowding rejected this concept, shrewdly recognising that Britain's salvation in the predictable clash with Germany would rely on the capability of her home defences, and he put in place what came to be known as the 'Dowding System', which enabled, through the use of radar and a dedicated telephone network, the direction of fighter aircraft and anti-aircraft artillery across the nation. This recognition of the importance of radar working in cooperation with fighter aircraft to tackle the Luftwaffe was a stroke of brilliance in Dowding that was appreciated by too few, including Winston Churchill, at the time.

Dowding became head of Fighter Command in 1936, but as late as 1938, the higher ranking RAF officers who supported the notion that the war would be won by bombers were very much in the majority. Only a handful of military chiefs, Dowding among them, were willing to question this.

Throughout the late 1930s as war clouds once again gathered over Europe, Dowding worked feverishly to bring together the disparate components of radar, ground observers, raid plotting, and radio control of aircraft into one unified system. Years later, the writer Leo McKinstry would point out that it was Dowding who urged for the speedy introduction of two new fighter designs, the Spitfire and the Hurricane, which would prove so devastatingly effective in the coming conflict, and would by 1940 make up most of

Fighter Command, Churchill was later to recognise the importance not just of the new fighter aircraft but of the 'Dowding System', writing in *The Second World War*, Vol. 2 (1949):

> All the ascendancy of the Hurricanes and Spitfires would have been fruitless but for this system which had been devised and built before the war. It had been shaped and refined in constant action, and all was now fused together into a most elaborate instrument of war, the like of which existed nowhere in the world.

Eventually, Dowding succeeded in his reorganisation of Fighter Command just as Hitler threatened to invade Poland. The new set-up had Fighter Command for the whole of Britain being administered through his headquarters at RAF Bentley Priory, London. In order to better control his aircraft, he divided the command into four sub-groups to cover all of the island. These sub-groups had their own command centres and the one for South East Britain (in Uxbridge, London) can still be visited today as the Battle of Britain bunker.

Air Chief Marshal Dowding was scheduled to retire in mid-1939, but he was asked to remain in his post due to the deteriorating international situation. As a result, Dowding was in charge of Fighter Command as the Second World War began.

Stunned by RAF fighter losses during the Battle of France to overwhelming numbers of German planes and superior pilot skills, Dowding upset Churchill by resisting pressure to commit the bulk of his command to support a collapsing France in 1940.

Hugh Dowding correctly foretold that France was already lost and therefore the looming battle for air superiority over Britain would determine the fate of the war. Only after France capitulated in early 1940 did the threat of a German invasion on Britain dawn as a distinct possibility. Thankfully the nervous pilots of Fighter Command took comfort in the fact that 'Stuffy' had prepared everything in readiness and was a steady, if distant leader.

The Battle of Britain began in June 1940 and would last four months. Though badly stretched during the course of the fighting, Air Chief Marshal Dowding's integrated system proved effective and at no point did he commit more than fifty per cent of his aircraft to the battle zone. During the course of the fighting a debate emerged between two of his officers immediately below him regarding tactics – Air Vice Marshals Park and Leigh-Mallory.

While Park favoured intercepting German raids with individual squadrons and subjecting them to continued attack, Leigh-Mallory advocated massed attacks by 'Big Wings' consisting of three or more squadrons. There were advantages and disadvantages with both tactics, but Dowding was not able to resolve the differences between his commanders. Dowding preferred Park's methods while the Air Ministry favoured the Big Wing approach.

Dowding was also criticised during these desperate times for again being too cautious, but ultimately his approach proved to be exactly the right tactic for victory. Nevertheless, the Battle of Britain was a very close-fought affair with the outcome never clear until the last. Over four desperate months the battle was fought in the summer skies of Britain. The German losses were mounting steadily at twice the rate of the RAF, but the Germans at the start had triple the number of planes as the RAF.

On 15 September 1940, the German Luftwaffe mounted one final climactic raid to lure the RAF out and destroy it. More than 1,000 German planes took to the air in wave after wave of attacks that were to last from dawn until well into the night. Facing them were the last 250 operational fighters of the RAF.

Air Chief Marshal Dowding was so skilful in husbanding his precious resources by constantly rotating his planes during the day, that the Germans were convinced the British had more fighters than previously thought possible. At the end of the day 60 German planes had been shot down for the loss of half that number of RAF fighters. Total German losses were estimated at over 1,600 planes during the four-month campaign, compared to British losses of around 900. The promised destruction of the Royal Air Force had not eventuated and the morale of the German pilots was broken.

Two days later, Hitler called off Operation 'Sea Lion', the German plans for the invasion of Britain. The Germans simply could not crush the RAF as the British were replacing their losses and pilots faster than the Germans.

The Battle of Britain ended when Germany's Luftwaffe failed to gain air superiority over the Royal Air Force despite months of targeting Britain's air bases, military posts and, ultimately, its civilian population. Britain's decisive victory saved the country from a ground invasion and possible occupation by German forces.

After the Battle of Britain had been won, Churchill decided that Dowding had to be removed from his positon as Commander in Chief of Fighter Command, believing he was not the right person to lead beyond this point of the War. It was a timely decision, for by then Dowding was physically and mentally exhausted. But it was also a convenient excuse because Churchill had had his own disagreements with the Fighter Command's Chief Air Marshal and was well acquainted with conflicts between his two second in commands.

Douglas Bader who famously flew in the RAF after losing both his legs in an aircraft crash in 1931, said of Hugh Dowding later, 'Without his vision, his planning, his singleness of purpose, and his complete disregard for personal aggrandisement, Fighter Command might have been unable to win the Battle of Britain in the summer of 1940.'

To his credit, Churchill was not going to let Air Marshal Dowding's removal occur without some reward being given to him for his sterling efforts at saving Britain. Dowding was awarded the Knight Grand Cross of the Order of the Bath and asked to make a lecture tour of the United States. Subsequently, he was asked to conduct some meaningless manpower study of the RAF before officially retiring in July 1942.

In 1943, he was created 1st Baron Dowding of Bentley Priory for his service to the nation and retired to live out the rest of his life at Tunbridge Wells, Kent. In his later years he became actively engaged in spiritualism and increasingly bitter regarding his treatment by the RAF.

In 1951, he married Muriel Whiting, the widow of an RAF pilot, who shared his eccentric beliefs. Under her influence, he gave up game shooting and became a strict vegetarian and campaigner for animal rights. In the House of Lords he spoke against vivisection and other abuses against animals.

During his retirement, Dowding pursued his interests in spiritualism, fairies and theosophy, he and his wife occasionally hosting séances during which he claimed to be communing with the dead. Dowding died at Tunbridge Wells in 1970 and was buried at Westminster Abbey.

Those months from June until the middle of September 1940, when the men of the RAF held the nation's destiny in their hands, were a unique moment in Britain's island history. As Winston Churchill famously put it during the height of the battle, 'Never in the field of human conflict has so much been owed by so many to so few.'

According to McKinstry, 'Dowding may not have been the most charismatic leader, but thanks in no small part to this strange man, [Britain's] darkest hour became [its] finest.'

JOHN LOGIE BAIRD (1888–1946)

SCIENTIST AND PIONEER
OF TELEVISION

Every time you switch on a television, you might like to know that it was a Scotsman who invented it first.

Born in Helensburgh on the west coast of Scotland, he was the youngest of the Reverend John Baird's four children. From an early age he showed an interest in electric devices and his tinkering led him to be trained as an electrical engineer at an early age. He enrolled first at the Royal Technical College in Glasgow (which was later renamed Strathclyde University), and then went on to Glasgow University, where the First World War curtailed his final year.

Baird tried to enlist for service in the war but was rejected due to ill health, a condition that would plague him most of his life. For the next few years he worked on many inventions, some useful but most failures and even spent some time in Trinidad for his health. While working for the Clyde Valley Electrical Power Company he tried to make diamonds out of a carbon rod, but he only succeeded in shorting out the company's electricity supply to parts of Scotland, which led to many unpleasant explanations – and no diamonds.

He also tried to make rust-free razor blades out of glass, which was predictably a failure as was a jam-making venture in Trinidad. On the other hand, Baird's invention of an undersock that reduced the incident of trench foot for soldiers in the Great War was definitely a significant success for him and the troops in the muddy trenches of Europe.

In 1923, he moved again, this time to the slightly warmer climate of southern England. There, he began work on the new medium of television which at the time was being actively pursued by several teams around the world.

In a rented attic and virtually penniless, he constructed the world's first television when he transmitted an actual picture, which he demonstrated before fifty scientists in 1926. He followed this up in 1927 with another first, by relaying a television signal over the telephone from London to Glasgow. In 1928 he then became the first person to transmit an image across the Atlantic.

In 1931, Baird married Margaret Albu in England. She was a concert pianist whose family originally came from South Africa. They had a daughter and a son.

So impressed were authorities in Britain that the BBC used his system from 1929 to 1937. However, after years of pioneering effort Baird could not keep up with successive innovations from later entrants into the field of television, especially followers who had deeper pockets to spend than Baird, and in 1938, the BBC adopted the Marconi-EMI system, the rival company offering a more flexible product that was technically superior.

This came straight after a disastrous fire in November 1937 at

Crystal Palace where Baird had his 'experimental station'. Much of his equipment was damaged or destroyed. Despite these setbacks, Baird continued to invent and innovate. His research projects included colour television, stereophonic sound and fibre optics. During the Second World War, the development of radar was a highly sensitive and secret project by the British authorities. Baird is thought to have played a vital part in the research and technical improvements to the system, but even today his contribution has never been officially acknowledged.

A worse setback was a heart attack in 1941, which slowed him down a little. Even so, he still managed to write his memoirs while convalescing in a nursing home to allay boredom. Later that same year he was hired by Cable and Wireless as consultant technical adviser, which helped to finance his continuing research.

Baird died from complications following a stroke at his home in England in 1946. It was his wish to be buried alongside his parents back in his place of birth in Helensburgh, Argyll, Scotland. He left behind a wife and two adolescent children in financial difficulties. Thankfully, Baird's older sister, Annie, a retired hospital matron in Scotland, took the family in.

Without John Logie Baird, we would not have television as we know it today. The annual television awards in Australia have been named the 'Logie Awards' since 1960 in honour of Baird's pioneering achievements in this field.

SIR JOHN 'JACKIE' STEWART (B.1939)

THREE-TIMES WORLD CHAMPION FORMULA ONE RACING DRIVER

Jackie was born into a car-loving and car-racing family in Milton, West Dunbartonshire, Scotland. The father, who was a motorcycle racer in his younger days, owned a successful car dealership. Jackie's older brother was competing at the top level of motorcar racing when Jackie was in his teens.

Jackie attended Hartfield primary school in Dumbarton, and then continued his secondary schooling at Dumbarton Academy. He experienced learning difficulties owing to undiagnosed dyslexia, which caused him to leave school at the age of sixteen. Stewart then began working at his father's garage and became a qualified mechanic. His parents discouraged him from becoming involved in motor racing when his brother was injured at Le Mans. Instead, blessed as he was with exceptional eye–hand co-ordination, he took up shooting and won several Scottish clay pigeon shooting competitions, just failing to get on to the Olympic team in 1960.

Then a customer of the family business encouraged him to try out as a racing car driver.

At the age of twenty-three, Jackie drove at several minor race meetings in England and excelled. He was noticed by Ken Tyrell, then manager of Cooper Car Company, who signed him on as a driver in his Formula Three team. He debuted for Tyrell in 1964 and was dominant from the start, easily taking the Championship in his first year. Three years later, he reluctantly left Tyrell, which he regarded as the best time of his life, to step up to Formula One racing with Graham Hill's BRM team.

In his first year he finished the season ranked third in the coveted world Drivers Championship. Also in his first year he experienced a crash which left him determined to improve driver safety in racing. On the first lap of the 1966 Belgium Grand Prix a sudden downpour of rain left the road surface greasy and dangerous.

Many cars slid off the track, including Stewart's. He found himself in a ditch pinned in his overturned vehicle, getting soaked by leaking – and highly combustible – fuel, and lay there for twenty-five minutes before finally being freed. Eventually he was transported in a rickety old ambulance to the closest hospital, getting lost on the way. He had fractured his collarbone and was in considerable pain, but it could have been far worse.

This life-threatening experience made him a determined campaigner for improvements in driver and track safety, in a sport that up to then was regarded as one of the most dangerous professions in the world.

Stewart's performances over the next three years driving for Hill's BRM team did not improve, due to having to compete with higher-specification vehicles. In 1967, he reconnected with Ken Tyrell, who had by now established a Formula One team of his own, and in his first year with Tyrell, Stewart came second in the Drivers Championship.

Over the next five years, Jackie Stewart won an unprecedented three Drivers Championships. He was at the top of his game and beloved by all. Then he unexpectedly announced his retirement at the end of the 1973 season. In explanation, the thirty-four-year-old Stewart said, 'The key in life is deciding when to go into something and when to get out if it.' He had also witnessed too many of his fellow drivers die needlessly in the sport.

He left Formula One racing with 27 wins from 99 starts, a record that stood for almost two decades.

However, motorsport at the elite level was still in his blood and in 1974, Stewart shifted seamlessly from driver to advocate and media commentator the year following his retirement as Formula One driver. He became a consultant for Ford Motor Company while continuing to be a spokesman for safer cars and circuits in Formula One. Stewart pressed for a number of safety improvements; including mandatory seat belt usage, full-face helmets for drivers, removal steering wheels to get better access to drivers in case of an emergency and fuel cut-off switches to avoid crashes ending up in catastrophic fire explosions. Today, Formula One racing would be unthinkable without these improvements. Likewise, he pressed track owners to modernise their tracks with the addition of barriers, run-off areas, fire crews, and medical facilities.

Stewart became a commentator covering motorsport for American television for the next fourteen years, up to 1986. His insightful analysis, Scottish accent, and rapid delivery caused him to become a household name to a new generation of motor enthusiasts.

Much admired throughout Great Britain, Stewart was honoured by Queen Elizabeth with a knighthood in 2001. He was also inducted into both the International Motorsports Hall of Fame and the Sports Hall of Fame.

Outside the world of racing, Stewart and his wife Helen, whom he married in 1962, raised two sons, Paul – who was a racing driver and then ran a racing team with his father – and Mark, a television and film producer.

Thanks to Jackie Stewart's tireless advocacy, motor racing is a far safer sport today than it was when he entered it in the 1960s. His accomplishments as a Formula One driver continue to be so highly regarded, that in 2009 he was ranked as the fifth greatest Formula One driver of all time, alongside such other giants of the sport as Juan Fangio, Ayrton Senna and Michael Schumacher.

Sir Jackie Stewart's portrait hangs proudly in the Grand Prix Hall of Fame along with other great legends of Formula One motor racing. When being interviewed by the Hall of Fame, he said 'If I have any legacy to leave the sport I hope it will be seen to be as an area of safety, because when I arrived in Grand Prix racing so-called precautions and safety measures were diabolical'.

SIR ALEX FERGUSON (B. 1941)

ONE OF FOOTBALL'S MOST SUCCESSFUL MANAGERS

Born to working-class parents in a poor suburb of Glasgow, Alex showed little interest in schooling, preferring to kick a football around the alleyways of the surrounding tenement housing. Guided by his father, Ferguson made his amateur football debut as a striker for Queen's Park FC (Glasgow) in 1958 when he was sixteen.

He scored a number of winning goals, but failed to get engaged on a regular basis so moved to St Johnstone FC (Perth) in 1960; there the story was much the same, but he turned professional when he joined Dunfermline Athletic in 1964. Over the next twelve years he played with several clubs, such as Rangers, Falkirk and Ayr United.

In 1974 he made the switch from player to manager (coach) and after a few faltering steps with East Stirlingshire and then St Mirren (Paisley), his career took off when he became the manager of Aberdeen Football Club. He was fiery and competitive, with an eye for detail and for nurturing new talent. He took Aberdeen to three Scottish Premier League titles, four Scottish Cups, a League Cup, a Super Cup and a European Cup Winner's Cup in the course of eight glorious years.

His growing reputation did not go unnoticed south of the Scottish border and in 1986 he took over the reins of Manchester United, which was then a well-respected but underperforming club in the English manufacturing centre.

His early years were undistinguished until the 1998–99 season when he became the first manager of a British side to win the coveted 'treble' (the Premier League championship, the FA Cup and the European Cup). With his successful formula in place, it was the start of a phenomenal run of achievements which saw Manchester United win four Premier League titles in five years.

Success seemed to follow Sir Alex and Manchester United almost every year thereafter. By the time he finally retired from professional coaching in 2013 he had accumulated an unprecedented forty-nine trophies for the clubs he had managed and been awarded more than a dozen personal honours, including a well-deserved knighthood in 1999.

While he was busy developing Manchester United into one of the most successful football clubs in history, others were busy converting Manchester United into a global brand. Once limited to Europe and South America, the game now captivates audiences and players throughout the world.

Sir Alex Ferguson, who was raised in humble surrounds in Glasgow, made Manchester United one of the most respected clubs in the world and in doing so helped turn the game of Association football (or soccer as it is sometimes known) into the world's most popular football code.

ANN GLOAG (B. 1942)

BUSINESSWOMAN AND MAJOR CHARITY DONOR

Born in Perth the daughter of a local bus driver, Ann Souter was educated at the Perth High School. She then entered nursing, where for the next twenty years she focused on treating burns victims at the Bridge of Earn Hospital, Perthshire. During her time at the hospital, she met her future husband, Robin Gloag, while he was there as a patient. Ann rose to become the sister in charge of the burns unit, but after marrying Robin in 1965, she retired to devote herself full time to raising a young family of two and operating a small caravan sales business with her husband.

In 1980, the couple, along with Ann's brother Brian Souter, bought a bus for £425. Their original intention was to take the trip of a lifetime to China but the plan failed through visa problems. Instead, the entrepreneurs were invited by a construction company to provide transport for workers travelling to building sites. The three realised the potential and after pooling their own savings of

£12,000 with an equal sum from their father's timely redundancy payment, they bought two more buses and started operating a service from Dundee to London. Robin Gloag was the driver and maintenance man, while Ann made sandwiches and tea and Brian Souter took the bookings. They called this enterprise Stagecoach.

The company was one of the prime beneficiaries of the privatisation of public transport and of the deregulation of bus services in the 1980s by the Thatcher government. The business took the opportunity to expand and started buying up small operators throughout Britain. From the mid-1980s, Stagecoach acquired operations in Scotland, Newcastle, London and Manchester, expanding rapidly to become one the largest transport companies in Britain.

Unfortunately, constant business growth put the Gloag marriage under pressure and the couple separated, divorcing soon after. Robin acrimoniously exited Stagecoach only to set up a rival coach company, called Highwayman, covering some of the same routes. The two companies then engaged in a price war which eventually resulted in Stagecoach dropping its fares altogether. Highwayman went bust and Stagecoach promptly swallowed up most of the ruined business, leaving Robin Gloag feeling a much-humiliated ex-husband. This corporate battle earned Ann a reputation for being a hardnosed businesswoman.

When Stagecoach eventually floated on the London Stock Exchange in 1993 it was valued at £134 million and catapulted Mrs Gloag into multimillionaire status. Stagecoach Group is now an international transport company operating buses, trains, trams and ferries in the UK, US and Canada, which is today conservatively valued at £2.5 billion and employs more than 30,000 people.

For decades, Mrs Gloag has devoted a significant amount of her time to charitable causes, including support for Mercy Ships, which operates the largest non-governmental hospital ship in the world. She was awarded an OBE in the 2004 New Year Honours list for her services to charity and has received numerous other awards, such as an honorary doctorate from Edinburgh's Napier University, the Eleanor Roosevelt Award, as well as Businesswoman of the Year Award and European Women in Achievement Award.

Her life has not been without tragedy however. Her son, Jonathan, was found dead in woodland in Perthshire in 1999. He was just twenty-eight and a father of three, but was suffering from depression at the time. In honour of her late son she runs a charitable school in Nairobi, Kenya, called the Jonathan Gloag Academy.

Just eight years later, ex-husband Robin Gloag was killed in a car crash in Perth. No other vehicle was involved.

In 2013, Scotland's second wealthiest woman (after J. K. Rowling; *see* p. 255) was approached to join the 'Giving Pledge' campaign by Bill and Melinda Gates. Subsequently Ann Gloag vowed to give away half of her fortune (estimated at £500 million in 2013) to charity before she dies. She was already helping thousands of women and children in Africa and the UK, but Gloag stated that 'It is so important for those of us who have enjoyed fortune . . . to empower people to help themselves.'

HAZEL COSGROVE,
LADY COSGROVE (B. 1946)

SCOTLAND'S FIRST FEMALE
SUPREME COURT JUDGE

azel Aronson was born in the upper-class suburb of Newlands,
Glasgow, the daughter of a successful businessman. She
attended Glasgow High School for Girls (changed to the High
School of Glasgow which is still selective, but now co-educational)
and went on to study Law at Glasgow University, graduating LLB
in 1966.

There was no tradition of practising law in the Aronson
household, but Hazel felt drawn instinctively to this profession.
In time, her younger sister, Danielle, would also graduate as a
lawyer. Despite her university professor advising her against it,
Hazel Aronson chose to become a barrister rather than a solicitor
(meaning to plead cases in court instead of preparing paperwork).
'The Bar is no place for women,' the professor told her, according to
Scotland's *Herald* newspaper's interview with her in January 2003.

In 1967, Aronson married John Cosgrove, an Edinburgh-based

dental surgeon, and from that point on she wanted to be known as Hazel Cosgrove in the legal profession. However, to appear before the courts in Scotland, barristers needed to be registered first with the Faculty of Advocates. The Dean of the Faculty decreed she should use her maiden name as it was not considered normal for women to practise under their married name at the time.

Aronson had joined approximately 350 other barristers practising in Scotland, of whom there were probably fewer than fifty women. Barristers – known as advocates in Scotland – needed to keep their profile current to attract new cases to represent. This environment was highly competitive for men. It was even more difficult for women. To maintain her profile in this male-dominated environment of advocacy, Aronson worked late into her pregnancies and returned to work shortly after giving birth. Later in her career, she would say, 'In those days there was no such thing as maternity leave, and at the Bar it was assumed when you had your first baby you would go away and not come back. If you were away for a long period, there was a chance that people would forget about you.'

After two years as Standing Junior Counsel to the Department of Trade, Aronson was appointed to the Sheriff Court (Local Court) in Glasgow where, as the first woman Sheriff, she worked from 1979 to 1983. The Sheriff Court in Glasgow was then, and still is, the busiest court in Scotland, frequently dealing with hundreds of cases each day. In 1983, she was promoted to Senior Sheriff of the Lothian and Borders and transferred to the Sheriff Court in Edinburgh. Aronson held this position until 1996.

In 1991, Aronson was elevated to Queen's Counsel (a senior barrister), a process quaintly known as 'taking silk' for the distinctive silk gowns they are entitled to wear in court. Now she was one of no more than a hundred Queen's Counsel, of whom perhaps fewer than ten were women, seeking employment in the legal system of Scotland.

Aronson made legal history again in 1992, when she was appointed as a temporary judge to the High Court of Justiciary jointly with the Court of Session bench. These two courts were and still are mainly held in Edinburgh and deal with the most serious criminal and civil cases under the Scottish legal system. When not required as a judge, she would resume her duties in the lower courts, where there were approximately 140 colleagues across Scotland dispensing justice.

In 1996 she was appointed Scotland's first full-time Supreme Court judge, breaking 500 years of male-only exclusivity to this illustrious and powerful position. Upon their appointment, as is the tradition in the British legal system, judges can choose a title by which they wish to be known. It was assumed that Hazel Aronson would choose to be known as Lady Aronson, but when the announcement was made, she shocked the establishment by declaring she would henceforth be known as Lady Cosgrove. She wanted to honour her husband of twenty-nine years and whose family name she had wanted to use professionally, but could not during that time. She was now one of approximately thirty top lawyers in Scotland.

Lady Cosgrove was one of the seven judges who, in 2001, re-wrote the 150-year-old law of rape, by removing the element of 'force' as an essential ingredient of the crime. As one of the appellant judges, she said, 'Our law should be like a living tree, not only growing but shedding dead wood as it does so. . . the rights of modern women include the right to refuse to consent to sexual intercourse, at any time and for any reason.'

Lady Cosgrove's next and final promotion occurred in 2003,

when she was appointed to the Inner House of the Court of Session. This is the highest court in Scotland and the pinnacle of the Scottish legal system. The appointment to this court made Hazel Cosgrove one of the top lawyers in the country and one of only ten of the most senior judges ultimately presiding over all criminal and civil appeals. Again, this position had never been held by a woman before and when asked how she felt being appointed to this unprecedented position, Lady Cosgrove said she was very honoured, adding, 'My sincere hope is that the day will come when women's appointments to such positions are so commonplace that they will not be newsworthy.'

In 2004, Lady Cosgrove received the title Commander of the Most Excellent Order of the British Empire (CBE) for her services to the justice system of Scotland. Retired from full-time work in 2006, on her sixtieth birthday, Lady Cosgrove said she was looking forward to spending time with her husband, two children Abigail (born 1970) and Nick (born 1972) and five grandchildren. From time to time, she is called upon to return to court and sit on the bench when there is a shortage of judges.

The Cosgrove family are practising Jews and John Cosgrove was President of the Edinburgh Hebrew Congregation for a time, but Lady Cosgrove never let her religion interfere with her profession. It therefore came as a great shock to her when one aggrieved litigant lodged an appeal claiming Lady Cosgrove's religion caused her to be biased. Lady Cosgrove had dismissed an appeal by a Palestinian woman objecting to her deportation as a failed asylum seeker. The matter was roundly dismissed by several appellant judges. There was not one scintilla of evidence that Lady Cosgrove was or had ever been biased in dealing with the Palestinian woman's refugee appeal. "'

Outside the courtroom, Lady Cosgrove held several extra-judicial appointments. She was a member of the Parole Board for Scotland from 1988 to 1991, Chairman of the Mental Welfare Commission from 1991 to 1996, and Chairman of the Expert Panel on Sex Offending from 1998 to 2001. Her report on sexual crimes in Scotland resulted in the creation of the National Sex Crimes Unit. Lady Cosgrove has been Deputy Chairman of the Boundary Commission for Scotland since 1997.

Currently, Scotland has five women judges out of thirty-four places in the Supreme Court. A move welcomed by most people in Scotland, but Lady Cosgrove was the first.

All through her almost forty years in Law, Lady Cosgrove kept breaking through progressively higher levels of the 'glass ceiling', right up to the very highest court in the land. She has remained coy whether this was an objective she deliberately set out to achieve. Nevertheless she was acutely aware that each barrier she was breaking was another milestone for women who wanted to follow.

The situation today is that more women are graduating with degrees in law from Scottish universities than men. In the last half-century, the percentage of women qualifying as solicitors, barristers and judges in Scotland has gradually increased, though unfortunately it is still a predominantly male bastion at the uppermost levels of the legal system.

With Lady Cosgrove's elevation to the very top of the Scottish legal system, it is hoped that she is a role model for many other women to reach for the stars. 'I have just been in the right place at the right time, part of a generation of women for whom there have been no barriers and . . . have been able to reach the heights in their chosen profession,' she recalled in an interview with *The Scotsman* in 2006.

Lady Cosgrove broke down the barriers of gender and religion to become a powerful force for good in Scotland's highest court.

SUSAN BOYLE (B. 1961)

INTERNATIONAL SINGING SENSATION AND INSPIRATION

In 1961, Susan Magdalane Boyle was born into a working-class family in the modest Scottish town of Blackburn, West Lothian, about 40 kilometres from Glasgow. Her parents were originally from Ireland and she was the youngest of four brothers and five sisters. It was a difficult birth and Susan had to be delivered by emergency caesarean. The doctors gravely told the mother that the child was deprived of oxygen during the operation and she had possibly suffered some degree of brain damage.

From the start her parents noticed that Susan was somehow different from other children, but they fell back on the words of the doctors who said that Susan would 'never come to anything, so don't expect too much of her'.

At school, further aptitude tests appeared to confirm the doctors' original diagnosis and as a child Susan was officially labelled with a learning difficulty and as intellectually handicapped. She was bullied at school and often called 'Simple Susie', but the truth was that the difficult birth had nothing to do with her behaviour, as she was to learn only many years later.

Labelling can often have lifelong effects and Susan grew up in a household determined to protect her from what they believed was an intellectual disability. When schooling finished, she had minimal qualifications and little job prospects. Yet there was one talent that Susan Boyle exhibited from an early age – she was a naturally gifted singer.

Growing up in a musical family, Susan was surrounded by the voices of her parents who went about their daily lives singing the popular tunes and melodies from the radio. There was a piano in the front room of the house and while her mother played, her father would sing in a fine tenor voice.

After graduating from school with few qualifications, she was employed as a trainee cook in the kitchen of West Lothian College for six months and took part in government training programmes. And she continued to sing at church and karaoke at pubs in her village.

In 1997, Boyle's father passed away, and she decided to put her life on hold to become the prime carer of her ailing mother. Her mother had always recognised her daughter's musical talent and constantly encouraged her to take part in singing competitions to develop her career. Apart from a few unsuccessful attempts at sending demonstration tapes away to record companies, Susan largely ignored the advice of her mother for years.

Then in 2007 her mother died and her loss crushed Susan. For a long time after the funeral she stayed at home for days at a time, refusing to show herself in the village. Family and friends rallied around her, and slowly Susan began to emerge from the deep depression she found herself in.

Boyle's singing coach urged her to try out for the popular TV show *Britain's Got Talent* as a final tribute to her mother. Susan would later say she entered the talent show, 'to show her I could do something with my life'. She set off for Glasgow, but became confused in all the excitement, eventually catching six different buses before arriving at the auditions. She filled out the registration form and waited over twelve hours before being called for her audition.

Susan's appearance on *Britain's Got Talent* in 2009 stunned the audience and fired the public imagination. She appeared disoriented and somewhat dowdy when she first came on stage. The judges smirked and the audience was initially hostile, but after this awkward introduction she opened her mouth and begun to sing 'I Dreamed a Dream' from the musical *Les Misérables*. This was the moment her life changed.

Susan became an instant internet sensation on YouTube and within weeks her performance had been downloaded over ten million times. Subsequently her audition has been viewed by more than 300 million people globally.

Although she was widely expected to win the £100,000 prize, she ended up coming second to dance troupe Diversity. After the series ended, she checked into the Priory, rehabilitation clinic to the stars, to be treated for nervous exhaustion.

Susan released her debut album *I Dreamed a Dream* in late 2009 worldwide. The studio project sold more than 400,000 copies across the UK in its first week, making it the fastest-selling album and achieving the largest first-week sales for a debut album in UK chart history. Her reign extended across the world and the album became No.1 in the many countries, including, Canada, the US and Australia. To date, the album has sold over ten million copies worldwide.

Next, she embarked on a gruelling promotional tour in Europe, America, Australia and Asia, but her fears and anxiety before a live audience led to a few embarrassments and poor performances when nerves got the better of her.

Back in Scotland it was decided that she needed professional counselling if her stellar career as a global singing super star was to continue. It was during sessions with a psychiatrist in Edinburgh that it was revealed Susan was not brain damaged at all. Instead, she was diagnosed with Asperger's Syndrome, which affects communication and social interaction. Sufferers have difficulty picking up on social cues and gauging appropriate behaviour. She was also told that she had an 'above average' IQ.

Even though she was relieved with the new diagnosis, there was still a long way for Susan to learn new ways to cope with the world. 'It's just a condition that I have to live with and work through', she said.

Slowly, she gained enough confidence to embark on a sell-out live tour of Scotland, followed by a sell-out tour of the rest of the UK in 2014. Her first tour of the USA followed in late 2014 to rapturous reviews, adoring crowds and standing ovations everywhere. A musical of her life has been performed to packed audiences and rave reviews throughout the United Kingdom and Ireland. More albums and tours are in the pipeline, and there is even talk of a film about Susan's extraordinary life.

People have purchased Susan Boyle's records and attended her concerts not only to hear the wonderful gift of her voice, but to also connect with Susan on a personal level. Here was a woman who was misdiagnosed at birth and condemned to a severely limiting future. Yet, she took an opportunity that led directly to a second chance to live a more fulfilling life.

From a shy, withdrawn girl who believed she was retarded, Susan Boyle blossomed into a singing superstar. She has performed before Queen Elizabeth II and the Pope. Her records – five albums so far – have collectively sold more than 22 million copies worldwide. Yet, for all the fame, she has remained a humble person grateful for the diagnosis that changed the way she thinks about herself.

In Susan Boyle, people see a woman who has triumphed over adversity and for that she is a role model and a hero to thousands.

JOANNE ROWLING (B. 1965)

BESTSELLING AUTHOR, WHO INSPIRED YOUTH TO READ FOR PLEASURE

Joanne Rowling was born in Yate in Gloucestershire, England. Her childhood was uneventful, secure and happy. Her father worked as an engineer in the Rolls-Royce factory in Bristol, and her mother as a laboratory assistant, after raising two children. At an early age, Rowling fell in love with writing. According to one biography, she can remember writing a short story for her family at the age of six about a rabbit with measles. Her mother Anne, who was a passionate reader, was quite impressed and encouraged her daughter to continue.

When she was nine the family moved to Tutshill on the England-Wales border alongside the Severn River. It was during this time that Kathleen, her favourite grandmother died. Between the ages of eleven and seventeen, she attended the nearby Wyedean School where she performed well academically, but poorly in sport.

After finishing school she went to the University of Exeter, where her parents encouraged her to study French and Classics, which she did. She slightly regretted the choice, saying she would have preferred to study English but it was her parents' wish that she study something 'more useful' than English, and French would help secure work as a bilingual secretary.

After having spent a year in Paris, Rowling graduated from university and took a number of jobs in London. One was as a researcher and bilingual secretary for Amnesty International, the charity which campaigns against human rights abuses throughout the world. Rowling was attracted to Amnesty International then and has generously supported Amnesty since becoming wealthy.

It was in 1990, that Rowling first conceived the idea of Harry Potter. As she recalls, it was on a long train journey from Manchester to London when she suddenly began forming in her mind, the characters of the series. At the forefront, was a young boy, at that time not aware that he was a wizard. The train was delayed for over four hours, but she didn't have a pen and was too shy to ask to borrow one.

When she eventually arrived home at her flat in London's Clapham Junction, Rowling started furiously writing down all the thoughts that had accumulated in her head. However, it would still take several years for the characters and story to be fully developed on paper. Later in the same year, Rowling lost her mother Anne to multiple sclerosis. Many years later she was proud to fund the creation of the Anne Rowling Clinic in Edinburgh with a donation of £10 million, in association with the University of Edinburgh. It is not only a living tribute to Joanne's mother, but a serious attempt to unlock the medical mysteries of multiple sclerosis, so that other people, especially young mothers like Anne Rowling, might not succumb to a disease that currently has no known cure.

JOANNE ROWLING (B. 1965)

The loss of her mother, whom she was very close to, caused a deep depression in Joanne. For a change of scenery, or perhaps to escape, she left England and got a job as an English teacher in the bustling city of Porto, Portugal. It was here that she met her first husband, Jorge Arantes, a television journalist, and together they had a child, Jessica. Within thirteen months, the couple had separated, with Joanne having full custody of the six-month-old Jessica. A full divorce followed in late 1994.

In December 1993, Rowling returned to the UK and moved to Edinburgh to stay briefly with her two-years-younger sister Dianne for support before she found a small flat to rent. It was the most vulnerable time of her life; a young, single mother of a twelve-month-old baby, without a job and with virtually no employment prospects. Somehow she managed to survive on state benefits on her own in a tiny flat while she completed the story of the boy who went to a magician's school. But it would still take another three years before the public would actually get to read the fruits of her work.

For two more years Rowling struggled to realise her idea as a writer and she was almost at the end of her rope. Her sister had been wonderful but Rowling felt she could not continue to live off her sister's charity and from part-time teaching French.

Eventually, she completed the manuscript of her book, which like all her subsequent books, was initially handwritten. Rowling then typed it, made copies and sent it to a number of literary agents. She secured an agent, Christopher Little, who spent the next year searching for a publisher. Eventually, after rejections by a dozen major publishers, in 1996 Bloomsbury, a small London-based publishing house made an offer for the book. The book was titled *Harry Potter and the Philosopher's Stone*.

Wisely, Rowling held onto the e-book rights rather than hand them over to her publishers. In 2012, she started selling copies of her Harry Potter series in electronic form exclusively through her own dedicated website, Pottermore. It is estimated that over 5 million electronic versions of her books have been sold (downloaded) so far. It is believed Rowling is the only author to have negotiated such an arrangement with a publisher to date.

The editor at Bloomsbury agreed to pay Rowling an advance of £1,500 and said the decision to publish the book was mainly due to his eight-year-old daughter's enthusiastic reception of the first few sample chapters. Also, the publisher suggested that a woman's name would not appeal to the target audience of young boys and requested Rowling publish under her initials. Since she only had one given name, Joanne added the initial of her beloved grandmother, Kathleen, to become J. K. Rowling, the name that she is more widely known by today.

Anxious to stabilise her chaotic finances, Rowling applied for and was awarded an £8,000 grant from the Scottish Council of the Arts, which allowed her to purchase writing equipment and pay off outstanding bills. She even found time to start the second novel of Harry Potter. The initial print run of Rowling's first novel was 1,000 copies only, but from the date of its publication in 1997 sales figures started to climb quickly. Within months, the book had been reprinted several times and was selling at a rate of 1,000 copies a week.

Harry Potter and the Philosopher's Stone won Rowling the 1997 British Book Awards Children's Book of the Year and received glowing reviews in both Europe and North America. On the back of highly successful sales figures in the UK, an American company, Scholastic, agreed to pay a remarkable £100,000 for the rights to publish in America. In 1998, barely a year after her first book had been published, Warner Brothers secured the film rights for the books, reportedly paying Rowling a seven-figure sum, making her a millionaire overnight.

The second book in the series *Harry Potter and the Chamber of Secrets* followed in 1998 to outstanding reviews and popularity. Rowling was becoming an international bestselling author. Next, *Harry Potter and the Prisoner of Azkaban* (1999) broke all sales records for a children's book. J. K. Rowling and her creation, Harry Potter, were becoming a worldwide phenomenon.

The fourth book in the series, *Harry Potter and the Goblet of Fire* (2000) was released simultaneously in the UK and the US. It sold an unprecedented 372,775 copies on the first day of its release in the UK and 3 million copies in the first 48 hours in the USA. Three more novels followed to complete the series, each outselling the last. *Harry Potter and the Order of the Phoenix* (2003), *Harry Potter and the Half-Blood Prince* (2005) and *Harry Potter and the Deathly Hallows* (2007). The final book of the series, *Deathly Hallows*, became the fastest-selling book in history.

By now, tens of millions of children and young adults were hooked on reading about Harry Potter, many of whom had not voluntarily picked up a book previously. *Harry Potter and the Order of the Phoenix* was a staggering 870 pages long for a children's book containing over 255,000 words. Some people thought young people would not be able to finish such a long and complex novel. The first print run in the USA was 8.5 million copies. It was sold out in weeks.

Since the end of her Harry Potter series, Rowling has branched out by writing novels for the adult reader. *Casual Vacancy* was published in 2012 and *Cuckoo's Calling* in 2013 under the pseudonym of Robert Galbraith. When it was discovered who the real author was, sales went ballistic. It was followed in 2014 by *The Silkworm*. All have been very well received.

Her novels have sold more than 400 million copies worldwide, have been translated into sixty-seven languages and have won numerous awards. The Harry Potter books have also been adapted to screen in a series of blockbuster films. Ranked as one of the richest women in the United Kingdom with a net worth of £600 million, it is said Rowling is wealthier than Queen Elizabeth II.

Rowling remarried in 2001 and lives with her husband, Dr Neil Murray, an anaesthetist, and three children in Edinburgh.

Even though Rowling has enjoyed a rags-to-riches life with her meteoric rise in prosperity, she has never forgotten her roots or the humble times when she lived on welfare as a single mother. It is estimated that she has so far given away almost £100 million in charities that are close to her heart, such as research into multiple sclerosis, helping one-parent families and improving the future of impoverished children in Eastern Europe.

In terms of international prestige, national influence and ability to change daily lives, it is hard to ignore Rowling's incredible affect. No other woman in Scotland commands the level of power, nor uses it so wisely. For example, within twenty-four hours of her writing to the Czech President Vaclav Klaus in 2004, complaining about barbaric 'caged beds' being used for young children in Czech psychiatric institutions, the President had ordered their immediate removal.

For a number of years J. K. Rowling has been named one of the one hundred most powerful women on the planet by *Forbes* magazine and, more importantly, is credited with encouraging a new generation of young people to read.

BIBLIOGRAPHY
AND SOURCES

GENERAL REFERENCES

Collins English Dictionary (10th ed. 2010)

Oxford English Dictionary (11th ed. 2008)

Macquarie Dictionary (2nd revision, 1988)

Oxford Dictionary of National Biography (2004)

Wikipedia at www.wikepedia.com

Lynch, M., *Scotland: a new History*, Pimlico, London, 2007

Devine, T., *The Scottish Nation: A History, 1700–2007*, Penguin, London, 2006

Royle, T., *The Flowers of the Forest: Scotland and the First World War*, Birlinn, Edinburgh, 2007

Macleod, I., (ed.) *The Illustrated Encyclopaedia of Scotland*, Lomond Books, Edinburgh, 2004

Undiscovered Scotland: The Ultimate Online Guide to Scotland at http://www.undiscoveredscotland.co.uk

Encyclopaedia Britannica online available at http://www.britannica com/

SPECIFIC REFERENCES

Calgacus

Dark, K., *Britain and the End of the Roman Empire*, The History Press, Stroud, 2011

Brabbs, D., *Hadrian's Wall*, Frances Lincoln Ltd., London, 2008

De Souza, P. (ed.) *The Ancient World at War*, Thames & Hudson, London, 2008

Ammianus Marcellinus *Res Gestae* (Book XX, chapter 1) in *The Later Roman Empire (AD 35–378),* trans. W. Hamilton, Penguin Classics, 1986; found in Vortigern Studies at www vortigernstudies.org.uk/artsou/ammian.htm

Publius (or Gaius) Cornelius Tacitus, *De vita Iulii Agricolae* (*The Life of Agricola*), *c.* AD 98, (29–32)

Tytler, P. F., *History of Scotland*, William Tait, Edinburgh, 1829; found in Internet Archive at https://archive.org/stream historyscotland12tytlgoog/historyscotland12tytlgoog_djvu.txt

Woodman, A. J., and Kraus, C. S. (eds), Tacitus: *Agricola*, Cambridge University Press, Cambridge, 2014

Sir William Wallace

Fisher, A., *William Wallace*, Birlinn, Edinburgh, 2007

Ross, D. A., *On the trail of William Wallace*, Luath Press, Edinburgh, 1998

BIBLIOGRAPHY AND SOURCES

Robert the Bruce

Penman, M., *Robert the Bruce: King of the Scots*, Yale University Press, New York, 2014

Scott, R. M., *Robert the Bruce: King of Scots*, Canongate Books, Edinburgh, 1996

John Knox

Forbes Gray, W., and Jamieson, J. H., *A Short History of Haddington*, Spa Books Ltd., Stevenage, England, 1988

Marshall, R. K., *John Knox*, Birlinn, Edinburgh, 2008

Greatsite.Com is the online showroom of The Bible Museum, Inc.: http://www.greatsite.com/timeline-english-bible-history/john knox.html

Mary, Queen of Scots

Edinburgh Castle: Official Souvenir Guide, Historic Scotland, 2008

Fraser, Lady A., *Mary, Queen of Scots*, Phoenix Press (Orion Books), London, 2009

John Napier

Napier, J., *Mirifici logarithmorum canonis descriptio (A Description of the Wonderful Canon of Logarithms)* sourced at http://www johnnapier.com/

Michael Caulfield, 'John Napier: His Life, His Logs, and His Bones' on the Mathematical Association of America website: http://www.maa.org/publications/periodicals/convergence/john napier-his-life-his-logs-and-his-bones-introduction

James VI of Scotland and I of England

Edinburgh Castle: Official Souvenir Guide, Historic Scotland, 2008

Stewart, A., *The Cradle King: The Life of James VI and I, the First Monarch of a united Great Britain*, St. Martin's Press, New York, 2003

King James I Biography found in http://www.jesus-is-lord.com kingbio.htm

David Hume

Baier, A. C., *The Pursuits of Philosophy: An Introduction to the Life and Thought of David Hume*, Harvard University Press, Cambridge MA, 2011

Morris, Ted, *David Hume's Life and Works*, found in the Hume Society website: http://www.humesociety.org/about/humebiography.asp

Mossner, E. C., *The Life of David Hume*, Oxford University Press, Oxford, 2001

Flora MacDonald

'Woman of Scottish Descent: Flora MacDonald' found at http:/www.electricscotland.com/history/women/wih9.htm

Martin J., (North Carolina History Project), *Flora MacDonald (1772–1790)*, found in http://www.northcarolinahistory.org encyclopedia/804/entry

Adam Smith

Cannan E., (ed.), *An Inquiry into the Nature and Causes of the Wealth of Nations,* University of Chicago Press, Chicago, 1976. Available online at: http://www.econlib.org/library Smith/smWN.html

The Concise Encyclopedia of Economics: Adam Smith (1723–1790), available online at Library of Economics and Liberty at http:/www.econlib.org/library/Enc/bios/Smith.html

Phillipson, N., *Adam Smith: An Enlightened Life*, Penquin, London, 2011

Adam Smith, *The Wealth of Nations (An Inquiry into the Nature and Causes of the Wealth of Nations)*, 1776; quotation from Book 1 Chapter 2

John Witherspoon

Craven, F. C., (1978) *John Witherspoon* found in http://etcweb princeton.edu/CampusWWW/Companion/witherspoon_john html

Declaration of Arbroath (1320), found in Constitution Society at http://www.constitution.org/scot/arbroath.htm

'John Witherspoon', (2014) found in http://www.biography.com people/john-witherspoon-21261997

John Witherspoon ('There is a tide in the affairs of men …'), quoted in Briggs, C. A., *American Presbyterianism*, Charles Scribner's Sons, New York, 1885; found in Foundation for Economic Education at http://fee.org/freeman/detail/john-witherspoon animated-son-of-liberty

Niel Gow

'Niel Gow, a family portrait', originally published in *The Celtic Monthly* magazine Vol. VII 1899, pp.171–4 found online at http:/www.amaranthpublishing.com/gowfamily.html

Duncan, A., 'Niel Gow', *The Living Tradition*, Issue 28, August September 1998, found at http://www.folkmusic.net/htmfiles inart441.htm

Lockhart, J., et al., *The Life of Robert Burns*, J.M, Dent & Sons, London, 1907, found at http://oudl.osmania.ac.in/bitstream handle OUDL/12204/216172_Life_Of_Robert_Burns.pdf?sequence=2

Robert Adam

Graham, R., *An Arbiter of Excellence: A Biography of Robert Adam*, Birlinn, Edinburgh, 2009

National Trust for Scotland, *Culzean Castle & Country Park*, National Trust for Scotland, 2013

James Watt

Lira, C. T., Biography of James Watt, (2013), found at http://www egr.msu.edu/~lira/supp/steam/wattbio.html

John Paul Jones

Thomas, E., *John Paul Jones: Sailor, Hero, Father of the American Navy,* Simon & Schuster, New York, 2003

'John Paul Jones' originally in *National Cyclopaedia of American Biography.* vol. 2. New York: James T. White & Co., (1893), and reprinted in *Biographies of Naval History,* found in http://www history.navy.mil/research/histories/bios/jones-john-paul/jones jpa.html

Sir Henry Raeburn

'Henry Raeburn', the Biography.com website (2014). Found at http://www.biography.com/people/henry-raeburn-9450510

'Sir Henry Raeburn', found at http://www.electricscotland.com history/other/raeburn_henry.htm

Thomas Telford

Rolt, L.T.C., *Thomas Telford*, The History Press, Stroud, UK, 2007 (new edition)

BIBLIOGRAPHY AND SOURCES

Robert Burns

Bowditch, Lindsey, *Robert Burns Birthplace Museum*, National Trust for Scotland, Edinburgh, 2013

Coutts, H., and Finnie, E., *The Writers' Museum Edinburgh*, City of Edinburgh Museum and Art Galleries, 1993

Robertson, J. L., (ed.) *The Poetical Works of Robert Burns*, Oxford University Press, London, 1921

Lachlan Macquarie

Parker, D., *Governor Macquarie: His Life, Times and Revolutionary Vision for Australia*, Woodslane Press, Sydney, 2010

Australian Dictionary of Biography: http://adb.anu.edu.au/biography macquarie-lachlan-2419.html

'The Governor: Lachlan Macquarie 1810 to 1821' at http:/ www.sl.nsw.gov.au/events/exhibitions/2010/governor/docs/the governor_guide.pdf

Sir Alexander Mackenzie

Dictionary of Canadian Biography, 'Sir Alexander Mackenzie', found in http://www.biographi.ca/en/bio/mackenzie_alexander_5E.html

Charles Macintosh

'Charles Macintosh', Today in Science History: http://todayinsci com/M/Macintosh_Charles/MacintoshCharlesBio.htm

Carolina Oliphant

'The Life of Carolina Oliphant (Lady Nairne) 1766–1845', found at http://www.musicanet.org/robokopp/bio/nairnela.html

Sir Walter Scott

Buchan, J., *Sir Walter Scott,* Cassell, London, 1932

Coutts, H., and Finnie, E., *The Writers' Museum Edinburgh*, City of Edinburgh Museum and Art Galleries, 1993

Scott, Sir W., *The Complete Works of Sir Walter Scott: With a Biography and his last Additions and Illustrations* (Volume 1), Conner & Cooke, New York, 1833; for the 1814 poem 'Pharos Loquitur' see p. 631. Found in Google Books at https://play google.com/store/books/details?id=yRMeAAAAMAAJ&rdid book-yRMeAAAAMAAJ&rdot=1

Sutherland, J., *The Life of Walter Scott: A Critical Biography.* Blackwell, Oxford, 1995

Robert Stevenson

Robert Stevenson, found in Northern Lighthouse Board: https:/www.nlb.org.uk/HistoricalInformation/StevensonEngineers Robert-Stevenson/

Thomas Cochrane

Cordingly, D., *The Life and Legacy of Lord Cochrane*, found in NPR Books: http://www.npr.org/templates/story/story php?storyId=14505058

'Thomas Cochrane, the real "Master and Commander"', found in National Maritime Museum: http://www.nmm.ac.uk/explore sea-and-ships/facts/explorers-and-leaders/thomas-cochrane

Sir David Brewster

Sir David Brewster (1761-1868), found in http://www preteristarchive.com/StudyArchive/b/brewster-david.html

BIBLIOGRAPHY AND SOURCES

David Livingstone

'David Livingstone's Life', found in Livingstone online: http:/
www.livingstoneonline.ucl.ac.uk/biog/dl/bio.html

Roye, G. B., *David Livingstone: Africa's Great Missionary and Explorer*,
found in http://www.wholesomewords.org/missions/bliving2
html

Worcester, Mrs J. H., *The Life of David Livingstone*, Forgotten
Books, London, 1888; found in Forgotten Books online at http:/
www.forgottenbooks.com/readbook_text/The_Life_of_David
Livingstone_1000153667/85

Margaret Oliphant

Husemann, Mary M., 'Margaret Oliphant Wilson Oliphant (1828
1897): a Brief Biography'. 2003, found in http://www
victorianweb.org/authors/oliphant/bio.html

Williams, M., *Margaret Oliphant: A Critical Biography*, St. Martin's
Press, New York, 1986. Found on line at https://archive.org
details/MargaretOliphantACriticalBiography

Isabella Elder

'Isabella Elder', found at the University of Glasgow Story: http:/
www.universitystory.gla.ac.uk/biography/?id=WH0024&type=P

Fraser, W. H., 'The Glasgow Story: Isabella Elder', found in http:/
www.theglasgowstory.com/story.php?id=TGSDH13

Andrew Carnegie

Carnegie, A., *Autobiography of Andrew Carnegie*, Houghton Mifflin
Company, Boston and New York, 1920, found online at http:/
cw.routledge.com/textbooks/9780415531948/data
webdocument3.pdf

'People and Events: Andrew Carnegie', found in http://www.pbs org/wgbh/amex/carnegie/peopleevents/pande01.html

Biographies: Andrew Carnegie, found in http://www.history.co.uk biographies/andrew-carnegie

John Muir

Gifford T., (editor), *John Muir: His Life and Letters and Other Writings*, Bâton Wicks Publications, London, 1996

'John Muir: A brief Biography', found in Sierra Club: http://vault sierraclub.org/john_muir_exhibit/life/muir_biography.aspx

Muir, J., *The Yosemite*, Century Company, New York, 1912

'Discover John Muir', John Muir Trust, with Scottish Natural Heritage and Year of Natural Scotland: thttp://discoverjohnmuir com/muir-info/

Stegner W., 'The Best Idea We Ever Had' in *Marking the Sparrow's Fall: The Making of the American West*. Edited by Page Stegner. New York: Henry Holt and Company, 1998

Sir James Dewar

James F.A.J.L., 'British Chemist and Physicist: James Dewar (1842–1923)', found in http://www.chemistryexplained.com/Co Di/Dewar-James.html

'James Dewar', NNDB (Notable Names Database), Soylent Communications 2014: http://www.nndb.com people/094/000099794/

Alexander Graham Bell

Surtees, L., 'Bell, Alexander Graham', found in *Dictionary of Canadian Biography*, available online at http://www.biographi.ca en/bio/bell_alexander_graham_15E.html

BIBLIOGRAPHY AND SOURCES

Kate Cranston

Blair, Anna (ed.), *Tea at Miss Cranston's: A Century of Glasgow Memories*, Birlinn, Edinburgh, 2013

Robert Louis Stevenson

Booth B. and Mehew E., *The Letters of Robert Louis Stevenson* (8 Volumes), Yale University Press, New York 1994-95. For Stevenson's letter to fellow novelist S. R. Crockett see Volume 5, page 81

Coutts, H., and Finnie, E., *The Writers' Museum Edinburgh*, City of Edinburgh Museum and Art Galleries, 1993

Sir Patrick Geddes

Ballater Geddes Project 2004, 'Sir Patrick Geddes (1854–1932)', a .pdf document found in http://metagraphies.org/Sir-Patrick Geddes/university-militant/geddesexhib04web.pdf

Sir Patrick Geddes Memorial Trust, Scotland: http://www patrickgeddestrust.co.uk/index.htm

Douglas Haig

Scottish National War Memorial: Official Guide, 2004

Hart, P., *The Somme*, Weidenfeld & Nicolson, London, 2005

'The Cavalry Arm: Lord Haig on Value in War', article in *The Times* (UK) dated 5 June 1925, p. 8, col. 4

Winter, J. M., *The Great War and the British People,* 2nd Edition, Palgrave Macmillan, Basingstoke, 2003

Elsie Maud Inglis

Inglis, Lucy, 'The Art of Medicine: Elsie Inglis, the Suffragette Physician', *The Lancet* Perspectives, (Vol. 384, Nov 2014), found in the online version of *The Lancet* at http://www.thelancet.com pdfs/journals/lancet/PIIS0140-6736%2814%2962022-5.pdf

McLaren, Eva Shaw, *Elsie Inglis: The Woman with the Torch*, Macmillan Press, New York, 1920 retrieved in http://www gutenberg.org/files/18530/18530-h/18530-h.htm

McLean, D., 'Lost Edinburgh: Elsie Inglis Memorial Hospital', in *The Scotsman* newspaper,13 May 2013, found online at http:/ www.scotsman.com/lifestyle/heritage/lost-edinburgh-elsie inglis-memorial-hospital-1-2927046

Charles Rennie Mackintosh

McKean, J., and Baxter, C., *Charles Rennie Mackintosh Pocket Guide*, Colin Baxter Photography, Grantown-on-Spey, 2011

Charles Rennie Mackintosh biography, listed in *Directory of Scottish Architects*, found online at http://www.scottisharchitects.org.uk architect_full.php?id=200362

'Fire Crews Leave Glasgow Arts School Mackintosh Building', *BBC News*, 30 May 2014, found at http://www.bbc.com/news uk-scotland-glasgow-west-27638803

John Buchan

Kimble, R., 'Catching up with John Buchan', published in *The Fortnightly Review* (new online series), 27 June 2012, found at http://fortnightlyreview.co.uk/2012/06/catchin-buchan/

http://www.johnbuchansociety.co.uk/theman.html

Daniel Laidlaw

Stewart, I., Victoria Cross and Campaign Medals awarded to Sergeant Piper Daniel Laidlaw, online article published 25 September 2005, found at http://www.victoriacross.org.uk/bblaidla.htm,

'The Pipes of War: Piper of Loos, Daniel Laidlaw V.C.' found at http://www.pipesofwar.com/piper-of-loos/history.php

Sir Alexander Fleming

Fleming, A., 'On the Antibacterial Action of Cultures of a Penicillium' *British Journal of Experimental Pathology*, 1929, 10 (3), pp. 226–36; found online at the National Library of Medicine http://www.ncbi.nlm.nih.gov/pmc/articles/PMC2048009/

'Sir Alexander Fleming – Biographical', found online at http:/www.nobelprize.org/nobel_prizes/medicine/laureates/1945 fleming-bio.html

Hugh Dowding

Chanter, A., 'Hugh Dowding', found in World War II database at http://ww2db.com/person_bio.php?person_id=543

The Battle of Britain – 1940: 'The Leaders, Air Chief Marshal Hugh Dowding', found in http://www.battleofbritain1940.net document-8.html

McKinstry, L., 'A Most Unlikely Hero: Dowding: Odd Man Out but the Right Man at the Right Time', *Daily Mail* (UK), sourced online at http://www.highbeam.com/doc/1G1-171672673.html

John Logie Baird

Baird Television: http://www.bairdtelevision.com/

'John Logie Baird, Scientist and Inventor', found in Scotlandspeople website on Famous Scots Archives at http://www.scotlandspeople gov.uk/content/help/index.aspx?r=546&1077

Sir Jackie Stewart

Donaldson, G., 'Jackie Stewart – Profile', found at Drivers' Hall of Fame feature in http://www.formula1.com/teams_and drivers/hall_of_fame/127/

'Sir Jackie Stewart: The Wee Boy at the Back', found in http://www.talkf1.co.uk/guides/sir_jackie_stewart.html

Grand Prix Hall of Fame, found at http://grandprixhistory.org stew_bio.htm

Sir Alex Ferguson

'Sir Alex Ferguson: Manager Manchester United', found at http://www.siralexferguson.net/

Alex Ferguson, Biography, found in biography online at http://www.biographyonline.net/sport/football/alex-ferguson.html

Ann Gloag

Barnes, J., 'Stagecoach Billionaire celebrates 70th Birthday', *Daily Mail*, 18 December 2012, found online at http://www.dailymail co.uk/femail/article-2249899/Stagecoach-millionaire-Ann Gloag-celebrates-70th-birthday-party-Scottish-castle-Lulu Neil-Sedaka.html

O'Sullivan, J., 'Jonathan Gloag had it all. It wasn't enough', *The Independent,* 21 September 1999, found online at http://www independent.co.uk/arts-entertainment/jonathan-gloag-had-it all-it-wasnt-enough-1120829.html

Hazel Cosgrove

The University of Glasgow Story: Lady Cosgrove, found online at http://www.universitystory.gla.ac.ukbiography/ ?id=WH1312&type=P

'The new She who must be Obeyed . . .', *The Herald* Scotland, 18 January 2003, found online at http://www.heraldscotland.com sport/spl/aberdeen/the-new-she-who-must-be-obeyed-profile lady-cosgrove-she-is-a-fervent-champion-of-women furthering-their-careers-particularly-in-law-but-jennifer cunningham-discovers-there-is-much-more-to-scotland-s-first and-formidably-successful-legal-lady-1.128801

'Fair Ladies, first ever all-female bench', *The Scotsman*, 30 May 2008, found online at http://www.scotsman.com/news/fair ladies-first-ever-all-female-bench-1-1170513

Susan Boyle

Flynn, P., 'Susan Boyle: Her Story', found online at http://www susanboylemusic.com/us/story

Pukas, A., 'Bullies made my life hell: But I've had the last laugh', *The Express*, 7 December 2013, found online at http://www express.co.uk/life-style/life/447277/Susan-Boyle-Bullies-made my-life-hell-but-I-ve-had-the-last-laugh

Withnall, A., 'Susan Boyle "relieved" after Asperger's Syndrome Diagnosis', *The Independent*, 8 December 2013, found online at http://www.independent.co.uk/news/people/news/susan-boyle relieved-to-discover-aspergers-syndrome-diagnosis-8991416.html

Joanne Rowling

'About J. K. Rowling', found at http://www.jkrowling.com/en GB/#/about-jk-rowling/

Famous Authors: J. K. Rowling, found online at http://www famousauthors.org/j-k-rowling

J. K. Rowling Biography, found at http://www.thefamouspeople com/profiles/j-k-rowling-4295.php

J. K. Rowling: Biography, Books and Facts, found online at http:/
education-portal.com/academy/lesson/jk-rowling-biography
books-facts.html